Aspects of Time in Jewish and Christian Exegesis

CHRONOI

Zeit, Zeitempfinden, Zeitordnungen

Time, Time Awareness, Time Management

Edited by
Eva Cancik-Kirschbaum, Christoph Markschies and
Hermann Parzinger

on behalf of the Einstein Center Chronoi

Volume 21

Aspects of Time in Jewish and Christian Exegesis

Edited by
Maren R. Niehoff and Christoph Markschies

DE GRUYTER

ISBN 978-3-11-222597-4
e-ISBN (PDF) 978-3-11-222598-1
e-ISBN (EPUB) 978-3-11-222599-8
ISSN 2701-1453
DOI https://doi.org/10.1515/9783112225981

Library of Congress Control Number: 2026930241

Bibliographic information published by the Deutsche Nationalbibliothek
The Deutsche Nationalbibliothek lists this publication in the Deutsche Nationalbibliografie; detailed bibliographic data are available on the internet at http://dnb.dnb.de.

www.degruyterbrill.com
Questions about General Product Safety Regulation:
productsafety@degruyterbrill.com

Contents

Maren R. Niehoff and Christoph Markschies

Introduction

This collection of articles is based on a workshop at CHRONOI, Berlin, which took place in July 2023, concluding a two-year exploration on "Creationism and the Calculation of Time in Late Antiquity: Between Alexandria and the Land of Israel" (1/2022–12/2023). The collection seeks to contribute to the exponentially growing body of literature on notions of time in antiquity, which is typically situated at the juncture of the humanities and the natural as well as the social sciences. Kattan Gribetz and Kaye (2019) even identify a "Temporal Turn in Ancient Judaism and Jewish Studies." In their edited volume *Time. A Multidisciplinary Introduction* (2023) they look back on the fruits of a blossoming field of research and propose an approach particularly apt for the humanities:

> This book seeks to understand time. It does so by changing the question from 'what is time?' to 'who' and 'how:' who interprets, defines, or creates time and how do they do it? Apposing methods and questions of scholars of different subjects and from diverse cultures demonstrates that time is not just 'relative' to an observer's physical position, as Einstein described. What time may be depends on who is asking the question and how they engage the topic. The multiple approaches of many disciplines and cultures offer us a chance to grasp time with a unique sense of depth and dimension.[1]

Kattan Gribetz and Kaye consequently seek to show that all notions of time, even those seemingly natural, such as periods of menstruation, are "culturally constructed and historically contingent."[2] To study any particular reference to time, they urge us to take into account the diversity of its constructions in changing historical circumstances. Kattan Gribetz further contributes to the field with a monograph on *Time and Difference in Rabbinic Judaism* (2020), which shows the rabbis' awareness of Roman and Christian notions of time as well as their endeavor to carve out distinct Jewish time. Women's time, even though described in bodily terms, emerges as equally constructed rather than naturally given. Kaye in turn wrote a monograph on *Time in the Babylonian Talmud* (2018), which shows the rabbis' acute awareness of different forms of time which they negotiate in their roles as both legislators and narrators.

Similar insights were reached in the ERC advanced grant 2013–18 "Calendars in Late Antiquity and the Middle Ages: Standardization and Fixation," led by

1 Kattan Gribetz and Kaye (2023, 2).
2 Kattan Gribetz and Kaye (2023, 21).

 https://doi.org/10.1515/9783112225981-001

Sacha Stern, now to be supplemented by a second ERC grant called "Astronomy, Calendar, and Related Sciences in Near Eastern Cultures, Third–Eight Centuries CE" (2024–2029). Stern writes at the conclusion of his first project that he "attempts, above all, to make a statement about the 'making' and 'origins' of calendars. In spite of their claim to accuracy and exactitude, it is evident that calendars have always been man-made and [are] the outcome of a process of making."[3] The institution and standardization of calendars, he further explains, is almost always a political act, often attributed to a political ruler, to which is often added a religious dimension, especially if instigated by a priest or priesthood. Stern himself has contributed to the field with studies of particular calendar disputes among ancient Jews and an investigation into robust concepts of time which are visible beyond particular chronologies or instruments of measurements, such as calendars.[4] He concludes that the rabbis were diametrically opposed to the Greco-Roman world, lacking a pristine notion of time, which was, however, intensely investigated among pagans.

The present collection is built on these insights and draws attention to the social and ideological contingency of time. Rather than attempting a definition of time, it asks who is addressing issues related to time and how, when and why this is being done. All of the studies presented here investigate junctures, when debates about time emerged and shaped religious identities. The literary corpora studied here all belong to the field of exegesis and thus to a type of literature which is explicitly or professionally focused on time. Such literature has so far been marginal in studies of time in antiquity. During our collaborations between Berlin, Jerusalem and L'Aquila, however, we became increasingly aware of the importance of non-professional genres for the shaping of notions of time and their dissemination among wider audiences.

In particular, this collection of articles focuses on Jewish and Christian Bible exegesis in Alexandria, Rome and the Land of Israel, and especially on their interactions with each other. Disciplinary boundaries are crossed in each contribution, and pagan, Christian and Jewish exegetes are shown to be interacting with each other and responding to each other. Defining one's own notions of time always implied positioning oneself vis-à-vis alternatives and competing with rival approaches. This holds true for the rabbis as well as for Origen and Philo of Alexandria. The latter plays a particular role in this collection, being discussed by four of the contributors at varying degrees of length. He serves in a way as a bridge between Judaism and the Greco-Roman world as well as between Hellenistic and rabbinic Ju-

3 Stern (2021, 5).
4 Stern (2007; 2019).

daism, which can no longer be seen as diametrically opposed entities, one fading into Christianity, the other constituting authentic Judaism.[5]

* * *

Brief introductions into each of the contributions will provide an overview of the overall achievement. The collection opens with Glenn Most's essay "Some Aspects of Time and Eternity in Philo's *De aeternitate mundi*," which investigates the relation between these two concepts from a comparative angle, namely in view of Plato. Most identifies a curious discrepancy between Philo's explicit praise of Plato in this particular treatise and his lack of engagement with the Platonic notion of eternity as something entirely different from temporality (*Timaeus* 37c–38a, 38b–c). Philo nowhere asserts the same opposition. For him, time and the cosmos may well be unlimited but they do not belong to different dimensions. Remarkably, he applies Plato's discussion of eternity not to the eternal as opposed to time, but instead to time as unlimited. In his summary of the *Timaeus* at *Aet.* 4.15, Philo thus substitutes "intelligible" for Plato's "eternal." This transformation is striking and reflects Philo's theological interests.

Ludovica De Luca, "God's Clock and the First Hours of the World. Philo of Alexandria and John Philoponus on 'Day One' as the Measure of Creation," conducts a comparative analysis of the exegeses of the Christian John Philoponus (5th–6th century CE) and the Jewish Philo of Alexandria (1st century BCE—1st century CE) on what, according to the LXX, is considered the day "one" of creation and on the role of time. Both authors deal with the subject in works on the creation of the world (*De opificio mundi*), preserved in the same manuscript (*Vind. theol. gr.* 29). Among the points of contact is the fact that both authors regard the first ἀρχή of Gen 1:1 as timeless and 'day one' as that instant in which the measure of time is fixed. Philo, however, understands the concept of measure as a synonym for 'idea' and, in his view, the imperishable model, created by God, comes to life on 'day one.' For Philoponus, on the other hand, 'measure' indicates the number that expresses the nature of time and determines time as the product of the astronomical recurrence of 'day one.' In his *Commentary on Physics*, 'day one' is presented by Philoponus as that νῦν (i.e. the 'now') which gives rise to the beginning of time and which—unlike what Aristotle said about the 'now'—remains part of time as its beginning and as its unit of measurement. According to Philo, who is more influenced by the *Timaeus*, time begins to flow on the second day, with the formation of the heavens and the stars, when from the stasis of the intelligible world, created on 'day one,' we enter the sense-perceptible dimension. Both

5 See Niehoff (2024) for more details.

Philo and Philoponus, proponents of theologically oriented cosmologies, also propose a helical vision of time. This is made up of days which, once begun, constantly repeat themselves, and whose periodicity becomes a guarantee of the existence of God: the cosmic 'clockmaker.' A comparison of Philoponus' *De opificio* with that of Philo may be useful in considering Philo as a possible source for the Philoponian hexameron: an idea that has so far received little attention. Moreover, such a comparison may also reveal possible Aristotelian echoes in the Philonian conception of time, which are usually obscured by the predominant references to Plato and the Stoics.

Maren Niehoff, in her essay "The Conflagration of the World in Philo, Josephus and Rabbi Abbahu. Responses to a Circular Model of Time Advocated by the Stoics" studies three Jewish authors, who shed light on vivid debates about the Stoic notion of the conflagration in different cultural and historical contexts. Josephus, who declares himself a Pharisee and associates with the Stoic school, avoids the philosophical notion of a conflagration in first century Rome. He never mentions it, probably because it does not fit his views of the Biblical demiurge and Divine providence. Philo of Alexandria, as an ambassador to Gaius Caligula, addresses Roman readers with remarkable openness to Stoicism. His treatise *De Aeternitate Mundi* provides a hitherto overlooked window into lively first century debates. His report represents the missing link between Cicero and Seneca, providing crucial information on the shift from an attenuated to a radical interpretation of the conflagration. Rabbi Abbahu, even though a native Hebrew or Aramaic speaker and thus seemingly distanced from Greco-Roman debates, expressed the updated Stoic view of a conflagration initiated to improve the world. It is perhaps somewhat paradoxical that this third century rabbi was a keener adept of the Stoic idea than Philo of Alexandria, who was immersed all his life in Greco-Roman culture and expressed himself in Greek. Abbahu's views are preserved in *Genesis Rabbah* even though later rabbis and the redactor of the Midrash seem to have become rather more ambivalent about them and tried to subordinate them to Biblical verses, which actually convey contrary assumptions about the world. This reception is of special interest in view of Origen, who shared Abbahu's basic interpretation of the conflagration in the context of Christian theology.

Christoph Markschies addresses the topic of "The Concept of Time in Origen," pleading for an approach that seriously addresses the different literary genres in which Origen expressed himself. Biblical exegesis rather than abstract theology or philosophy was Origen's main venue of expression and therefore his different commentaries are investigated in the chronological order of their composition. Embedded in them is a grammar of ideas. Origen is found to make a strict distinction between the timelessness of God, on the one hand, and the duality of time and eternity on the other. This, for example, distinguishes him from Plato and many thinkers of the Platonic tradition.

Oz Tamir, in his paper "The Time and Context of the Consolation Prophecies: Preliminary Insights into Historical Interpretations in Late Antique Judaism," examines a rarely attested Jewish exegetical tradition preserved in Jerome's commentaries that reads the biblical consolation prophecies as referring to a concrete historical event: the return of Zerubbabel, Ezra, and Nehemiah to Jerusalem following the Edict of Cyrus. While rabbinic literature typically interprets these prophecies through a future messianic lens, Jerome records an alternative, historically grounded Jewish reading. Through a close analysis of Jerome's citations, the article shows that his record preserves a coherent and distinctive Jewish tradition, centered on the fulfillment of prophecy in the Persian period, which has not survived within the rabbinic corpus. The paper concludes by suggesting that the historical reading may reflect a broader response to contemporary realities in fourth-century Palestine, especially the collapse of renewed messianic hopes and the growing dominance of Christian power.

Bibliography

Kattan Gribetz, S. 2020. *Time and Difference in Rabbinic Judaism.* Princeton: Princeton University Press.

Kattan Gribetz, S., and L. Kaye. 2019. "The Temporal Turn in Ancient Judaism and Jewish Studies." *Biblical Research* 17: 332–395.

Kattan Gribetz, S., and L. Kaye, eds. 2023. *Time. A Multidisciplinary Introduction.* Berlin/Boston: De Gruyter.

Kaye, L. 2018. *Time in the Babylonian Talmud: Natural and Imagined Times in Jewish Law and Narrative.* Cambridge: Cambridge University Press.

Niehoff, M. R. 2024. *Judentum und Hellenismus*, Tübingen: Mohr Siebeck.

Stern, S. 2007. *Time and Process in Ancient Judaism.* Atlanta: Littman Library of Jewish Civilization.

Stern, S. 2019. *Calendars in Antiquity: Empires, States and Societies.* Oxford: Oxford University Press.

Stern, S., ed. 2021. *Calendars in the Making: The Origins of Calendars from the Roman Empire to the Later Middle Ages.* Leiden: Brill.

Glenn W. Most

Some Aspects of Time and Eternity in Philo's *De aeternitate mundi*

1 Preliminaries

The central research question I address in this essay is that of the relation between the concepts of time and eternity in Philo's essay *De aeternitate mundi*; along the way it will turn out to be pertinent to consider the larger issue of Philo's general faithfulness to Plato. But before entering into the body of my remarks in this article, I owe the reader two clarifications regarding its title.

First, I refer in it to the essay *De aeternitate mundi* as a work of Philo's. To be sure, since Bernays' seminal study (Bernays 1883) the authenticity of this treatise, which is transmitted among the works of Philo, has often been doubted.[1] My own view is that the arguments against Philo's authorship are not convincing and that they can be answered: above all, the objections do not take sufficient account of the fact that the treatise as it survives is incomplete, so that all we have is the first, dialectical presentation of views that Philo himself opposes, while the defense of his own views has been lost. Hence it misses the point to take exception to the fact that a number of the positions and formulations found in the surviving treatise stand in contradiction with views that Philo himself is known or likely to have held. But in any case, the question is probably destined to remain open—yet it is not essential to the argumentation of this paper, which is directed to the essay itself, not to its author: when I use the term "Philo" in this article, I mean by it "the author of the treatise *De aeternitate mundi*, whoever that might be," but in fact I think that that author is really likely to be Philo.

And second, the Latin title *De aeternitate mundi* might suggest to someone who has not read the essay that it is about the eternity of the world. But this title is a misnomer: the Greek title is Περὶ ἀφθαρσίας κόσμου, and ἀφθαρσία, deriving from φθείρω "to destroy or corrupt," denotes not "eternity" (whether we mean by this time that is unlimited with respect both to the past and to the future or something that is essentially different from time) but "indestructibility" or "incorruptibility" (in the sense of something that is unlimited in time only with respect to the future)—a concept which is not easy to express in a single common

1 Among older discussions of this issue, see especially Leisegang (1937) and Runia (1981); Niehoff (2018, 77–81) provides a balanced recent discussion.

 https://doi.org/10.1515/9783112225981-002

Latin word. But under this trivial problem of the title there lie two other, more difficult and interesting problems: what is eternity and what is its relation to time?

2 Time and Eternity in Plato's *Timaeus*

The foundational text on what eternity is and how it is related to time is Plato's *Timaeus*. At least since that text, and because of that text, time and eternity have been defined in terms of one another. The passage in question is so important, in general for the history of philosophy and in particular with regard to Philo,[2] that it is worth quoting in full despite its length (I set in boldface the terms in Plato's text that are central to my argument here):

> Ὡς δὲ κινηθὲν αὐτὸ καὶ ζῶν ἐνόησεν τῶν **ἀιδίων** θεῶν
> γεγονὸς ἄγαλμα ὁ γεννήσας πατήρ, ἠγάσθη τε καὶ εὐφρανθεὶς
> ἔτι δὴ μᾶλλον ὅμοιον πρὸς τὸ παράδειγμα ἐπενόησεν ἀπερ-
> **(37d)** γάσασθαι. καθάπερ οὖν αὐτὸ τυγχάνει ζῷον **ἀίδιον** ὄν, καὶ
> τόδε τὸ πᾶν οὕτως εἰς δύναμιν ἐπεχείρησε τοιοῦτον ἀποτελεῖν.
> ἡ μὲν οὖν τοῦ ζῴου φύσις ἐτύγχανεν οὖσα **αἰώνιος**, καὶ τοῦτο
> μὲν δὴ τῷ γεννητῷ παντελῶς προσάπτειν οὐκ ἦν δυνατόν·
> εἰκὼ δ' ἐπενόει κινητόν τινα **αἰῶνος** ποιῆσαι, καὶ διακοσμῶν
> ἅμα οὐρανὸν ποιεῖ μένοντος **αἰῶνος** ἐν ἑνὶ κατ' ἀριθμὸν
> ἰοῦσαν **αἰώνιον** εἰκόνα, τοῦτον ὃν δὴ χρόνον ὠνομάκαμεν.
> **(37e)** ἡμέρας γὰρ καὶ νύκτας καὶ μῆνας καὶ ἐνιαυτούς, οὐκ ὄντας
> πρὶν οὐρανὸν γενέσθαι, τότε ἅμα ἐκείνῳ συνισταμένῳ τὴν
> γένεσιν αὐτῶν μηχανᾶται· ταῦτα δὲ πάντα μέρη χρόνου, καὶ
> τό τ' ἦν τό τ' ἔσται χρόνου γεγονότα εἴδη, ἃ δὴ φέροντες
> λανθάνομεν ἐπὶ τὴν **ἀίδιον** οὐσίαν οὐκ ὀρθῶς. λέγομεν γὰρ
> δὴ ὡς ἦν ἔστιν τε καὶ ἔσται, τῇ δὲ τὸ ἔστιν μόνον κατὰ τὸν
> **(38a)** ἀληθῆ λόγον προσήκει, τὸ δὲ ἦν τό τ' ἔσται περὶ τὴν ἐν
> χρόνῳ γένεσιν ἰοῦσαν πρέπει λέγεσθαι—κινήσεις γάρ ἐστον,
> τὸ δὲ ἀεὶ κατὰ ταὐτὰ ἔχον ἀκινήτως οὔτε πρεσβύτερον οὔτε
> νεώτερον προσήκει γίγνεσθαι διὰ χρόνου οὐδὲ γενέσθαι ποτὲ
> οὐδὲ γεγονέναι νῦν οὐδ' εἰς αὖθις ἔσεσθαι, τὸ παράπαν τε
> οὐδὲν ὅσα γένεσις τοῖς ἐν αἰσθήσει φερομένοις προσῆψεν,
> ἀλλὰ χρόνου ταῦτα **αἰῶνα** μιμουμένου καὶ κατ' ἀριθμὸν
> κυκλουμένου γέγονεν εἴδη [...]
> Χρόνος δ' οὖν μετ' οὐρανοῦ γέγονεν, ἵνα ἅμα γεννηθέντες
> ἅμα καὶ λυθῶσιν, ἄν ποτε λύσις τις αὐτῶν γίγνηται, καὶ
> κατὰ τὸ παράδειγμα τῆς **διαιωνίας** φύσεως, ἵν' ὡς ὁμοιότατος
> **(38c)** αὐτῷ κατὰ δύναμιν ᾖ· τὸ μὲν γὰρ δὴ παράδειγμα πάντα

2 See for example Reydams-Schils (1999).

αἰῶνά ἐστιν ὄν, ὁ δ' αὖ διὰ τέλους τὸν ἅπαντα χρόνον
γεγονώς τε καὶ ὢν καὶ ἐσόμενος. ἐξ οὖν λόγου καὶ διανοίας
θεοῦ τοιαύτης πρὸς χρόνου γένεσιν, ἵνα γεννηθῇ χρόνος,
ἥλιος καὶ σελήνη καὶ πέντε ἄλλα ἄστρα, ἐπίκλην ἔχοντα
πλανητά, εἰς διορισμὸν καὶ φυλακὴν ἀριθμῶν χρόνου γέγονεν.

(Plato, *Tim.* 37c–38a, 38b–c)

And when the Father that engendered it perceived it in motion and alive, a thing of joy to the **eternal** gods, He too rejoiced; and being well-pleased He designed to make it resemble its Model (37d) still more closely. Accordingly, seeing that that Model is an **eternal** Living Creature, He set about making this Universe, so far as He could, of a like kind. But inasmuch as the nature of the Living Creature was **eternal**, this quality it was impossible to attach in its entirety to what is generated; wherefore He planned to make a movable image of **Eternity**, and, as He set in order the Heaven, of that **Eternity** which abides in unity He made an **eternal** image, moving according to number, even that which we have named Time. (37e) For simultaneously with the construction of the Heaven He contrived the production of days and nights and months and years, which existed not before the Heaven came into being. And these are all portions of Time; even as "Was" and "Shall be" are generated forms of Time, although we apply them wrongly, without noticing, to **Eternal** Being. For we say that it "is" or "was" or "will be," whereas, in truth of speech, "is" alone (38a) is the appropriate term; "was" and "will be," on the other hand, are terms properly applicable to the Becoming which proceeds in Time, since both of these are motions; but it belongs not to that which is ever changeless in its uniformity to become either older or younger through time, nor ever to have become so, nor to be so now, nor to be about to be so hereafter, nor in general to be subject to any of the conditions which Becoming has attached to the things which move in the world of Sense, these being generated forms of Time, which imitates **Eternity** and circles round according to number. [...]
Time, then, came into existence along with the Heaven, to the end that having been generated together they might also be dissolved together, if ever a dissolution of them should take place; and it was made after the pattern of the **Eternal** Nature, to the end that it might be as like thereto as possible; for whereas the pattern is existent through all **eternity**, (38c) the copy, on the other hand, is through all time, continually having existed, existing, and being about to exist. Wherefore, as a consequence of this reasoning and design on the part of God, with a view to the generation of Time, the sun and moon and five other stars, which bear the appellation of "planets," came into existence for the determining and preserving of the numbers of Time.
(trans. R. G. Bury, Loeb edition)

Plato is describing here the creation of the World Soul and of the universe. The whole account is structured in terms of the opposition between model and image: the World Soul is the model, prior and autonomous and essential, while the material universe that is created in its image is secondary, dependent, and contingent. To the former belongs eternity, which knows no past or future but exists forever as a timeless present; to the latter is assigned time as a moving image of eternity, something that was and is and will be. Time is divided into portions, which are generated forms devoid of eternal being; it is created and is capable of being destroyed together with the heavens, for the portions of time are determined numerically by the heavenly bodies.

For Plato, eternity is not the same as unlimited time. Time is created by the Demiurge and it can be destroyed if the heavens that measure it are destroyed. But even if it happened to be unlimited in both directions, towards the future as towards the past, it would still not be identical with eternity, which is something completely different from time. Time is derivative and secondary; eternity is primary. Time moves; eternity stands still. Time is a mere image; eternity is the model. Thus eternity stands outside of time.

3 Time in Philo's *De aeternitate mundi*

Philo provides a doxographical series of definitions of 'cosmos' or world in paragraph 4 of his treatise. The third one is attributed to the Stoics, and in its course Philo cites the Stoic definition of time:

> [...] κατὰ δὲ τρίτον,
> ὡς δοκεῖ τοῖς Στωικοῖς, διῆκον ἄχρι τῆς ἐκπυρώσεως, οὐσία τις
> ἢ διακεκοσμημένη ἢ ἀδιακόσμητος, οὗ τῆς κινήσεώς φασιν εἶναι τὸν
> χρόνον διάστημα. (Philo, *Aet.* 4)
>
> [...] the third sense, which is approved by the Stoics, is something existing continuously to and through the general conflagration, a substance either reduced or not reduced to order, and time, they say, is what measures its [i.e. the cosmos'] movement. (trans. F. H. Colson, Loeb edition)[3]

As far as time is concerned, this is not a particularly interesting definition; it is not focused on time and does not really tell us what time is in itself but speaks only about the question of its continuity through the cosmic conflagration and its relation to the cosmos. Elsewhere Philo discusses Stoic views about the relation between the cosmos and the conflagration, suggesting that for these philosophers the world is in one regard perishable and in another eternal (8–9), and he considers at some length the growth and progress of the world (58, 70, 133–138) and its decline and destruction (11, 125). But the subject of all of these passages is not the nature of time itself but rather the nature of the cosmos which may or may not undergo certain changes in the course of time.

---

3 My quotations from Philo's Greek text are taken throughout from Cohn and Reiter (1915) and are indicated by paragraph number, the translations from the Loeb edition of F. H. Colson.

But in one passage Philo does indeed discuss the nature of time, using it as evidence in an argument about the indestructibility of the world:

> **(52)** Μεγίστην μέντοι παρέχεται πίστιν εἰς ἀιδιότητα καὶ ὁ χρόνος. εἰ γὰρ ἀγένητος ὁ χρόνος, ἐξ ἀνάγκης καὶ ὁ κόσμος ἀγένητος. διὰ τί; ὅτι, ᾗ φησιν ὁ μέγας Πλάτων, ἡμέραι καὶ νύκτες μῆνές τε καὶ ἐνιαυτῶν περίοδοι χρόνον ἔδειξαν. ἀμήχανον δέ τι τούτων συστῆναι δίχα ἡλίου κινήσεως καὶ τῆς τοῦ παντὸς οὐρανοῦ περιφορᾶς· ὥστ' εὐθυβόλως ἀποδεδόσθαι πρὸς τῶν εἰωθότων τὰ πράγματα ὁρίζεσθαι χρόνον διάστημα τῆς τοῦ κόσμου κινήσεως. ἐπεὶ δὲ τοῦθ' ὑγιές ἐστι, γίνεται ὁ κόσμος ἰσῆλιξ τοῦ χρόνου καὶ αἴτιος. **(53)** πάντων δ' ἀτοπώτατον ὑπονοεῖν, ὅτι ἦν ποτε κόσμος, ἡνίκα οὐκ ἦν χρόνος· ἄναρχος γὰρ καὶ ἀτελεύτητος ἡ τούτου φύσις, ἐπεὶ καὶ αὐτὰ ταῦτα, τὸ ἦν, τὸ ποτέ, τὸ ἡνίκα, χρόνον συνεμφαίνει. τούτῳ δ' ἀκόλουθον τὸ μηδὲ χρόνον ὑποστῆναι καθ' ἑαυτόν, ἡνίκα κόσμος οὐκ ἦν· τὸ γὰρ μὴ ὑπάρχον οὐδὲ κινεῖται· διάστημα δὲ κοσμικῆς κινήσεως ἐδείχθη ὁ χρόνος ὤν. ἀνάγκη τοίνυν ἑκάτερον ἐξ ἀιδίου ὑφεστάναι γενέσεως ἀρχὴν μὴ λαβόντα· τὰ δ' ἀίδια φθορᾶς ἀνεπίδεκτα. **(54)** τάχα τις εὑρεσιλογῶν Στωικὸς ἐρεῖ, τὸν χρόνον ἀποδεδόσθαι διάστημα τῆς τοῦ κόσμου κινήσεως οὐχὶ τοῦ νυνὶ διακεκοσμημένου μόνον ἀλλὰ καὶ τοῦ κατὰ τὴν ἐκπύρωσιν ὑπονοουμένου. πρὸς ὃν λεκτέον· τὴν ἀκοσμίαν, ὦ γενναῖε, μετατιθεὶς τὰ ὀνόματα κόσμον καλεῖς· εἰ γὰρ οὗτος ὃν ὁρῶμεν ἐτύμως καὶ προσφυέστατα κόσμος κέκληται, διατεταγμένος καὶ διακεκοσμημένος ἀνεπανορθώτου τέχνης ἀκρότητι, τὴν πρὸς τὸ πῦρ αὐτοῦ μεταβολὴν δεόντως ἄν τις ἀκοσμίαν ὀνομάσαι. (Philo, *Aet.* 52–54)
>
> (52) Another very weighty proof to show its [i.e. the cosmos'] perpetuity is supplied by time. If time is uncreated, the world also necessarily must be uncreated. Why? Because as great Plato says time is indicated by days and nights and months and successions of years, and none of these can subsist without the movement of the sun and the revolution of the whole heaven. Thus people who are accustomed to define things have correctly explained time as what measures the movement of the universe, and since this is sound, the world is coeval with time and its original source. (53) But nothing can be so preposterous as to suppose that there was a time when the world was when time was not. Time by its nature has no beginning or end, since these very terms "was, time when, when," involve the idea of time. From this it follows that time also did not exist of itself when the world was not, for what does not subsist does not move either and time has been shown to be what measures the cosmic movement. It is necessary therefore that both should have subsisted from everlasting without having any beginning in which they came into being and things which are from everlasting are not susceptible of destruction. (54) Possibly some argumentative Stoic quibbler will say that time is explained as the measurement of the movement not only of the world of the present cosmic order but of that postulated at the conflagration. The answer to this is, "My friend. you are transferring your terms and give the sense of Cosmos to the negation of Cosmos, for if this world which we see is very fitly called Cosmos in the proper sense of the word being ordered and disposed with consummate craftsmanship, which admits of no improvement, one may rightly describe its change into fire as the negation of Cosmos."

This argument is based upon the postulate of the interdependence of time and the cosmos: without the world there would be no time, because the units of time are measured by the motions of the heavenly bodies (Philo refers to Plato here); but without time there would be no world, for time is nothing other than the measurement of the motion of the parts of the world. So time and the world must be coeval: both must exist or not exist simultaneously. Hence if time has no beginning or end, then the world too must have no beginning or end. But that which has no beginning must also have no end; and since time and the world have no beginning, they have no end either. Philo concludes by dismissing as an abuse of terms the suggestion by some Stoics that time can be applied not only to the movement of the parts of the present cosmos but also to that at the conflagration.

The argument Philo reports here can hardly be considered very satisfactory. To be sure, the claim that just as it is impossible to strip the cosmos from its motion, so too it is impossible to strip the cosmos from time, does seem to provide some support for the proposition that time, just like motion, is a feature of the cosmos; but the support is only specious, since the parallel invoked does not prove even that time and motion are substantially correlated with one another, let alone that the cosmos is imperishable, which is the basic point that the argument claims to be designed to prove. But what is graver are the facts (1) that the claim that the units of time are measured by the motions of the heavenly bodies does not prove that time is dependent upon the world, for to be measured by something is not to be dependent upon or identical with it; (2) that the claim that time measures the motions of the parts of the world does not prove that the world is dependent upon time, for to measure something is not to determine its being; and (3) that the claim that that which lacks a beginning must also be without an end is unsupported by evidence or argument and in itself is not particularly plausible. It might be considered remarkable that Philo's argumentation is so fallacious in this case—were it not that a certain degree of logical sloppiness is in fact quite typical of the polemical parts of the whole of the *De aeternitate mundi.*

4 Plato's *Timaeus* in *De aeternitate mundi*

Plato's influence upon this passage in *De aeternitate mundi* is manifest: as we have seen above, Philo refers here to Plato eulogistically and by name as ὁ μέγας Πλάτων, "great Plato" (52); he quotes Plato's phrase ἡμέρας γὰρ καὶ νύκτας καὶ μῆνας καὶ ἐνιαυτούς (*Timaeus* 37e, quoted above) with only the slightest of variations as ἡμέραι καὶ νύκτες μῆνές τε καὶ ἐνιαυτῶν περίοδοι (52); and his discussion of the meaning of the tense terms "was, time when, when" is obviously indebted to Plato (37e–38a).

But so too throughout this essay the author's dependence upon Plato's *Timaeus* is made deliberately and programmatically clear by numerous allusions and references. The very opening of the treatise (1) is clearly modeled upon a celebrated passage in *Timaeus* 27c); soon thereafter Philo provides a doxographical list of views on the question of whether or not the world is uncreated and imperishable (7), and the first element of this list quotes exactly the very same passage from *Parmenides* (D8.8 Laks/Most = B8.3 Diels/Kranz) which Plato also quotes verbatim in the same dialogue (53a); and Philo's treatise contains a number of direct attributed quotations from Plato's dialogue.[4] Beyond these many individual references, Philo at one point also provides a laudatory summary of the key concepts of the *Timaeus* as a whole:

> [...] διὰ παντὸς τοῦ συγγράμματος πατέρα μὲν καὶ ποιητὴν καὶ δημιουργὸν τὸν θεοπλάστην ἐκεῖνον καλεῖ, ἔργον δὲ καὶ ἔγγονον τουτονὶ τὸν κόσμον, ἀπ' ἀρχετύπου <καὶ> νοητοῦ παραδείγματος μίμημα αἰσθητόν, πάνθ' ὅσα ἐν ἐκείνῳ νοητὰ περιέχοντα αἰσθητὰ ἐν αὑτῷ, τελειοτάτου πρὸς νοῦν τελειότατον ἐκμαγεῖον πρὸς αἴσθησιν [...] (*Aet.* 15)

> [...] throughout the whole treatise he speaks of the great Framer of deities as the Father and Maker and Artificer and this world as His work and offspring, a sensible copy of the archetypal and intelligible model, embracing in itself as objects of sense all which that model contains as objects of intelligence, an impress for sense perception as absolutely perfect as that is for the mind.

But with regard to the conception of time, this ostentatious display of the presence of Plato's *Timaeus* in Philo's treatise creates a difficulty. For as we saw above, Plato in that dialogue sharply opposes time to eternity; but in *De aeternitate mundi* Philo nowhere asserts the same opposition. For Philo, time and the cosmos may well be unlimited but they do not belong to different dimensions; eternity as something which would be entirely different from temporality is simply missing in the treatise. Remarkably, Philo applies Plato's discussion of eternity at *Timaeus* 37c–38a, 38b–c, quoted above, not to the eternal as opposed to time, but instead to time as unlimited. So too, in Philo's summary of the *Timaeus* at *Aet.* 15, Philo substitutes "intelligible" for Plato's "eternal." Such striking transformations (or indeed deformations) in Philo's treatment of an author like Plato, whom he obviously knew very well and to whom he was strongly committed, raise interesting and potentially disturbing questions about the degree to which we can confidently rely upon his quotations and summaries of other sources as well.

---

4 E.g., for *Aet.* 13 cf. *Tim.* 41a, for *Aet.* 25–26 cf. *Tim.* 32c, for *Aet.* 38 cf. *Tim.* 33c.

Philo's motivation for these changes from his Platonic source is easy to explain: after all, the object of his treatise is not some non-temporal or supra-temporal dimension but rather this temporal cosmos here, and his question is whether it is unlimited in time or not. So it is not difficult to understand why he has apparently played down the supra-cosmical, metaphysical aspect of Plato's discussion. This could also have resulted not only from the immanent argument of the treatise but also from external factors as well, for example from Stoic influence upon Philo, as Maren Niehoff has suggested.[5]

5 ἀίδιος in *De aeternitate mundi*

These observations can be corroborated by consideration of the use of ἀίδιος and related words in Philo's treatise. As we saw above, this term is used by Plato in the *Timaeus* precisely in order to characterize eternity in its difference from the time of this world. But in Philo it is applied to what is or would be unlimited in the temporal dimension of this world itself. So for example in the following instances:

> Μεγίστην μέντοι παρέχεται πίστιν εἰς **ἀιδιότητα** καὶ ὁ χρόνος. (*Aet.* 52)
>
> Another very weighty proof to show its **perpetuity** is supplied by time.
>
> Τριτταὶ δὲ περὶ τοῦ ζητουμένου γεγόνασι δόξαι, τῶν μὲν **ἀίδιον** τὸν κόσμον φαμένων, ἀγένητόν τε καὶ ἀνώλεθρον [...] (*Aet.* 7)
>
> Three views have been put forward on the question before us. Some assert that the world is **eternal**, uncreated and imperishable.

For other examples of passages in which Philo uses ἀίδιος in this temporal sense, see e.g. *Aet.* 9, 69, 113, 116, 130, and 131. In fact, it is remarkable that there is not a single instance in this treatise in which the term occurs with reference to eternity as opposed to time.

Is this simply a matter of terminological looseness on the part of Philo? I do not think so. For one thing, this is a perfectly acceptable usage of the word in ancient Greek.[6] Alternatively, might Philo simply have misunderstood the Platonic treatise which according to all evidence he has studied so closely? This seems like an uncharitable interpretation. It would surely be more plausible to suppose that Philo knows the *Timaeus* inside out but does not feel obliged to follow exactly Plato's own terminology. Perhaps Philo is reading Plato through the lens of some

---

5 See now Niehoff (2024).

6 See LSJ, s.v. "ἀίδιος."

later Greek philosophers, maybe even including some of the very same Stoic thinkers whom he otherwise takes pleasure in attacking.[7]

6 God in *De aeternitate mundi*

In the preceding section we considered from a lexical perspective the question of the relation between time and eternity in Philo's treatise. But this issue also has an evident theological dimension. For eternity is a feature that is commonly attributed to god, especially but not only in the Judeo-Christian tradition; and in Plato's *Timaeus* the opposition between time and eternity is closely linked to the question of the relation between the creator god and the world that he has created. So it is pertinent to ask in the present context what Philo's view of god is in *De aeternitate mundi.*

There can be no doubt that in Philo's discussions of god in this treatise his emphasis is consistently upon god's moral qualities. God is asserted to be good (1) and the cause of good (39, 106); he is skilled and knowing (1, 41, 43); he is active (84). By contrast, the discussions of his ontological qualities are few and far between: once he is said to be intelligible and non-sensible (1), and twice to be imperishable (44, 46–47)—it seems rather odd that in a treatise devoted to the question of the imperishability of the world the imperishability of god should be mentioned so rarely. All in all, Philo seems to envision god as working within the cosmos, not as transcending it. This raises the interesting question of the relation between *De aeternitate mundi* and Philo's earlier treatise *Quod deus sit immutabilis* on the unchangeableness of god.

Indeed, in one celebrated and controversial passage Philo goes so far as to call the cosmos a "visible god:"

> Ἀριστοτέλης δὲ μήποτ' εὐσεβῶς καὶ ὁσίως ἐνιστά-
> μενος ἀγένητον καὶ ἄφθαρτον ἔφη τὸν κόσμον εἶναι, δεινὴν δὲ ἀθεότητα
> κατεγίνωσκε τῶν τἀναντία διεξιόντων, οἳ τῶν χειροκμήτων οὐδὲν ᾠήθησαν
> διαφέρειν τοσοῦτον **ὁρατὸν θεόν**, ἥλιον καὶ σελήνην καὶ τὸ ἄλλο τῶν
> πλανήτων καὶ ἀπλανῶν ὡς ἀληθῶς περιέχοντα πάνθειον (10)
>
> But Aristotle surely showed a pious and religious spirit when in opposition to this view he said that the world was uncreated and indestructible and denounced the shocking atheism of those who stated the contrary and held that there was no difference between handmade idols and that great **visible God** who embraces the sun and moon and the pantheon as it may be truly called of the fixed and wandering stars.

7 See again Niehoff (2024).

It was above all on the basis of this phrase that Bernays (1883, 45) claimed that this treatise could not have been written by Philo, on the grounds that no orthodox Jew could possibly have written these words about the visible world. My own view, as I indicated earlier, is that *De aeternitate mundi* may or may not be authentic (I incline to believe that Philo is its author), but that in any case this phrase cannot suffice to decide the issue definitively. For one thing, what counted as orthodoxy for a Jew in 19th century Germany and what counted in 1st century CE Alexandria are surely likely to have been two different things. For another, the passage quoted forms part of a report on the views of Aristotle, and it is at least as likely that the words in question, or at least the views that they represent, are to be attributed to Aristotle as they are to Philo. Furthermore, a close analogue to this phrase recurs later in the course of a polemic against the Stoics:

> κατ' ἀνάλογον οὖν εἰ φθείρεται ὁ οὐρανός, φθαρήσεται μὲν ἥλιος καὶ σελήνη, φθαρήσονται δ' οἱ λοιποὶ πλάνητες, φθαρήσονται δ' οἱ ἀπλανεῖς ἀστέρες, ὁ τοσοῦτος **αἰσθητῶν θεῶν** εὐδαίμων τὸ πάλαι νομισθεὶς στρατός. (14.46)
>
> On the same analogy, if heaven is destroyed, the sun and moon will be destroyed, so also the other planets, so also the fixed stars, that mighty host of **perceptible gods** whose blessedness from of old has been recognized. (translation modified)

And finally, we should not exclude the possibility that the language of this passage has been influenced by Plato *Timaeus* 41a, in which Plato emphasizes the fact of the visibility of the created gods (in the form of the heavenly bodies) and discusses the question of their indestructibility.[8]

7 Conclusion

In summary, we might well expect Philo's treatise to consider eternity as something that essentially transcends the physical world—after all, this is the understanding of eternity in Plato's *Timaeus*, a text to which Philo makes frequent and detailed reference and upon which in certain key aspects his own views clearly depend. But instead Philo's treatise locates time within the cosmos rather than assigning it a transcendent role. (What is more, the same applies to the conception of god in this treatise as well.) Eternity as a non-temporal dimension does not really enter at all into the purview of Philo's argumentation; eternity is included

8 My thanks to Sharon Weisser for this suggestion.

only as an unlimited form of the time that is characteristic of and immanent within this world.

Bibliography

Bernays, J. 1883. *Über die unter Philon's Werken stehende Schrift Über die Unzerstörbarkeit des Weltalls.* Berlin: Königliche Akademie der Wissenschaften.

Cohn, L., and S. Reiter, eds. 1915. *Philonis Alexandrini Opera quae Supersunt.* Vol. 6. Berlin: Georg Reimer.

Diels, H., and W. Kranz, eds. 1951–1952. *Die Fragmente der Vorsokratiker*, 6th ed., 3 vols. Berlin: Weidmann.

Laks, A., and G. W. Most, eds. 2016. *Early Greek Philosophy*, Vol. 5: Western Greek Thinkers, Part I. Cambridge, MA/London: Harvard University Press.

Leisegang, H. 1937. "Philons Schrift über die Ewigkeit der Welt." *Philologus* 92: 156–176.

Liddell, H. G., and R. Scott, and H. S. Jones. 1940. *A Greek–English Lexicon.* 9th ed. Oxford: Clarendon Press. Online at the Perseus Digital Library. https://www.perseus.tufts.edu/hopper/text?doc=Perseus%3Atext%3A1999.04.0057%3Aentry%3Da)i%2F%252Bdios. Accessed September 17, 2025.

Niehoff, M. R. 2018. *Philo of Alexandria. An Intellectual Biography.* New Haven/London: Yale University Press.

Niehoff, M. R. 2024. "Philons und Origenes' Interpretation von Platons Zeitvorstellung in *Timaeus* 38b–d. Ein Plädoyer für zeitgenössische Kontextualisierung." In *Platon und die Zeit*, edited by K. Corcilius and I. Männlein, 59–76. Tübingen: Mohr Siebeck.

Reydams-Schils, G. 1999. *Demiurge and Providence: Stoic and Platonist Readings of Plato's Timaeus.* Turnhout: Brepols.

Runia, D. T. 1981. "Philo's *De aeternitate mundi:* The Problem of Interpretation." *Vigiliae Christianae* 35: 105–151.

Ludovica De Luca

God's Clock and the First Hours of the World

Philo of Alexandria and John Philoponus on 'Day One' as the Measure of Creation

1 Introduction

Cicero, giving voice to the Stoic Balbus, rhetorically wondered how one could look at a sundial or a water-clock and not infer that it tells the time 'by virtue of art' and not by chance (*arte non casu*), as the fruit of an intelligent and divine reason.[1] Despite their different philosophical and theological orientations, Philo of Alexandria (1st century BCE – 1st century CE) and John Philoponus (5th–6th century CE) share a vision of the world which in their hexamerons appears as a precise 'clock,' set in motion by God. At the stroke of the world's first hour, on the border of a dimension that is still timeless, with 'day one,' the measure by which time is to be reckoned comes into existence: an intelligible measure for Philo, a sense-perceptible measure for Philoponus.

A necessary premise to make before we begin our analysis is to answer the question: why make a comparison between Philo of Alexandria and John Philo-

Note: This study was carried out within the postdoctoral fellowship conducted at the Hebrew University of Jerusalem and funded by the Einstein Center CHRONOI of the Freie Universität Berlin, as part of the project 'Creationism and the Calculation of Time in Late Antiquity: Between Alexandria and the Land of Israel,' directed by Prof. Maren R. Niehoff. My research on the relationship between John Philoponus and Philo of Alexandria began during a previous postdoctoral fellowship conducted at the University of L'Aquila as part of the PRIN 2017 project 'Racconti di creazione come luoghi di interculturalità dinamica,' directed by Prof. Angela Longo. I would like to thank the members of this research group, with whom I have been in constant dialogue since 2020, the participants of the seminar at the Mandel Scholion Research Center of the Hebrew University, where I presented a first version of this study in January 2023, and finally the participants of the CHRONOI workshop in July 2023, whose comments were decisive for me. I would also like to thank Prof. E. Vimercati for reading this paper and for all his comments and corrections, which were indescribably fruitful for me. I am very grateful to Profs. Longo and Niehoff, to whom my scientific and human debt is immeasurable.

1 Cic., *Nat. d.* 2.87. For an analysis of this Ciceronian paragraph in relation to the use that Philo made of it, taking up the Stoic tradition, see De Luca (2024a, 19–20).

 https://doi.org/10.1515/9783112225981-003

ponus? Among the various authors who have written commentaries or homilies on the Book of Genesis (Origen, Basil or John Chrysostom, for example), Philoponus and Philo, although relatively distant in time and, as we shall see, partially different in perspective, share more than other authors a common focus on the relationship of the creation of the world with the temporal dimension. This relationship is justified by both in connection with their philosophical exegesis of the 'day one' of creation. Our analysis will be conducted retrospectively, dealing first with Philoponus' point of view and only in the second instance with that of Philo, because this reversal of perspective, which may seem counterintuitive at a historical level, in our opinion has the merit of highlighting the main philosophical-exegetical *loci* for which Philoponus could be seen as dependent on Philo. On the other hand, Philo's works circulated widely in Christian circles and, either directly or mediated by other authors, may have reached Philoponus, who may have become aware of Philo's rational explanation of the *incipit* of creation at the boundary of atemporality and temporality and been inspired by it. What immediately aroused our interest is the fact that both of them wrote works, not only *de aeternitate mundi*, denying the eternity of the cosmos, but also *de opificio mundi*, in favor of a creationist perspective, presenting the cosmogony of the Book of Genesis in a philosophical manner.[2] Furthermore, the two *De opificio mundi* by Philo and Philoponus, handed down under the same Latin title, are preserved in the same manuscript, the *Vindobonensis theologicus graecus* 29, within which Philo's *De opificio*, preserved here up to paragraph 91, seems to play the role of a 'prototype' philosophical hexameron in relation to Philoponus' *De opificio.*[3] Indeed, the

2 In particular, the Greek titles of Philo's two works in favor of the creation of the cosmos and against an eternalist perspective are: Περὶ τῆς κατὰ Μωυσέα κοσμοποιίας (*On the Creation of the Cosmos according to Moses*) and Περὶ ἀφθαρσίας κόσμου (*On the Incorruptibility of the World*). Philoponus' *De aeternitate mundi* was titled by the editor H. Rabe as Κατὰ τῶν Πρόκλου περὶ ἀιδιότητος κόσμου ἐπιχειρημάτων (*Against Proclus' Proofs about the Eternity of the World*) because the manuscript in which the work is preserved is acephalous. While the Greek title of his hexameron is Τῶν εἰς τὴν Μωυσέως κοσμογονίαν ἐξηγητικῶν λόγοι ἑπτά (*The Seven Books of the Exegetical Interpretations to Moses' Cosmogony*). For the other works that Philoponus wrote in favour of creationism and against eternalism, see Giardina (2011, esp. 483–487).

3 On the ms *Vind. th. gr. 29* and the two *De opificio* it contains, see respectively Cohn/Wendland (1962[2], xxxvi) on the work of Philo, and Reichardt (1897, xiii–xvi) and Scholten (1997, 67) on that of Philoponus, which is extant only in this manuscript. In addition to the two *De opificio*, within *Vind. th. gr. 29* we find the *Eclogae propheticae* by Eusebius of Caesarea, the *Disputatio de tempore celebrandi Paschatis* by Philoponus and the *Catecheses* by Cyril of Jerusalem. As one of the two anonymous reviewers pointed out to me, there is no strict distinction in the manuscript between a text presenting a Jewish point of view and the other texts presenting Christian points of view. Moreover, as has been shown by Runia (1999, or. ed. 1993, 11–42), several Christian authors

presence of such Philonian paragraphs leads the reader of the manuscript to make a comparison between the two different interpretations of the same verses. Both Philo and Philoponus focus on the cosmogony expounded in Gen 1–3 and, as we shall see in relation to 'day one,' face the same exegetical questions, although they often arrive at different solutions.

Philo and Philoponus, both natives of Alexandria, were writing some five centuries apart, and there may be more points of distance between them than points of contact between them. But, as I hope to show in my study, there is a certain 'family resemblance' between their two *De opificio* that cannot have escaped the compiler of the manuscript.[4] To comment on the Genesis cosmogony, it is well known that Philo mainly turns to Platonism and Stoicism, while Philoponus turns to the works of Aristotle, whose works he had long commented on at the school of Ammonius in Alexandria.[5] He is best known as a commentator on Aristotle, but less so for his *De opificio mundi.* One is Jewish, the other is Christian, both are driven by the need to affirm the creation of the world: a thesis they defend against the detractors of creation, among whom both recognize Aristotle. In fact, Philoponus, who thinks and argues like an Aristotelian, finds himself almost reluctantly lashing out at the Stagirite whose thesis that the world has neither a beginning nor an end he, as a Christian, cannot accept.[6]

In order to defend a creationist position, both Philo and Philoponus make extensive use of Plato's *Timaeus*, which is their constant 'foothold' to show how the cosmos was the work of a God whom they both metaphorically call 'demiurge' and whose creation they describe using the lexicon of demiurgy.[7] Philo plays a pioneering role in interpreting the Book of Genesis through the *Timaeus*, and, by

---

appropriated Philo's works not by contextualising them within the Jewish tradition but by making their author a *Philo christianus.*

4 I have conducted a comparative analysis of the two *De opificio* by Philo and Philoponus in some of my earlier studies, dealing in particular with their different recourse to astronomy within their exegesis (De Luca 2022), their use of urban imagery and cosmopolitanism in relation to the cosmogony of Genesis (De Luca 2025a), and a comparison of their interpretations of Gen 1:5 and 1:26–27 (De Luca 2024b). The latter study also includes a first, preliminary analysis of Philop., *De op.* 2.23.

5 On Philo's recourse to Platonism and Stoicism within his *De opificio* and the synthesis he makes of them from a Jewish perspective, I will refer to De Luca (2021a), where the main bibliography on the subject is discussed, including at least Runia (1986) and Niehoff (2018, 96–102). For Philoponus' recourse to Aristotelianism in his *De opificio*, see instead Ottobrini (2023a) and Sorabji (2010), whose essays there focus on the Commentaries and on the *De aeternitate mundi contra Proclum* rather than on the *De opificio.*

6 Other points where Philoponus differs from Aristotle include his rejection of the existence of aether. In his view, the stars are not made of aether but of fire. See Wildberg (1988).

7 On demiurgical lexicon in Philo see De Luca (2023a); in Philoponus see De Luca (2023b).

the time of Philoponus this exegetical practice has become quite standard.[8] Philo and Philoponus, however, make different use of the Platonic dialogue and often refer to different pages for different purposes.[9] While Philo, as is well known, prefers those pages of the *Timaeus* where the demiurge is said to have created the sense-perceptible cosmos by looking at the noetic paradigm, Philoponus avoids any reference to the intelligible world. Indeed, in Philoponus' work the existence of an intelligible model to contemplate during creation is never envisaged, and the only noetic reality that exists is the hypercosmic dimension of the angels.[10] Therefore, for Philoponus, who thinks as a Christian, the cosmos has an end as well as a beginning, while for the Philo of *De opificio* the question is more ambiguous: in line with the *Timaeus*, he seems to accept the perspective of a generated and incorruptible cosmos, unless the God-Demiurge decides otherwise. The two authors have two different eschatological points of view and propose two different scenarios for that eternity which they both attack. While Philo attacks an eternity *a parte ante*, Philoponus doubles down on his criticism of eternalism by turning against those who, like Aristotle and Proclus, had argued for an eternity *a parte post*, thus foreseeing the existence of a cosmos not only without a beginning but also without an end.

My analysis will focus on how Philo and Philoponus understood 'day one' (ἡμέρα μία) of Gen 1:5b, which in the Septuagint version states:

---

8 Several Christian writers have referred to the *Timaeus* in order to interpret Scripture (see Köckert 2009). Justin comes to mind, who was often critical of the Platonic dialogue. See, for instance, 1 *Apol.* 59, in which Justin relates Gen. 1:1–3 with *Tim.* 29e–30b, 51a–b and 69b–c to affirm the divine creation of matter (but his position on whether matter existed already before creation or not is not entirely clear: cf. 1 *Apol.* 67.8). For how Christian authors addressed the question of pre-existent matter, see Wolfson (1966). Niehoff (2007) emphasizes the authority of the *Timaeus* and how a 'textual community' was formed in the pagan sphere around this dialogue: a textual community that Christian authors could not ignore and with which they were constantly confronted.

9 See, for example, how both refer with different purposes to *Tim.* 41b, which describes the formation of the young gods. In *Opif.* 75, Philo resorts to this Platonic page in order to justify the use of the plural in Gen 1:26 in relation to the creation of man ('let us make man') and in order to affirm the existence of divine collaborators, which justifies the predisposition of human beings not only to virtue but also to vice. Philoponus, on the other hand, in *De op.* 1.2 quotes this page of the *Timaeus* verbatim to show the precedence of Moses over Plato, while in *De op.* 5.9 he quotes it to affirm the incorruptibility of the heavens. For Philoponus' quotations from *Tim.* 41b, see De Luca (2023b, esp. 69–70, 75–76, and 90–91).

10 On angels in Philoponus' *De opificio*, see in particular *De op.* 1.8–12 and, more generally, Ottobrini (2023c).

καὶ ἐγένετο ἑσπέρα καὶ ἐγένετο πρωΐ, ἡμέρα μία.

And there came into being the evening and there came into being the morning, day one.

In this case, the Septuagint agrees with the Hebrew text, since in the latter we find the cardinal number *echad* and not the ordinal number *rishon.* In addition to the Septuagint, Philoponus also quotes the later translations of Aquila, Theodotion and Simmachus, which he sometimes prefers for their more literal rendering of the Hebrew text, in this case with the expression ἡμέρα μία. In particular, I will show how Philoponus may have wanted to refer implicitly to Philo when he mentions this Jewish tradition, which had already attempted to clarify the use of the cardinal number in the Septuagint.

There is no lack of similarities in the way the two authors interpret the ἡμέρα μία of Gen 1:5b. As we shall see, among the points of contact is the fact that both authors regard the first ἀρχή of Gen 1:1 as timeless and 'day one' as that instant in which the measure of time is fixed. Philo, however, understands the concept of measure as a synonym for 'idea' and, in his view, the imperishable model, created by God, comes to life on 'day one.' For Philoponus, on the other hand, 'measure' indicates the number that expresses the nature of time and determines χρόνος as the product of the astronomical recurrence of 'day one.' In his *Commentary on Physics*, we will see how 'day one' is presented by Philoponus as that νῦν (i.e. the 'now') which gives rise to the beginning of time and which – unlike what Aristotle said about the 'now' – remains part of time as its beginning and as its unit of measurement. According to Philo, who is more influenced by the *Timaeus*, time begins to flow on the second day, with the formation of the heavens and the stars, when from the stasis of the intelligible world, created on 'day one,' we enter the sense-perceptible dimension. Both Philo and Philoponus, proponents of theologically oriented cosmologies, also propose a helical vision of time. This is made up of days which, once begun, constantly repeat themselves, and whose periodicity becomes a guarantee of the existence of God: the cosmic 'clockmaker'. A comparison of Philoponus' *De opificio* with that of Philo may be useful in considering Philo as a possible source for the Philoponian hexameron: an idea that has so far received little attention. Moreover, such a comparison may also reveal possible Aristotelian echoes in the Philonian conception of time, which are usually obscured by the predominant references to Plato and the Stoics.[11]

---

11 On Philo's philosophical eclecticism, see Runia (2007). On the concept of time in Philo's *De opificio* in relation to his main philosophical sources, see De Luca (2025b), where the main bibliography on this topic is discussed. In particular, I will recall Niehoff (2026) in this volume for the relationship with Stoicism, Strauss (2022) for divine acronyms, Alesso (2004) for the rela-

2 At the Dawn of the World: ‘Day One’ in *De opificio mundi* 2.23 by John Philoponus

As our analysis will show, Philoponus opens up three temporal perspectives, one propaedeutic to the other. The first perspective is that inaugurated by ‘day one,’ which represents what brings time into existence. By widening the perspective, the second angle he proposes is that of the cosmological week, which turns out to be the product of the astronomical repetition of ‘day one’ seven times and which corresponds to the moment in which time is fixed and organized. It is precisely within the cosmological week that the heavens and the stars are created, to which, as we shall see, the flow of time is bound. On the other hand, according to an even broader view, the third perspective emphasizes the presence of a time of the cosmos, which consists in the continuous repetition of the cosmological week, which, by repeating itself, constitutes the month and the year. In such a view, ‘day one’ is that cause which, only in potency but not in act, is free from causation, since it actually remains within time and must be counted with it. Thus, ‘day one’ has a causal role in Philoponus because he sees it as a unit of measurement: as the μέτρον by which cosmic time is measured.

In *De op.* 2.23 (266.10–270.15 Scholten) (= 107.3–109.14 Reichardt), Philoponus states:

> Διὰ τί Ἑβραῖοι τὴν πρώτην τῆς ἑβδομάδος ἡμέραν μίαν καλοῦσι καὶ τὴν πρώτην τοῦ μηνὸς ὁμοίως, οὐκέτι δὲ ἐπὶ τῶν μηνῶν τὸν μῆνα τοῦ ἐνιαυτοῦ τὸν πρῶτον λέγουσιν ἕνα.
>
> ‘Καὶ ἐγένετο ἑσπέρα καὶ ἐγένετο πρωΐ, ἡμέρα μία’· ἐζήτησαν διὰ τί μὴ εἶπεν ἡμέρα πρώτη, μέλλων ἐπάγειν δευτέραν καὶ μέχρι τῆς ἕκτης· καλῶς δέ τινες ἐπετήρησαν, ὅτι ἰδίωμα τοῦτο τῆς Ἑβραΐδος ἐστὶ διαλέκτου τὴν πρώτην μίαν καλεῖν, ὡς ἐπὶ τὸ πλεῖστον, καὶ τὸν πρῶτον ἕνα. [...]
>
> Καλλίστης οὖν καὶ ἀληθοῦς οὔσης τῆς παρατηρήσεως περιττὸν οἶμαι τὸ ζητεῖν διὰ τί καὶ νῦν τὴν πρώτην μίαν ὠνόμασεν. εἰ μή τις ἄρα φιλοτιμώτερον προσθείη τοῦ ἔθους τὴν αἰτίαν, ἥντινα οἶμαι ταύτην· τὸ πρῶτον καὶ δεύτερον καὶ τρίτον ἐπὶ διαφόρων λέγεται πραγμάτων, ὡς ὅταν εἴπω· πρῶτος ἐν προφήταις ἐστὶ Μωϋσῆς, δεύτερος φέρε Σαμουὴλ καὶ ἑφεξῆς· ὁμοίως πρώτη ἐστὶν ἡ Γένεσις, δευτέρα ἡ Ἔξοδος. ἡμέραν δὲ καλοῦμεν τὴν ἀπὸ τοῦ ἀνατολικοῦ ὁρίζοντος εἰς τὸν αὐτὸν πάλιν τοῦ ἡλίου ἀποκατάστασιν, καὶ ἕτερόν τι ποιητικὸν ἡμέρας οὐκ ἔστι. πάλιν οὖν ἡ αὐτὴ περιδίνησις ἄλλην ἡμέραν ποιεῖ καὶ πάλιν ἄλλην. μία οὖν ἐστιν ἡμέρα ἡ τοῦ ἡλίου ἀπὸ τοῦ αὐτοῦ εἰς τὸ αὐτὸ ἀποκατάστασις, ἐφ’ ἑαυτὴν πολλάκις ἀνακυκλουμένη καὶ τὸ τῶν ἡμερῶν ποιοῦσα πλῆθος· ἐπεὶ οὖν τῶν ἡμερῶν οὐκ ἔστι διαφορά,

---

tionship with *Tim.* 37–38 and Neo-Pythagoreanism, Crepaldi (1985) for that with the biblical tradition, and Lauer (1958), which is a point of reference for all the above-mentioned studies and where some Aristotelian echoes are also highlighted.

ἀλλ' ὡς εἶπον μία ἡ πρώτη τὰς ἄλλας ἀνακυκλουμένη ποιεῖ, εἰκότως ἄρα μίαν αὐτὴν καὶ οὐ πρώτην ὠνόμασε Μωϋσῆς, ἅτε δὴ τῶν ἑξῆς ἁπασῶν οὖσαν γεννητικήν, ὡς καὶ ἡ μονὰς μία ἐστὶ τῇ ἰδίᾳ ἀνακυκλήσει τοὺς ἑξῆς ἀριθμοὺς γεννῶσα.

Εὔλογον οὖν τὸ αἴτιον μὴ ποιεῖν τοῖς αἰτιατοῖς σύστοιχον, ἀλλ' ἐκεῖνα μὲν ἐκ τῆς πρὸς αὐτὸ σχέσεως ἔχειν τὸ δεύτερα εἶναι καὶ τρίτα, τοῦτο δὲ ὡς ἐκείνων ἐξῃρημένον τῇ δυνάμει ἄσχετον πρὸς αὐτὰ τὴν προσηγορίαν ἔχειν, ἓν λεγόμενον καὶ μία καὶ εἷς, οὐχὶ δὲ πρῶτος καὶ πρώτη καὶ πρῶτον. ὥσπερ δὲ μία τῶν σαββάτων ἐστὶν ἡ πρώτη τῆς ἑβδομάδος, ἧς κατὰ ἀνακύκλησιν ἡ ἑβδομὰς συμπληροῦται, οὕτω καὶ μία τοῦ μηνὸς κατὰ τὴν αὐτὴν ἀναλογίαν, ἧς ἡ ἀνακύκλησις εἰς ἑαυτὴν τὸν μῆνα ποιεῖ. τοῦτο δὲ λέγω οὐκ ἀναιρῶν παντελῶς παρ' αὐτοῖς τὴν προσηγορίαν τοῦ πρώτου καὶ πρώτης, μόνον δὲ τὸ Ἑβραϊκὸν αἰτιολογῶν ἔθος, ὡς οὐκ ἄλογον ἔσχε τὴν ἐπιτήρησιν.

Τούτῳ δὲ κἀκεῖνό ἐστι σύμφωνον ἐπὶ τῆς τῶν μηνῶν ἀπαριθμήσεως. οὐδέποτε τὸν μῆνα τὸν πρῶτον ἕνα λέγουσιν ἀλλὰ μόνως πρῶτον. 'ὁ μὴν οὗτος ὑμῖν ἀρχὴ μηνῶν, πρῶτός ἐστιν ὑμῖν ἐν τοῖς μησὶ τοῦ ἐνιαυτοῦ' καὶ πάλιν 'ἐν τῷ πρώτῳ μηνὶ ἐν τῇ τεσσαρεσκαιδεκάτῃ ἡμέρᾳ τοῦ μηνός'· ἐπειδὴ καὶ ὁ τριακονθήμερος τοῦ μηνὸς χρόνος καὶ αὐτὸς κατὰ ἀνακύκλησιν τῆς μιᾶς ἡμέρας γίνεται, οὐ μὴν ὁ ἐνιαυτὸς κατὰ ἀνακύκλησιν ἑνὸς μηνός. τὸ γὰρ μέτρον ἐστὶν ἐλάχιστον, ὧν ἐστι μέτρον· ἐλαχίστη δὲ πασῶν ἡ τῆς ἀπλανοῦς κίνησις, ἧς ἡ ἀπὸ τοῦ αὐτοῦ εἰς τὸ αὐτὸ ἀποκατάστασις ἡμέρα ἐστίν· διὸ ταύτῃ καὶ ὁ πᾶς χρόνος μετρεῖται. τούτου δὲ καὶ ἐπὶ τῶν ποταμῶν ἢ γυναικῶν ἢ ἑτέρων τινῶν τοιούτων ἡ τοῦ ἔθους μετῆλθε κατάχρησις.

Why the Hebrews call the first day of the week Day One and the first of the month the same, but in the case of months they no longer call the first month of the year One.[12]

"And there was the evening and there was the morning, one day."[13] People have asked why he (Moses) did not say "the first day," since it was about to lead on to the second (and so on) up to the sixth. Some have well observed that this is an idiom of the Hebrew language, to call the first 'one,' for the most part, and the first thing 'one' (masculine). [...]

I think it extraordinary, since this observation is both excellent and true, that people enquire why even at present they call the first day 'One.' Lest anyone should add a more ambitious reason to the custom, I think it is something like this: "the first, second, third" are said in the case of different things, as when I say: the first among the prophets is Moses, the second Samuel, and so on. Likewise the first (book of the Bible) is Genesis, the second Exodus. We call 'day' the sun's recurring revolution from the eastern horizon back to the same (point) again, and there is nothing else constitutive of day. Again, the same revolution makes another day and another. 'One day' therefore is the sun's returning revolution from the same point to the same point, re-cycling many times upon itself and making the multitude of days. If, then, there is no difference of days, but, so to say, one, the first, in its re-revolving makes the others, then it makes sense that Moses called it 'one' and not 'first,' since it was the one that was generative of all the rest in succession, the way the monad is one and by its own repetition gives rise to the rest of the numbers in succession.

12 Note that each chapter of Philoponus' *De opificio* is introduced by a title, which summarizes the topic of the chapter.
13 Gen 1:5b LXX.

> It is right, then, not to make the cause co-ordinate with the effects, but they rather have their being second and third from their relation to it, and it as transcending them is unqualified in power vis-à-vis them and has as its proper term being called 'one' (in all three genders). Just as 'Day One of the seven' is the first day of the week, by the cyclic return of which the week is fulfilled, so too by the same analogy Day One of the month, the cyclic return of which back to itself makes the month. I say this not at all doing away with the terminology of 'first', only accounting for the cause in the Hebrew way of doing things, which makes the observation not without sense.
>
> The former agrees with the latter in the case of numbering the months. We do not call the first month 'One,' only first. 'This month shall be unto you the beginning of months it shall be the first month of the year to you.'[14] Although the thirty-day duration (span) of the month itself comes about through the recurrence of Day One, the year (does not do so) by the cyclic return of Month One. For a measure is smaller than the things it measures; and the movement of the fixed (sphere) is the smallest of all, whose cyclic return from the same point to the same point is a day: and so all of time is measured by this. So the analogical use of the term 'cycle' for this habitude is carried over to apply to rivers or women or other such things (that have cycles or cyclic phenomena).[15]

As can be deduced from *De op.* 2.23, we can speak of 'the first month' and not of 'month one,' because only 'day one,' but not the first month, is a unit of measurement of time. Philoponus refers to 'the Hebrew custom' (τὸ Ἑβραϊκὸν ἔθος), which should be contextualized not only with reference to a linguistic ἔθος justified on the basis of the Hebrew text of Gen 1:5b, but also with reference to an exegetical ἔθος, since Philoponus may have wished to refer to specific exegeses of Gen 1:5 developed in the Hebrew context either in his own day or earlier.[16] Such exegeses may have been seen as a unified voice, and it cannot be ruled out that Philoponus also intended to refer more generally to the Midrashic tradition. We do not know who the τινές (some) to whom he refers at the beginning of chapter 23 are, but they may be Jewish exegetes. An indication that Philoponus is referring to some exegetes can be found in his use of verbs such as ζητεῖν (to inquire), ἐπιτηρεῖν

14 The two Biblical quotations are from Exod 12:2 and Lev 23:5 (both LXX).
15 Transl. by Leslie S. B. MacCoull. The English translation of Philoponus' *De opificio* will soon be published by Brill, edited by U. M. Lang, to whom I am most grateful for sharing it with me.
16 See, however, Ottobrini (2019), who, in analyzing the concept of time in Philoponus' *De opificio*, also addresses the question of 'day one' and draws a comparison with Philo. Ottobrini shows how, unlike with Philo, who argues as a 'Greek,' this question is ignored in the Mishnaic, Talmudic, Targumic and Midrashic spheres because it does not pose any problems for Jewish exegetes. The term for the ordinal number 'first' (*rishon*) would have been coined in Hebrew only in the 3rd century (see p. 309, n. 51). In Ottobrini's view, it is therefore against this purely linguistic and grammatical background that Philoponus' reference to the Ἑβραϊκὸν ἔθος should be placed. In my view, however, a broadening of the perspective to include exegetical, conceptual and philosophical references should not be ruled out.

(to observe), and nouns like παρατήρησις and ἐπιτήρησις (observation): these are terms that refer to well-structured research and observation; to philosophical enquiry and empirical observation. On the other hand, from Philo to Flavius Josephus, who shows himself to be familiar with this exegetical issue, to the Midrash *Bereshit Rabbah*, it was common in Jewish circles to ponder why Moses spoke of day "one" in Gen 1:5 and did not use the ordinal number as in all other cases.[17]

Philoponus shows his appreciation of such an exegetical 'custom,' which he describes with the adverb καλῶς and as producing a καλλίστη and ἀληθής (the most beautiful and true) observation. This habit is also defined as οὐκ ἄλογον (not irrational). Nevertheless, he recognizes a limit to such Ἑβραϊκὸν ἔθος, and, for this reason, not without a polemical vein and some presumption, he juxtaposes his own point of view with it. Rhetorically, there is a τις— i. e. Philoponus himself—as opposed to the τινές quoted immediately before. In his view, the limitation of Jewish exegesis is that it has not identified the reason why 'day one' is mentioned in Scripture. Indeed, Philoponus shifts the question from a purely linguistic level to a causal one and, therefore, to the level of philosophical exegesis. 'Day one' is something unrelated (ἄσχετον)—totally isolated—with respect to what is caused (i. e. to the other days). Its isolation is emphasized by the excellence that characterizes 'day one', which is described with the participle ἐξῃρημένον in allusion to its 'transcending' the other days. But it is not an absolute 'solitude,' since 'day one' has a relationship (a σχέσις) with the other days, otherwise they could not be called the 'second,' 'third,' 'fourth' day etc. According to Philoponus, 'day one' represents the cause of the other days, which, on the other hand, are the αἰτιατά (i. e. what is produced by a cause) and so he describes 'day one' in terms of a transcendence which emphasizes its excellence but not its effective isolation.[18] With regard to the Ἑβραϊκὸν ἔθος, he speaks of αἰτιολογεῖν ('to inquire into causes'), using a verb that is proper to scientific research and is also attested in Ptolemy.[19] Such Jewish exegesis, to which Philoponus may be indirectly referring, did not go so far as his own in supporting interpretations of Scripture

17 Cf. Ios. *A.J.* 1.29, where Josephus promises to speak in another work (but there is no trace of this) about why Moses used the expression 'day one' in Gen 1:5. Cf. *Bereshit Rabbah* 3.9, which emphasizes the exceptionality of day one, which differs from the second, third etc. day because it is the day of creation. See De Luca (2024b). As Ottobrini (2019) suggests, it is possible that in *Bereshit Rabbah* this issue acquires importance mainly because of the influence of the Greek tradition on this writing. As Ottobrini shows, this is an issue that begins with the LXX and the Greek language, for in Hebrew the cardinal *echad* was actually commonly used as an ordinal.
18 The opposite is true of the month within the year, which is not called 'month one' since both month and year occur according to the recurrence of 'day one' and not of a 'month one.'
19 Ptol. *Harm.* 1.6.1; 2.10.7. This verb is widely used by the Neo-Platonists, from Plotinus to Porphyry, from Proclus to Simplicius.

with science and scientific observation, in a style characteristic of his hexameron, in which Christian tradition and natural philosophy meet.

In *De op.* 2.23, Philoponus sees the reason why Moses spoke of day 'one' and not of the 'first' in the poietic (ποιητικόν) and generative (γεννητικόν) character of the ἡμέρα μία. The cardinal number distinguishes this day from all the others, because they are derived from it. Indeed, all the days of the week are formed by the repetition of the cycle of sunset and sunrise that occurs for the first time on 'day one': as if what is repeated were the same ἡμέρα μία, understood from an astronomical point of view.[20] In order to show the relationship between 'day one' and the other days, Philoponus introduces the comparison of 'day one' with the monad (ἡ μονάς), which is one and 'which generates' (γεννῶσα) the numbers in succession with its own recurrence. This is an implicit reference to a tradition that can be traced back to the Neoplatonic one—but previously of Neopythagorean and Pythagorean origin—which we shall see is already present in Philo. Unlike the latter, however, Philoponus's use of arithmology to interpret the Book of Genesis is rare, although some arithmological digressions concerning the days of creation are not entirely absent from his *De opificio*.[21] No explicit dependence of Philoponus on Philo from the arithmological point of view has been attested so far, but in our opinion it cannot be ruled out that Philoponus was aware of the pioneering application of arithmology to the exegesis on the Book of Genesis conducted centuries earlier by Philo. Furthermore, we should bear in mind that Philoponus had also written a commentary on the *Introduction to Arithmetic* by Nicomachus of Gerasa, a Neopythagorean philosopher of the Imperial age.[22]

At the end of Philoponus' *De opificio*, in *De op.* 7.13 and 7.14, there are two examples of the application of arithmology to the Book of Genesis:

Philop., *De op.* 7.13 (632.2–23 Scholten) (= 304.7–305.8 Reichardt)

Διὰ τί ἐν ἓξ ἡμέραις τὸν κόσμον συνεπλήρωσεν ὁ θεός.

Διὰ τί ἐν ἓξ ἡμέραις τὸν κόσμον ἐποίησεν ὁ θεός, οὐ δίκαιον μὲν ἴσως περιεργάζεσθαι· —τί γάρ, εἰ καὶ ἐν πλείοσιν ἢ καὶ ἐλάττοσιν ἐγεγόνει, λέγειν εἴχομενἢ καὶ ἀθρόον καὶ ἅμα πᾶς; —

20 On the importance for Philoponus of a visual calculation of time, such as that provided by a sundial, see MacCoull (1989). On the other hand, we should not forget that Philoponus had dedicated a work to the use of the astrolabe (*De usu astrolabii eiusque constructione*), with which it was possible to calculate the position of the sun or the heavenly bodies. We are not surprised by MacCoull's hypothesis that in *De opificio* he used not only theoretical science but also technology to support his philosophical commentary on *Genesis*.

21 One is reminded of the extensive use of arithmology in Philo's *De opificio*, where the excursus on the number 7 alone occupies a large part of the work (*Opif.* 89–128). See Runia (2000).

22 See Giardina (1999, 36–94).

ἤρκει δὲ καὶ ἡ μέχρι νῦν τοῦ παντὸς διάταξις καὶ ἡ ὑπὸ πάντων ἀνθρώπων ἑβδοματικὴ τῶν ἡμερῶν ἀπαρίθμησις ἀπόδειξιν ἱκανὴν ἔχουσα τοῦ ἐν τοσαύταις ἡμέραις τὸν πάντα κόσμον δημιουργῆσαι τὸν θεόν, τῆς ἑβδόμης ὥσπερ ἑορτῆς ἐπὶ συμπληρώσει τῆς γενέσεως τοῦ παντὸς ὑπαρχούσης· τινὲς δὲ καὶ ἀριθμητικήν τινα τοῦ 'ἕξ' ἀριθμοῦ θεωρίαν οὐκ ἄκομψον παρειλήφασι ταύτην· τέλειος τῶν ἀριθμῶν ἐστιν ὁ ἕξ· τέλειον γὰρ ἀριθμόν φασι τὸν ἐξισάζοντα τοῖς ἰδίοις ἑαυτοῦ μέρεσι. πρῶτος δὲ τῶν τελείων ἐστὶν ὁ ἓξ καὶ μόνος τῶν ἐντὸς τῆς δεκάδος τέλειος ἐκ τοῦ ἡμίσεος τοῦ ἰδίου, τῶν τριῶν, καὶ τοῦ τρίτου, τῶν δύο, καὶ τοῦ ἕκτου, τοῦ ἑνός, συγκείμενος· τρία γὰρ καὶ δύο καὶ ἓν τὸν ἓξ συνάγουσιν. ἔπρεπεν οὖν τὸν τελειότατον καὶ ἐν ἑαυτῷ πάντα συνειληφότα κόσμον εἰς τὸ εἶναι παραγόμενον ὑπὸ θεοῦ, εἰ μὴ ἀθρόον ὁμοῦ τοῦτον ἐθέλοι παράγειν διὰ λόγους ἀγνοουμένους ἡμῖν, ἐν τοσούτῳ ἡμερῶν ἀριθμῷ, τῷ πρώτῳ τελείῳ, παραγαγεῖν [τὸν τέλειον κόσμον καὶ πρώτως νῦν ὑφιστάμενον, ἐξ ὧν καὶ ὁ χρόνος ἀνακυκλεῖται]. [...]

Why God finished the world in six days.

Why God made the world in six days, first of all it is perhaps not right to over-belabor the question—for what, if it had happened in more or fewer days, would we have to say, or (if it had happened) instantly and all at once? —but the disposition of the universe up to now and the weekly numbering of the days by all people are enough to provide a sufficient demonstration of the fact that God created the entire universe in so many days, with the seventh day being as a festival for the completion of the coming into being of the universe; but some have added some sort of arithmetical theory of the number six, which is not too unlearned, as follows: of the numbers, six is perfect: for they say a perfect number is one equal to the sum of its factors. Six is the first of the perfect numbers, and the only perfect one among the first ten, since it is made up of its half, three, plus its third, two, plus its sixth, one: for 3+2 +1=6. So it was fitting that the most perfect cosmos that also contains everything within itself was brought into being by God, even if for reasons unknown to us he did not want to accomplish that instantaneously, in such a number of days, the first perfect number; [i. e. to bring it about that the perfect universe also first came to subsist, from which also time cycles on.] [...].[23]

Philop., *De op.* 7.14 (636.1–23 Scholten) (= 306.5–307.3 Reichardt)

Διὰ τί ἐν τῇ ἑβδόμῃ ἡμέρᾳ κατέπαυσεν ὁ θεὸς ἀπὸ πάντων τῶν ἔργων αὐτοῦ.

Οὐκ ἄλογον ἴσως καὶ περὶ τοῦ ἀριθμοῦ τούτου βραχέα διελθεῖν, τίνος χάριν τῇ καταπαύσει τῶν ἔργων ἀποδέδοται τοῦ θεοῦ. φημὶ τοίνυν ὡς τῶν μέχρι τῆς δεκάδος ἀριθμῶν οἱ μὲν γεννῶσι τούτων τινὰς ἢ ἐφ' ἑαυτοὺς πολλαπλασιαζόμενοι ἢ ἐφ' ἑτέρους· ἐφ' ἑαυτοὺς μέν· ὁ μὲν δύο τὸν τέσσαρα—δὶς γὰρ τὰ δύο τέσσαρα—ὁ δὲ τρία τὸν ἐννέα—τρὶς γὰρ τὰ τρία ἐννέα—ἐφ' ἑτέρους δέ· ὁ μὲν δύο ἐπὶ τὸν τρία ποιεῖ τὸν ἕξ, ἐπὶ δὲ τὸν τέσσαρα τὸν ὀκτώ, ἐπὶ δὲ τὸν πέντε τὸν δέκα· οἱ δὲ γεννῶνται μὲν ἐξ ἑτέρων, ὡς οἱ εἰρημένοι, γεννῶσι δὲ ὅλως αὐτοὶ οὐδένα· μόνος δὲ ὁ ἑπτὰ οὔτε ἐξ ἑτέρων κατὰ πολυπλασιασμὸν ἐγεννήθη οὔτε ἕτερον ἐγέννησε· καὶ ἔστι κατὰ τοῦτο μονήρης καὶ διὰ τοῦτο μόνος τῶν ἀριθμῶν ἠρεμίας ἐστὶ σύμβολον. εὐλόγως οὖν ἀφώρισται μετὰ τὰς ἓξ τῶν ἔργων ἡμέρας τῇ καταπαύσει τῆς τοῦ κόσμου γενέσεως. τοῦτο μὲν οὖν κομψεία τίς ἐστιν ἀριθμητική.

23 Transl. by Leslie S. B. MacCoull.

> Εἰ δὲ καὶ δύναμιν ἔχει τινὰ φυσικὴν οὗτος ὁ ἀριθμὸς ἐν τοῖς πράγμασι, λέγειν οὐκ ἔχω· ἐκεῖνό γε μὴν συμπεφώνηται πᾶσιν ἀνθρώποις ἑπτὰ μόνας εἶναι τὰς ἡμέρας, αἵτινες εἰς ἑαυτὰς ἀνακυκλούμεναι τὸν ὅλον ποιοῦσι χρόνον. τίνα οὖν τούτου λόγον ἐστὶν εἰπεῖν ἕτερον, ἢ μόνον ὃν εἴρηκε Μωϋσῆς; [...]
>
> *Why on the seventh day God rested from all his works.*
>
> It is equally not irrational to make a short digression about this number (sc. seven) as well, on account of what is it attributed to God's rest from his works. Well now, I am talking about how, of the numbers up to ten, some give rise to some of these by being multiplied either by themselves or by other numbers: by themselves, two produces four (twice two is four), three produces nine (thrice three is nine); by others, two times three makes six, (two) times four makes eight, (two) times five makes ten; while some are made out of others, like the aforementioned, though they themselves do not produce any at all. But only seven is not made out of others via multiplication, nor does it produce another (number): and thusly it is alone, and thereby it only of the numbers is the symbol of rest. So it is well assigned, after the six days of the works, to resting from the creation of the cosmos. Indeed this is a kind of arithmetical fine point.
>
> But if this number possesses also in fact some kind of physical power I am not able to say: but all people agree that there are just seven days, which as they cycle back upon themselves produce all of time. Indeed what other account of this could there be to say if not the one Moses spoke? [...][24]

These two chapters recall leitmotifs of Pythagorean origin that, as we will see, are already accepted earlier by Philo. Philoponus uses two arithmetical theories concerning the number 6, which is considered to be the most perfect (τελειότατος) number, and the number 7 which is a symbol of the ἠρεμία (rest) that characterizes the seventh day of creation. In his view, these two theories are expressions of remarkable refinement (κομψεία). The first theory, expressed in *De op.* 7.13, shows that six is the most perfect number, because it is the sum of its own parts (2+3+1). Therefore, six is a symbol of a complete creation, which did not happen simultaneously, but according to the gradualness of the days. The second theory of *De op.* 7.14, on the other hand, shows the isolation of the number 7 as the only number within the series of 10 that was not generated from other numbers and did not in turn generate other numbers. For this reason, seven is considered the symbol of that rest that characterizes the seventh day of creation, called—as Philo also called it—ἑορτή (feast) for the completion of divine creation.[25] It is precisely with-

24 Transl. by Leslie S. B. MacCoull.

25 In *Opif.* 89 Philo states: Ἐπεὶ δ' ὁ σύμπας κόσμος ἐτελειώθη κατὰ τὴν ἑξάδος ἀριθμοῦ τελείου φύσιν, τὴν ἐπιοῦσαν ἡμέραν ἑβδόμην ἐσέμνυνεν ὁ πατὴρ ἐπαινέσας καὶ ἁγίαν προσειπών· ἑορτὴ γὰρ οὐ μιᾶς πόλεως ἢ χώρας ἐστὶν ἀλλὰ τοῦ παντός, ἣν κυρίως ἄξιον καὶ μόνην πάνδημον ὀνομάζειν καὶ τοῦ κόσμου γενέθλιον. When the entire cosmos had been completed in accordance

in this excursus on the number 7 that Philoponus concludes his *De opificio* and in which the generative character of the cosmological week itself is reaffirmed, since the repetition of the seven days gives rise to the calendarisation of the cosmos and the whole of time is produced.

Returning to *De op.* 2.23, Philoponus concludes his analysis with an Aristotelian coda recalling *De caelo*, where Aristotle states that the movement of the heavens is the unit of measurement for all other movements because it is continuous, uniform and eternal.[26] Similarly, Philoponus considers 'day one' as a unit of measurement because, in cyclically repeating itself, it ends up measuring all time. Therefore, in his view, such a procedure, which identifies 'day one' as a form of circular measurement, is also applicable to all those other cyclically repeating situations, such as the flow of a river or menstruation in women. To this end, Philoponus evokes the rhetorical figure of catachresis, by which a word or phrase is extended beyond the limits of its meaning, as happens, for instance, when we refer to the 'legs' of a table or to the 'neck' of a bottle.[27] The catachresis or extension of the Ἑβραϊκὸν ἔθος to the case of rivers and women seems to evoke a helical view of world time. It is a form of time which has a beginning in 'day one' and seems to consist of an infinitely repeated 'day one' until the end of the world. 'Day one' represents the first loop in the spiral of time, in which the other loops are nothing more than a recurrence of 'day one' and, therefore, of the second, third, etc. days, that depend on it.

3 'Day One' as a νῦν: What Happens After the ἀρχή in Philoponus' View

In accordance with Aristotle's well-known definition in *Phys.* 4.11, 219b1–2, for which 'time is a number of movement with respect to the before and after'

---

with the nature of the perfect number six, the Father proceeded to honour the seventh day which followed by praising it and calling it holy. For this day is a festival, not of a single city or country, but of the universe, the only day which rightly deserves to be called universal and the birthday of the cosmos. Transl. by Runia (2001, 70).

26 *Cael.* 2.4, 287a23–26.

27 Apart from the everyday use of catachresis, of which our common language is rich, this reference confirms the fact that Philoponus was known as Ἰωάννης ὁ γραμματικός (John the Grammarian), since he was also the author of grammar treatises such as the treatise on accents, known with the title *De vocabulis quae diversum significatum exhibent secundum differentiam accentus.* For a similar, metaphorical use of catachresis, see Philop. *In DA* (129.28–32 Hayduck) on *DA* 1.3, 407a11.

(τοῦτο γάρ ἐστιν ὁ χρόνος, ἀριθμὸς κινήσεως κατὰ τὸ πρότερον καὶ ὕστερον), Philoponus, when he speaks of 'day one' in terms of a 'monad;' presents that day precisely as the expression of a number.[28] Therefore, he does not seem to take up the criticisms of those who—for example, Plotinus—had railed against the Aristotelian definition of time, emphasizing the incompatibility of number and time, since one is a discrete quantity and the other is continuous.[29] In particular, Philoponus seems to apply his knowledge of the *Physics*, to which he had devoted a commentary before writing the *De opificio*, by considering the ἡμέρα μία as if it were the νῦν ('now'), placed at the dawn of creation, as a first fragment of time, which, however,—unlike in Aristotle—remains part of time for Philoponus. In the *Commentary on the Physics*, there is no trace either of 'day one' or, more generally, of explicit references to the biblical tradition, although it cannot be ruled out that Philoponus was a spokesperson for a Christian creationist position already in this work, which predates *De opificio.*[30] According to Philoponus, it is the νῦν that is considered to be τὸ γεννητικὸν τοῦ χρόνου ('generative of time,' *In Phys.* 17 (725.32 and 729.13–14 Vitelli), and not the ἡμέρα μία, as it appears in *De op.* 2.23. In particular, commenting on Arist., *Phys.* 4.11, 219b10–11, he states:

Philop., *in Phys.* 17 (724.30–725.13 Vitelli)

Ὁ δὲ ἅμα πᾶς χρόνος ὁ αὐτός· τὸ γὰρ νῦν τὸ αὐτὸ ὅ ποτε ἦν, τὸ δὲ εἶναι αὐτῷ ἕτερον.

Ἅμα πᾶς ὁ πανταχοῦ λαμβανόμενος χρόνος, οὗτος εἷς ἐστι καὶ ὁ αὐτός· πάσης γὰρ κινήσεως τὸ πρότερον μετρεῖ καὶ τὸ ὕστερον (οὐ μέντοι ὡς ἀλλοιώσεως ἢ ὡς αὐξήσεως), τὸ δὲ πρότε-

28 On time as number in Aristotle, see Annas (1975), according to whom time and number are interchangeable concepts in Aristotle if number is understood as 'measure.' According to Sorabji (2006, 84–97), on the other hand, number and measure are not interchangeable concepts and, in his view, Aristotle spoke of time as 'number' in the sense of the accounting aspect of change. See Cavagnaro (2002, 100–107) and Coope (2005, 85–109).

29 This is why Plotinus asked whether it would not be more appropriate to speak of time as a measure rather than as a number (Plot., *Enn.* 3.7.9). On this Plotinian criticism, see Trotta (1981). Cavagnaro (2002, 100) points out that a similar criticism had already been made before Plotinus by Strato. See more generally Sorabji (2006, 84–97) for a critique of the Aristotelian correlation of number and time. The latter two are considered by Aristotle in the same category as quantity and they, despite their differences, share certain characteristics such as not having parts with a reciprocal position (*Cat.* 6, 5a23–37).

30 I have examined this hypothesis in De Luca (2023b, 87–90), where I discuss his use of the demiurgical lexicon. Consider, for example, Philop., *In Phys.* 16.54 (31–55.8 Vitelli), where, defining the efficient cause as 'demiurgic,' he describes it as a creator who produces *ex nihilo* not only forms but also matter. Furthermore, on this occasion, Philoponus affirms the need to envisage an origin of the cosmos, which in his view is not eternal. See Giardina (2015) for the Philoponian position on divine providence in this commentary. We should bear in mind that the *Commentary on the Physics* was composed in 517 CE and the *De opificio* in 553–560 CE (Sorabji 2010, 82).

ρον καὶ ὕστερον τῶν ἅμα γινομένων κινήσεων τὸ αὐτό, ὥστε καὶ ὁ χρόνος ὁ αὐτός. τοῦτο μέντοιοὐκέτι καὶ ἐπὶ τῆς κινήσεως ἁρμόζει λέγειν· οὐ γὰρ ἅμα αἱ κινήσεις αἱ αὐταί, ἀλλ' αἱ μὲν οὐ μόνον τῷ ἀριθμῷ ἕτεραι ἀλλὰ καὶ τῷ εἴδει, αἱ δὲ εἰ καὶ τῷ εἴδει αἱ αὐταί, οἷον αἱ πλείους φοραί, ἀλλ' οὖν γε τῷ ἀριθμῷ οὐχ αἱ αὐταί. ὁ μέντοι χρόνος εἷς καὶ ὁ αὐτὸς ὁ πανταχοῦ τῷ ἀριθμῷ· ὥστε καὶ ταύτῃ δῆλον ὅτι οὐ κίνησις ὁ χρόνος, ἀλλ' ἀριθμὸς κινήσεως. ὅτι δὲ εἷς καὶ ὁ αὐτὸς χρόνος ὁ πανταχοῦ, κατασκευάζει ἐκ τοῦ νῦν. τὸ γὰρ νῦν, φησί, κατὰ τὴν ἑαυτοῦ φύσιν ἕν ἐστι πανταχοῦ, τῷ μέντοι λόγῳ διαφέρει (ἄλλως γὰρ λαμβάνεται ὡς πρότερον λαμβανόμενον, καὶ ἄλλως ὡς ὕστερον, ὡς μέντοι πρότερον ἕν ἐστι καὶ τὸ αὐτὸ πανταχοῦ, ὁμοίως δὲ καὶ ὡς ὕστερον), εἰ τοίνυν τὸ νῦν ἐστι τὸ γεννητικὸν τοῦ χρόνου, τοῦτο δὲ ἕν ἐστι καὶ τὸ αὐτὸ πανταχοῦ, δῆλον ὅτι καὶ ὁ χρόνος ἅμα πανταχοῦ εἷς ἂν εἴη καὶ τῇ φύσει καὶ τῷ ἀριθμῷ.

All time that is together is the same; for the now is the same whatever it was, although its being is different (Arist., *Phys.* 4.11, 219b10–11).

All time that is together, taken anywhere <in the world>, is one and the same. For it measures the prior and the posterior of every movement (not of alteration as such or of growth as such, however); but the prior and posterior of movements that occur together are the same, so that the time too is the same. However, it is not correct to go on and say this of movement too, for movements that are together are not the same; rather, some differ not only in number but also in form, and others, although the same in form, e.g. a plurality of locomotions, are still not the same in number. Yet time everywhere is one and the same in number. So from this consideration too it is clear that time is not movement but number of movement. That time everywhere is one and the same he proves on the basis of the now. The now, he says, in respect of its own nature is everywhere one, but it differs in description. For it is taken in one way when taken as prior, and in another way when <taken> as posterior; yet as prior it is one and the same everywhere, and so also as posterior. So if the now is what generates time, and <the now> is one and the same everywhere, clearly time too that is together will be everywhere one, both in nature and in number.[31]

Philoponus explains how all time together (ὁ ἅμα πᾶς χρόνος) is the same, since the 'now' is the same. First, he reiterates that time is the number 'of' movement and does not correspond to movement, because movements that occur together are not the same (since they may differ in number or form). Time, on the other hand, is always one and the same (εἷς καὶ ὁ αὐτός) in terms of number and, therefore, cannot be equivalent to movement, since there can be one or more movements together. Rather than movement, one has to look to the 'now' in order to show in what sense time is everywhere one and the same (εἷς καὶ ὁ αὐτὸς ὁ πανταχοῦ). By its very nature, the 'now' is πανταχοῦ (everywhere), even if it differs τῷ λόγῳ, i.e. because of its definition, which coincides with its 'account', since the anterior 'now' is different from the posterior 'now.' Philoponus concludes by stating that if the 'now' is generative of time, and this is everywhere one and the same,

31 Transl. from Broadie (2014, 28).

then time too, unlike movement, must be everywhere together one (ἅμα πανταχοῦ εἷς) by nature and number.

Shortly afterwards, however, Philoponus, this time commenting on *Phys.* 4.11, 219b26–28, specifies how to understand the fact that the 'now' is the same with respect to the substrate but it is different with respect to the definition (λόγος).

Philop., *in Phys.* 17 (729.7–23 Vitelli)

Ὥστε καὶ ἐν τούτοις, ὅ μέν ποτε ὂν νῦν ἐστι, τὸ αὐτό (τὸ πρότερον γὰρ ἢ ὕστερόν ἐστι τὸ ἐν κινήσει), τὸ δὲ εἶναι ἕτερον· <ᾗ> ἀριθμητὸν γὰρ τὸ πρότερον καὶ τὸ ὕστερον, τὸ νῦν ἐστιν.

Οὕτω λοιπὸν τὸ προκείμενον συνάγει, λέγω δὴ ὅτι τὸ νῦν τῷ μὲν ὑποκειμένῳ τὸ αὐτό ἐστι, τῷ δὲ λόγῳ ἄλλο καὶ ἄλλο. τὸ γὰρ ὥστε καὶ ἐν τούτοις ἀντὶ τοῦ ἐν τοῖς νῦν· ὥσπερ γὰρ καὶ τὸ σημεῖον τὸ γεννητικὸν τῆς γραμμῆς ἓν καὶ τὸ αὐτὸ τῷ ὑποκειμένῳ, καὶ τὸ φερόμενον τὸ γεννητικὸν τῆς κινήσεως, οὕτω δὲ καὶ τὸ νῦν τὸ τοῦ χρόνου γεννητικόν. ὅ μέν ποτε ὂν νῦν ἐστι, τουτέστιν ὁτιδήποτε κατὰ τὸ ὑποκείμενον ὑπάρχει τε καὶ ἔστι νῦν, ἕν ἐστι καὶ τὸ αὐτό. εἶτα καὶ τί ἐστιν ἐπάγει· τὸ πρότερον γάρ, φησίν, ἢ ὕστερον τὸ ἐν κινήσει· ταὐτὸν γὰρ τὸ ἐν κινήσει πρότερον καὶ ὕστερον κατὰ τὸ ὑποκείμενον, ἐπεὶ καὶ ἐπὶ τῆς κινήσεως τὸ φερόμενον. τὸ δὲ εἶναι ἕτερον, τουτέστι κατὰ τὸν λόγον· τὸ γὰρ ἐν τῇ κινήσει πρότερον καὶ ὕστερον, μὴ ὡς ἀριθμούμενον λαμβανόμενον μηδὲ ὡς πρότερον καὶ ὕστερον, τὸ ὑποκείμενόν ἐστι τοῖς νῦν, τοῦτο δὲ αὐτὸ ὅταν ὡς πρότερον καὶ ὕστερον ληφθῇ καὶ ὡς κατὰ διαφορὰν τῆς κινήσεως γινόμενον, τότε δὴ ἄλλο καὶ ἄλλο ἐστὶ κατὰ τὸν λόγον· ἄλλο γάρ ἐστιν αὐτῷ τὸ προτέρῳ εἶναι καὶ ἄλλο τὸ ὑστέρῳ.

Hence in these also that, whatever it is, by being which it is now is the same (for it is the prior and posterior in movement), but its being is different: for it is insofar as the prior and posterior is numerable that we get the now. (Arist., *Phys.* 4.11, 219b26–28).

In this way he now draws the intended conclusion – namely, that the now is the same in substrate but other and other in description. (Hence in these also is instead of '<Hence> in the case of the nows'.) Just as the point too that is generative of the line is one and the same in substrate, and likewise the body in locomotion that is generative of the movement, so it is with the now that is generative of time. That, whatever it is, by being which it is now – i. e. whatever it is that is there at the level of substrate, and is now – is one and the same. He then follows up with what <this> is. <It is>, he says, the prior and posterior in movement. For the prior and posterior in movement are the same in substrate, since so too is the body in locomotion. But its being is different: i. e. <it is different> in description. For the prior and posterior in movement, if not taken as numbered nor yet as prior and posterior, is the substrate of the nows; yet precisely this, whenever it is taken as prior and posterior and as occurring in accordance with the movement's different <stages>, is – then – other and other in description. For it is one thing for the prior itself to be, and another thing for the posterior.[32]

According to Philoponus, the anterior 'now' and the posterior 'now' are both 'now' because they have the same substrate. However, because of a difference in move-

32 Transl. from Broadie (2014, 33).

ment, they are located at different points on the time axis. Philoponus proposes to understand the expression ἐν τούτοις, at the beginning of the Aristotelian passage he is commenting on, as ἐν τοῖς νῦν ('in the nows'). In this way he shows how, if the 'now' is not specified on the basis of a difference of movement in the time axis (i.e. if it is not numbered and described as neither anterior nor posterior), it appears as the substrate of all other 'nows' and, therefore, we might add, as the substrate of time. In order to show in what sense the 'now' is to be understood as τὸ τοῦ χρόνου γεννητικόν, Philoponus makes the comparison with the point, which, being one and the same in the substrate, is generative of the line, and with the body in locomotion, which is generative of movement.

In these two passages of Philoponus' *Commentary on the Physics*, a meaning of νῦν as a 'principle' (as a beginning) that remains within what it originates seems to emerge, anticipating what will be stated in his *De opificio* regarding the 'day one' that must be included in the calculation of time.[33] The Philoponian account of νῦν in the *Commentary on the Physics* contrasts with Aristotle's statement in the *Physics* that the 'now' is not part of time because it is the limit (the πέρας) of time and, as such, is not time.[34] For Aristotle, it is precisely as a limit that the 'now' is not time, just as the point is not 'part' of the line. According to Philoponus, on the other hand, the now or 'day one,' at the boundary of creation is not only the beginning, that is the first limit from which time begins to flow, but the 'now' and 'day one,' although generative of time, remain part of time: 'day one' is a 'day,' so it is already time.

In the last Philoponian passage we will consider, Philoponus, interpreting the incipit of the Septuagint and thus the Ἐν ἀρχῇ of Gen 1:1, refers to Basil of Cae-

33 As was also shown in the arithmological excursuses in *De op.* 7.13–14, quoted above, Philoponus presents a 'day one' that does not represent an isolated principle: precisely because it is a monad, it remains part of the numerical series that it begins and is therefore related to it. Unlike Philo, when Philoponus speaks of the six days in relation to the number 6, he emphasizes the presence of the monad in the latter, focusing on its representation not so much in terms of the multiplication 2x3 as Philo does, but of the sum 1+2+3, where the number 1 remains part of the addition. The importance of νῦν as a unit of time also recurs in reference to celestial motion (Philop., *in Phys.* 16 [198.19–32 Vitelli]) since each 'instant' of circular motion is both the beginning and the end of movement. This observation serves Philoponus to justify the Aristotelian definition of nature as the 'principle of motion and stillness,' even in the case of celestial bodies (which, for Aristotle, enjoy perpetual motion).

34 See *Phys.* 4.10, 218a6–20; 11, 220a19.

sarea (*Hex.* 1.3–6), for whom he shows his esteem on several occasions in his work.[35]

Philop., *De op.* 1.3 (86.1–88.20 Scholten) (= 7.4–9.4 Reichardt)

Ποσαχῶς ἡ ἀρχή, καὶ ποῖα μὲν αὐτῆς σημαινόμενα παραληπτέον νῦν, ποῖα δὲ οὐ.

Ἐν ἀρχῇ ἐποίησεν ὁ θεὸς τὸν οὐρανὸν καὶ τὴν γῆν. Πολλὰ τὰ σημαινόμενα τῆς ἀρχῆς ὁ πολὺς ἀπαριθμεῖται Βασίλειος· καὶ πρῶτόν γε πάντων τὴν κατὰ χρόνον ἀρχήν. λέγω δὲ νῦν κατὰ χρόνον οὐχ οὗ τῆς γενέσεως προηγεῖται χρόνος ὡς ἡμῶν ἑκάστου ἀλλὰ τὸ πρῶτον τοῦ χρόνου νῦν, ἐν ᾧ τὸν οὐρανὸν καὶ τὴν γῆν παρήγαγεν ὁ θεὸς παντὸς χρονικοῦ χωρὶς διαστήματος. ἅπασα γὰρ ἀρχὴ ἑτέρα πάντως ἐστὶν οὗπερ ἀρχὴ λέγεται εἶναι, οἷον τῆς πηχυαίας φέρε γραμμῆς· τὸ πρῶτον αὐτῆς σημεῖόν ἐστιν ἀρχή, ὅπερ ἀμερέςτὸ πρῶτον αὐτῆς σημεῖόν ἐστιν ἀρχή, ὅπερ ἀμερές ἐστι παντελῶς. εἰ γὰρ βραχύ τι ταύτης ἀφέλοι τις μόριον, οὐκέτι ἔσται τοῦτο τῆς πηχυαίας γραμμῆς ἀρχή, ἀλλὰ μέρους αὐτῆς τοῦ μετὰ τὴν ἀφαίρεσιν ὑπολειφθέντος. οὕτως οὖν καὶ ἡ τοῦ χρόνου ἀρχή, εἴτε ὅλου εἴτε μερικοῦ τινος, οἷον τῆς σήμερον, οὔπω χρόνος· ὅταν γὰρ τοῦ πρώτου σημείου τοῦ ὑπὲρ γῆν ὁρίζοντος ὁ ἥλιος ἅψηται, τοῦτο τῆς ἡμέρας ἐστὶν ἀρχὴ οὐκ ὂν διάστημά τι καὶ μόριον τοῦ ἡμερησίου χρόνου. ὅλης γὰρ τῆς ἡμέρας τὴν ἀρχὴν ζητοῦμεν. Ὡς οὖν τὴν ἀρχὴν τῆς γραμμῆς σημεῖον καλοῦσιν οἱ περὶ ταῦτα σοφοὶ ἀδιάστατον καὶ ἀμερὲς ὂν οὐχὶ δὲ γραμμήν, οὕτω καὶ τὴν τοῦ χρόνου ἀρχὴν οὐ χρόνον ἀλλ' αὐτὸ τοῦτο χρόνου ἀρχὴν ὃ προσαγορεύουσι νῦν. εἰ γὰρ καὶ τοῦτό τις βραχύν τινα νομίσειε χρόνον, οὐκέτι τὴν ἀρχὴν εἴληφε τοῦ ζητουμένου χρόνου, ἀλλὰ μόριον αὐτοῦ δέκατον τυχὸν ἢ ὁποσονοῦν. οὕτω τοίνυν καὶ τοῦ ὅλου χρόνου τὸ πρῶτον νῦν ἀρχή ἐστιν ὅλης αὐτοῦ τῆς ὑποστάσεως, οὐκ ὂν οὔπω χρόνος. ἐπεὶ οὖν ὁ χρόνος μέτρον ἐστὶ τῆς τῶν οὐρανίων περιφορᾶς—ἡμέραι γὰρ καὶ μῆνες καὶ ἐνιαυτοὶ μέρη τοῦ χρόνου εἰσὶ καὶ οὐδέν ἐστιν ἕτερον παρὰ ταῦτα ὁ χρόνος, ἀλλ' αὐτῶν εἰς ἑαυτὰ τῶν εἰρημένων ἀνακυκλουμένων ὁ χρόνος αὔξεται, καθ' ὃν καὶ τὴν ἑκάστου γένεσιν ἀριθμοῦμεν—πρὶν δὲ οὐρανὸν γενέσθαι τούτων ἦν οὐδέν, οὐκ ἦν ἄρα χρόνος πρὶν οὐρανὸν ὑποστῆναι.

Ἐπεὶ οὖν ἅμα οὐρανῷ συνυπέστησε τὸν χρόνον ὁ θεός, ἐν τῷ πρώτῳ δὲ καὶ ἀμερεῖ τοῦ χρόνου νῦν ὅπερ ἐστὶν ἡ τοῦ χρόνου ἀρχή, τὸν οὐρανὸν καὶ τὴν γῆν ἐποίησεν ὁ θεός, ταύτην εἶναί φησι Βασίλειος κατὰ χρόνον ἀρχὴν τῆς τῶν εἰρημένων γενέσεως, τὴν ἀκαριαίαν καὶ ἀδιάστατον. ἐντεῦθεν ὁρμηθεὶς ὁ Πλάτων τὸ 'χρόνος δ' οὖν μετ' οὐρανοῦ γέγονε' κάλλιστα γέγραφεν 'ἵν' ἅμα γενόμενοι ἅμα καὶ λυθῶσιν, ἄν ποτε λύσις τις αὐτῶν γένηται.' μία μὲν οὖν σημασία τῆς ἀρχῆς, ἐν ᾗ τὸν οὐρανὸν καὶ τὴν γῆν ἐποίησεν ὁ θεὸς αὕτη, ἣ καὶ κυριωτάτη μοι τῶν ἄλλων καὶ ἀληθεστάτη φαίνεται [...].

In how many ways the beginning was, and which of its significations are to be understood as a 'now' and which not.

'In the beginning God created the heaven and the earth.'[36] The great Basil enumerates many significations of 'beginning'; and the first of all is beginning in time.[37] By 'in time' I mean, not

35 For instance, see *De op.* 3.6, where Basil is praised for considering astronomical rather than astrological observations to be rigorous. See De Luca (2022, 125–126). On Philoponus and Basil, especially in relation to *De op.* 1.3, see Giardina (2023) and Ottobrini (2023b).
36 Gen 1:1.
37 Cf. Bas., *Hex.* 1.5–6.

> that to the coming into being of which duration is added, as for each one of us, but the first point of time as it is now, in which God produced heaven and earth without any durative interval. For every beginning is completely different with respect to that of which it is called a beginning, such as that of a line a foot long. Its first element, its beginning, is a point, which is completely dimensionless. But if someone draws it out a short fraction, it is not yet the beginning of a foot-long line, but of the part of it that is left after the subtraction. So too is the beginning of time, in whole or in part, like that of this day, not yet time: for whenever the sun touches the first part of the horizon above the earth, this is the beginning of the day, not being an interval, yet being a segment of the diurnal duration. For it is the beginning of the whole day that we are looking for.
>
> So then, as those expert in these matters call a point, the beginning of a line, unextended and dimensionless, but not the line, so also they call the beginning of time not 'a time' but rather this thing itself, the beginning of time, which they term 'now.' For if someone were to think it a kind of short time, he would not grasp it as the beginning of the time in question, but as a part of it, a tenth or some such. And so the first element of all of present time is the beginning of its entire substance, but it itself is in no way a time. Since time is a measurement of the circular motion of the heavenly bodies – for days and months and years are portions of time, and time is in no way different with respect to that, but rather time increases as the aforementioned (days etc.) recur in their revolutions, and we count the coming into being of each accordingly – before heaven came into being none of the heavenly bodies existed, and so therefore time did not exist before the heavens subsisted.
>
> Since God caused time to subsist at the same time as heaven, in the first and dimensionless 'now' of time which is the beginning of time, 'God created heaven and earth' is what Basil calls the beginning in time of their (heaven and earth's) coming into being, which is momentary and unextended. Starting from there, Plato was very right to write 'Time came into being together with heaven, so that things might be both created and destroyed, that some sort of their ceasing to be might take place.'[38] So then this first signification of 'beginning', in which God created heaven and earth, seems to me more cogent and clearer than others [...].[39]

Of the four main meanings, highlighted by Basil, in which ἀρχή can be understood according to a temporal, pragmatic, productive and final sense, Philoponus focuses on the first, which is considered the most appropriate, namely the ἀρχὴ κατὰ χρόνον. Philoponus is careful to point out that ἀρχή should be understood as 'the first now of time' (τὸ πρῶτον τοῦ χρόνου νῦν) in which heaven and earth are created simultaneously without any interval (διάστημα). This principle, or πρῶτον νῦν, does not correspond to the νῦν that we have equated with 'day one,' because the πρῶτον νῦν (i.e. the ἀρχή), unlike 'day one,' is not part of time. As the literal quotation from *Timaeus* 38b also shows, time originates with the heavens, but before the creation of the heavens, there cannot be time.

38 Plat., *Tim.* 38b6–7.
39 Transl. by Leslie S. B. MacCoull.

The Ἐν ἀρχῇ of Gen 1:1, therefore, describes a timeless νῦν before the simultaneous creation of heaven and earth, which represents a stage that can be described as the 'antechamber' of time. It is a timeless dimension, which seems to be very short—as long as a νῦν—and which precedes the days (and therefore 'day one').

Although it must be remembered that Philoponus is driven by different exegetical needs in the two passages, if we compare this last chapter with *De op.* 2.23, 'day one' appears as a hybrid reality. The first day of creation occurs between the ἀρχή, understood as the timeless πρῶτον νῦν, and the νῦν, understood by Philoponus—but not by Aristotle—as 'part' of time and representing that instant in which time begins to be measured. Thus, for Philoponus, time comes into being between two νῦν: between an anterior 'now' and a posterior 'now,' in which time expresses a number of movement and, in particular, being at the origin of the world, the number 1: the monad.[40] As Philoponus affirms in *De op.* 1.3, the day is a 'part' (μέρος) of time and 'day one' represents a first step out of pre-creative timelessness: a quick step, starting from which time is generated.

4 Perpetuity and Time as Numbers in Philo

By analyzing the points of contact with the Philonian rational exegesis of the temporal dimension of the creation and the 'day one,' we can see how, before Philoponus, already according to his Jewish predecessor Philo the ἀρχή of Gen 1:1 is a timeless dimension, in which time has not yet come into existence:

Philo, *Opif.* 26–28

Φησὶ δ' ὡς "ἐν ἀρχῇ ἐποίησεν ὁ θεὸς τὸν οὐρανὸν καὶ τὴν γῆν", τὴν ἀρχὴν παραλαμβάνων οὐχ ὡς οἴονταί τινες τὴν κατὰ χρόνον· χρόνος γὰρ οὐκ ἦν πρὸ κόσμου, ἀλλ' ἢ σὺν αὐτῷ γέγονεν ἢ μετ' αὐτόν· ἐπεὶ γὰρ διάστημα τῆς τοῦ κόσμου κινήσεώς ἐστιν ὁ χρόνος, προτέρα δὲ τοῦ κινουμένου κίνησις οὐκ ἂν γένοιτο, ἀλλ' ἀναγκαῖον αὐτὴν ἢ ὕστερον ἢ ἅμα συνίστασθαι, ἀναγκαῖον ἄρα καὶ τὸν χρόνον ἢ ἰσήλικα κόσμου γεγονέναι ἢ νεώτερον ἐκείνου· πρεσβύτερον δ' ἀποφαίνεσθαι τολμᾶν ἀφιλόσοφον. εἰ δ' ἀρχὴ μὴ παραλαμβάνεται τανῦν ἡ κατὰ χρόνον, εἰκὸς ἂν εἴη μηνύεσθαι τὴν κατ' ἀριθμόν, ὡς τὸ "ἐν ἀρχῇ ἐποίησεν" ἴσον εἶναι τῷ πρῶτον ἐποίησε τὸν οὐρανόν· καὶ γὰρ εὔλογον τῷ ὄντι πρῶτον αὐτὸν εἰς γένεσιν ἐλθεῖν, ἄριστόν τε ὄντα τῶν γεγονότων κἀκ τοῦ καθαρωτάτου τῆς οὐσίας παγέντα, διότι θεῶν ἐμφανῶν τε καὶ αἰσθητῶν ἔμελλεν οἶκος ἔσεσθαι ἱερώτατος. καὶ γὰρ εἰ πάνθ' ἅμα ὁ ποιῶν ἐποίει, τάξιν οὐδὲν ἧττον εἶχε τὰ καλῶς γινόμενα· καλὸν γὰρ οὐδὲν ἐν ἀταξίᾳ. τάξις δ' ἀκολουθία καὶ εἱρμός ἐστι προηγουμένων τινῶν καὶ ἑπομένων, εἰ καὶ μὴ τοῖς ἀποτελέσμασιν, ἀλλά τοι ταῖς τῶν

40 When we speak of 'day one' in Gen 1:5, the heavens are actually seen as having already been created, as it is clear from Gen 1:1.

τεκταινομένων ἐπινοίαις· οὕτως γὰρ ἔμελλον ἠκριβῶσθαί τε καὶ ἀπλανεῖς εἶναι καὶ ἀσύγχυτοι.

When he says that "in (the) beginning God made the heaven and the earth,"[41] he does not take the (term) "beginning," as some people think, in a temporal sense. For there was no time before the cosmos, but rather it either came into existence together with the cosmos or after it. When we consider that time is the extension of the cosmos' movement, and that there could not be any movement earlier than or at the same time, then we must necessarily conclude that time too is either the same age as the cosmos or younger than it. To venture to affirm that it is older is unphilosophical. If "beginning" in the present context is not taken in the temporal sense, it is likely that its use indicates beginning in the numerical sense, so that the expression "in (the) beginning he made" is equivalent to "he" first "made the heaven." It is indeed reasonable that heaven should in fact be the first thing to enter into becoming. It is the most excellent of the things that have come into existence and is also composed of the purest substance, because it was to be the holiest dwelling-place for the gods whose appearance is perceived by the senses. Even if the maker proceeded to make all things simultaneously, it is nonetheless true that what comes into a beautiful existence did possess order, for there is no beauty in disorder. Order is a sequence and series of things that precede and follow, if not in the completed products, then certainly in the conceptions of the builders. Only in this way could they be precisely arranged, and not deviate from their path or be full of confusion.[42]

Philo specifies how the principle is to be understood οὐ κατὰ χρόνον: thus 'not' in a temporal sense. The expression κατὰ χρόνον is therefore intended differently from how Philoponus will understand it, while arriving at the same contextualisation of the ἀρχή beyond time. For Philo, κατὰ χρόνον indicates that the ἀρχή is 'in' time, which is why this is a perspective to be rejected. On the other hand, for Philoponus κατὰ χρόνον implies a consideration of the beginning of the world in relation to time, even if it does not entail its temporisation, since, as we have seen, the ἀρχή is not yet time. For Philo, the beginning of creation is not to be understood as κατὰ χρόνον, but as κατ' ἀριθμόν: in a numerical sense. The beginning is indeed to be placed in the context of a creation that, as in the *Timaeus*, follows a precise order (τάξις) in which the heavens are the first thing to have been created. Similarly to what happens in *Tim.* 38b, in the background of Philo's conception of time also, time begins to 'move' with the creation of the heavens and the stars, which are forged on the basis of the idea of noetic light created on 'day one' along with the other ideas.[43]

---

41 Gen 1:1.

42 Transl. from Runia (2001, 52).

43 On time in the *Timaeus*, among the extensive existing bibliography, see Thein (2020), which emphasizes that there is no unified theory of time in the Platonic dialogue and highlights the role of the planets within it.

In addition to the presence of Plato's *Timaeus*, we note that in these paragraphs Philo also draws on the Stoic definition of time as διάστημα τῆς τοῦ κόσμου κινήσεως (as the 'interval' of the movement of the world).[44] However, he does not apply this definition in an eternalist context, such as that proposed by Stoics like Chrysippus, according to whom the existence of the cosmos is marked by eternally recurring cycles of destruction and rebirth, with time appearing to be no more than an interval between one cosmic cycle and another.[45] What seems to be most important to Philo in the Stoic definition of time is the genitive τῆς κινήσεως, for it is here that movement is the aspect which seems to interest Philo most. Indeed, immediately after this definition, he specifies that movement cannot have come into existence before that which is moved, and that it must have been constituted either after or at the same time as that which is moved. In the same way, time too must be either as old as the world or younger than it: to say that time is older than the cosmos would be unphilosophical. Like the Stoics, Philo also links the existence of time to that of movement and, in particular, to the movement of the stars.

According to Philo, who seems to follow Aristotle, movement is linked to number, and for this reason the periodic revolutions (the περίοδοι) of the stars determine the days, months and years, which are the μέτρα χρόνου (the 'measures of time'), and they determine the ἀριθμοῦ φύσις (the 'nature of number').[46] He states:

Philo, *Opif.* 55–60

πρὸς δὴ τὴν τοῦ νοητοῦ φωτὸς ἰδέαν ἐκείνην ἀπιδών, ἣ λέλεκται κατὰ τὸν ἀσώματον κόσμον, ἐδημιούργει τοὺς αἰσθητοὺς ἀστέρας, ἀγάλματα θεῖα καὶ περικαλλέστατα, οὓς ὥσπερ ἐν ἱερῷ καθαρωτάτῳ τῆς σωματικῆς οὐσίας ἵδρυε τῷ οὐρανῷ, πολλῶν χάριν· ἑνὸς μὲν τοῦ φωσφορεῖν, ἑτέρου δὲ σημείων, εἶτα καιρῶν τῶν περὶ τὰς ἐτησίους ὥρας, καὶ ἐπὶ πᾶσιν ἡμερῶν μηνῶν ἐνιαυτῶν, ἃ δὴ καὶ μέτρα χρόνου γέγονε καὶ τὴν ἀριθμοῦ φύσιν ἐγέννησεν. [...] γεγόνασι δὲ καὶ πρὸς μέτρα χρόνων· ἡλίου γὰρ καὶ σελήνης καὶ τῶν ἄλλων τεταγμέναις περιόδοις ἡμέραι καὶ μῆνες καὶ ἐνιαυτοὶ συνέστησαν. εὐθύς τε τὸ χρησιμώτατον, ἡ ἀριθμοῦ φύσις, ἐδείχθη, χρόνου παραφήναντος αὐτήν· ἐκ γὰρ μιᾶς ἡμέρας τὸ ἓν καὶ ἐκ δυοῖν τὰ δύο καὶ ἐκ τριῶν τὰ τρία καὶ ἐκ μηνὸς τὰ τριάκοντα καὶ ἐξ ἐνιαυτοῦ τὸ ἰσάριθμον ταῖς ἐκ δώδεκα μηνῶν ἡμέραις πλῆθος καὶ ἐξ ἀπείρου χρόνου ὁ ἄπειρος ἀριθμός.

---

44 On time as διάστημα in Stoicism, see Sambursky (1959). See also Greene (2018, 46–54), which analyzes the implications of the different ways in which the term διάστημα can be translated. I would like to thank Dr. Francesca Alesse for bringing this study to my attention.
45 See *SVF* II 509 = Stob., *Ecl.* I, in which Stobeus shows how Chrysippus distinguishes between a 'particular' time as the διάστημα of every movement, and a 'universal' time as that διάστημα which derives from the movement of the world, since everything moves and subsists κατὰ τὸν χρόνον (according to time). See Sambursky (1959, 106) and Long (2006, 274–282).
46 On Philo and Aristotle, see Sharples (2008) and Lévy (2011).

> Using as his model that form of intelligible light which was discussed in connection with the incorporeal cosmos, he proceeded to create the sense-perceptible heavenly bodies, divine images of exceeding beauty. These he established in heaven, as in a temple made of the purest part of bodily substance, for many reasons: firstly to give light, secondly for signs, then to give the right times for the annual seasons, and finally for days and months and years, which indeed have come into existence as the measures of time and also have generated the nature of number. [...] They have also come into existence to serve as measures of time, for by the ordered revolutions of the sun and moon and other heavenly bodies days and months and years have been constituted. And immediately that most useful thing, the nature of number, was revealed because time makes it manifest. For from a single day the number one is derived, from two days two, from three days three, and from a month thirty, from a year the number equivalent to the days produced by twelve months, and from infinite time the number that is infinite.[47]

Philo clearly says that numbers are derived from days because the progression of numbers is derived from the passage and accumulation of time: as the days are counted, they reveal the nature of number.[48] Although Philo seems to resent Aristotle himself when he rails against those who showed the world to be ungenerated and imperishable (in *Opif.* 7 and 171), he seems to have adopted the well-known definition of time in the *Physics* more than one would expect, and he treats days—and hence time—as an expression of numbers. Furthermore, as Aristotle showed in the *De Caelo*, since time is bound to movement and, therefore, to a moving body, it is also peculiar to the cosmos, outside of which there is no body and thus no temporality. In a similar way, Philo relates time to the sense-perceptible world, since χρόνος came into existence on the second day, when God began to constitute its first component, i. e. the heavens (cf. *Cael.* 1.9, 279a11–18).

Within a particularly eclectic view of time, in which elements drawn from the philosophies of Plato, Aristotle and the Stoics are decisive, the constant reference to the *Timaeus* proves crucial for the Philonian description of 'day one.' Philo gives a different interpretation to that which Philoponus will give of 'day one,' because Philo contextualizes the ἡμέρα μία according to a different philosophical frame of reference: that of Platonic metaphysics. In the opening paragraphs of *De opificio* he states:

Philo, *Opif.* 12–15

ἀλλ' ὅ γε μέγας Μωυσῆς ἀλλοτριώτατον τοῦ ὁρατοῦ νομίσας εἶναι τὸ ἀγένητον – πᾶν γὰρ τὸ αἰσθητὸν ἐν γενέσει καὶ μεταβολαῖς οὐδέποτε κατὰ ταὐτὰ ὄν – τῷ μὲν ἀοράτῳ καὶ νοητῷ

---

47 Transl. from Runia (2001, 60–61).

48 Cf. *Tim.* 47a4–b4, where it is shown how the vision of day and night, of months and years, on the one hand made by art (μεμηχάνηνται) number (μὲν ἀριθμόν) and on the other hand provided the notion of time (χρόνου δὲ ἔννοιαν) and the study of the nature of the universe.

προσένειμεν ὡς ἀδελφὸν καὶ συγγενὲς ἀιδιότητα, τῷ δ' αἰσθητῷ γένεσιν οἰκεῖον ὄνομα ἐπεφήμισεν. ἐπεὶ οὖν ὁρατός τε καὶ αἰσθητὸς ὅδε ὁ κόσμος, ἀναγκαίως ἂν εἴη καὶ γενητός· ὅθεν οὐκ ἀπὸ σκοποῦ καὶ τὴν γένεσιν ἀνέγραψεν αὐτοῦ μάλα σεμνῶς θεολογήσας. Ἓξ δὲ ἡμέραις δημιουργηθῆναί φησι τὸν κόσμον, οὐκ ἐπειδὴ προσεδεῖτο χρόνων μήκους ὁ ποιῶν – ἅμα γὰρ πάντα δρᾶν εἰκὸς θεόν, οὐ προστάττοντα μόνον ἀλλὰ καὶ διανοούμενον –, ἀλλ' ἐπειδὴ τοῖς γινομένοις ἔδει τάξεως. τάξει δὲ ἀριθμὸς οἰκεῖον, ἀριθμῶν δὲ φύσεως νόμοις γεννητικώτατος ὁ ἕξ· τῶν τε γὰρ ἀπὸ μονάδος πρῶτος τέλειός ἐστιν ἰσούμενος τοῖς ἑαυτοῦ μέρεσι καὶ συμπληρούμενος ἐξ αὐτῶν, ἡμίσους μὲν τριάδος, τρίτου δὲ δυάδος, ἕκτου δὲ μονάδος, καὶ ὡς ἔπος εἰπεῖν ἄρρην τε καὶ θῆλυς εἶναι πέφυκε κἀκ τῆς ἑκατέρου δυνάμεως ἥρμοσται· ἄρρεν μὲν γὰρ ἐν τοῖς οὖσι τὸ περιττόν, τὸ δ' ἄρτιον θῆλυ· περιττῶν μὲν οὖν ἀριθμῶν ἀρχὴ τριάς, δυὰς δ' ἀρτίων, ἡ δ' ἀμφοῖν δύναμις ἑξάς. ἔδει γὰρ τὸν κόσμον τελειότατον μὲν ὄντα τῶν γεγονότων κατ' ἀριθμὸν τέλειον παγῆναι τὸν ἕξ, ἐν ἑαυτῷ δ' ἔχειν μέλλοντα τὰς ἐκ συνδυασμοῦ γενέσεις πρὸς μικτὸν ἀριθμὸν τὸν πρῶτον ἀρτιοπέριττον τυπωθῆναι, περιέξοντα καὶ τὴν τοῦ σπείροντος ἄρρενος καὶ τὴν τοῦ ὑποδεχομένου τὰς γονὰς θήλεος ἰδέαν. ἑκάστῃ δὲ τῶν ἡμερῶν ἀπένειμεν ἔνια τῶν τοῦ παντὸς τμημάτων τὴν πρώτην ὑπεξελόμενος, ἣν αὐτὸς οὐδὲ πρώτην, ἵνα μὴ ταῖς ἄλλαις συγκαταριθμῆται, καλεῖ, μίαν δ' ὀνομάσας ὀνόματι εὐθυβόλῳ προσαγορεύει, τὴν μονάδος φύσιν καὶ πρόσρησιν ἐνιδών τε καὶ ἐπιφημίσας αὐτῇ. λεκτέον δὲ ὅσα οἷόν τέ ἐστι τῶν ἐμπεριεχομένων, ἐπειδὴ πάντα ἀμήχανον· περιέχει γὰρ τὸν νοητὸν κόσμον ἐξαίρετον, ὡς ὁ περὶ αὐτῆς λόγος μηνύει.

But the great Moses considered that what is ungenerated was of a totally different order from that which was visible, for the entire sense-perceptible realm is in a process of becoming and change and never remains in the same state. So to what is invisible and intelligible he assigned eternity as being akin and related to it, whereas on what is sense-perceptible he ascribed the appropriate name becoming (genesis). Since, therefore, this cosmos is both visible and sense-perceptible, it must necessarily also be generated. Hence he was not off the mark in also giving a description of its becoming, thereby speaking about God in a truly reverent manner.

He says that the cosmos was fashioned in six days, not because the maker was in need of a length of time—for God surely did everything at the same time, not only in giving commands but also in his thinking—, but because things that come into existence required order. Number is inherent in order, and by the laws of nature the most generative of numbers is the six. Of the numbers (proceeding) from the unit, six is the first perfect number. It is equal to (the product of) its parts and is also formed by their sum, namely the three as its half and two as its third and the unit as its sixth. It is also, so to speak, both male and female by nature, forming a harmonic union out of the product of each of them, for among existing things the odd is male and the female is even. The first of the odd numbers is the three, of the even numbers it is the two, and the product of both is the six. So it was right that the cosmos, as the most perfect of the things that have come into existence, be built in accordance with the perfect number six, and, because births resulting from coupling would take place in it, also be formed in relation to a mixed number, the first even-odd number which contains both the form of the male who sows the seed and the form of the female who receives it. To each of the days he assigned some of the parts of the universe, making an exception for the first, which he himself does not actually call first, in case it be counted together with the others. Instead he gives it the accurate name one, because he perceived the nature and the appellation of the unit in it, and so gave it that title. We must now state as many as we can of the things that are contained in it, since it is impossible to state them all. It contains as pre-eminent item the intelligible cosmos, as the account concerning it (day one) reveals.[49]

In *Opif.* 12–15, Philo, interpreting *Tim.* 27d–28c literally, is careful to distinguish between two temporal dimensions.[50] On the one hand, we find the perpetuity (the ἀιδιότης) of the model, created simultaneously on 'day one,' and on the other, the dimension of time, which comes into existence with the heavens and the stars and begins to flow from the second day of creation, characterizing the sense-perceptible cosmos and the six days of creation. Since—says Philo—number is 'of the same household' (οἰκεῖον) as the τάξις, two brief arithmological excursuses, neo-Pythagorean in style, are introduced to show how to understand the order of creation. In particular, by appealing to the laws of nature, which are the logical-causal laws expressed by the nature of numbers, Philo focuses on the number 6 and the number 1. In his view, these two numbers help to reveal the nature of the days in which creation was articulated. Philo places himself in continuity with the Neo-Pythagorean tradition by describing the number 6 as the pairing of an even number, 2, and an odd number, 3, although this is an association already highlighted in the Pythagorean pairs of opposites mentioned by Aristotle in *Metaph.* 1.5, 986a25, where the even/odd numbers are implicitly associated with the feminine/masculine pair. In particular, the reference to 6 as the product of the pairing of 2 and 3 recalls what was said after Philo by Theon of Smyrna (1st–2nd cent. CE) and Anatolius of Laodicea (3rd cent. CE), proponents of the ancient Pythagorean tradition.[51] Philo's arithmological digressions differ from those of Philoponus because in Philo the generative character that makes a number γεννητικώτατος, is not attributed to the number 1, as in Philoponus, but to the number 6, a number characteristic of the γένεσις and of the created world. Unlike Philoponus, Philo associates 'day one' with the generation not of time, but of perpetuity: of that ἀιδιότης which has a beginning but is without an end. As is clear from these paragraphs of Philo's, 'day one' is not the 'first' ἵνα μὴ ταῖς ἄλλαις συγκαταριθμῆται (so as not to be counted with the other

49 Transl. from Runia (2001, 49–50).

50 Philo takes an intermediate position between the κατὰ λέξιν and διδασκαλίας χάριν interpretations of the *Timaeus:* on the one hand, like the literalists, he regards the Platonic dialogue as a 'real' account of a temporal origin of everything (cf. Arist., *Cael.* 1.10, 280a7–8; on the other hand, like those who understood the *Timaeus* as having been written for didactic purposes, he 'interprets' it metaphorically, viewing it within his Jewish cosmogony, but nevertheless avoiding an eternalist reading of it like that of Pseusippus and Xenocrates. See Centrone (2015), Ferrari (2001) and Petrucci (2015) and (2019).

51 See Runia (2001, 127–129).

<days>): it is 1 because it expresses the isolation of the intelligible model, separated from sense-perceptible reality.

For Philo's association of 'day one' with noetic creation, the *Timaeus* is fundamental, but Philo distances himself from this dialogue when he envisages the existence of a model that is not eternal (αἰώνιος) but perpetual (ἀΐδιος), since it is a paradigm that in Philo—but not in Plato—has a beginning ordained by the divine will.[52] In particular, in the background of Philo's paragraphs on time, we can clearly detect an echo of the well-known Platonic description of *Tim.* 37d5 where χρόνος is presented as the εἰκὼ κινητὴ αἰῶνος (the 'moving image of eternity'). According to Philo, too, time is an 'image,' because it represents the copy of that perpetuity which characterizes the perpetual model. In his account of 'day one,' Philo seems particularly influenced by the fact that in the *Timaeus* eternity is described as abiding 'in one' (ἐν ἑνί) and that the resulting image—i. e. time—moves according to number (κατ' ἀριθμόν).[53] In the wake of the *Timaeus*, Philo, by specifying the distinction between 'day one' and the other six days, recovers these two Platonic characterizations according to which perpetuity is stationary and associated with the number 1, while time is in motion and associated with a series of numbers.

5 'Day One' as an Intelligible Measure

Although the two authors understand the concept of measure differently, 'day one' already appears in Philo as a 'measure,' as it later does in Philoponus. As can be

52 The eternal timelessness described as αἰώνιος in the *Timaeus*, and which characterizes the model, becomes in the Philonian universe what distinguishes God more than the intelligible world. Philo seems to distinguish conceptually between two types of 'eternity' and thus makes a varied use of the lexicon related to αἰών and ἀιδιότης. On the one hand, the αἰών refers to an eternal life that has not only has no end but also no beginning, like that of God; on the other hand, ἀιδιότης refers to the permanence of the intelligible world that, once it has been created, is imperishable. What we have, then, is an *aeternitas a parte ante et a parte post* that characterizes God and an *aeternitas a parte post* that characterizes the noetic cosmos, beyond which χρόνος flows. In the *Timaeus*, however, I believe that the adjectives ἀΐδιος and αἰώνιος are used as synonyms and it seems to me that the latter term is a metaphorical expression for the former, since, as part of the broader imagery of the noetic ζῷον, it denotes the eternal life of the model. I address this question in De Luca (2025b). On eternity in the *Timaeus*, see De Bianchi (2022) and, more generally on the literary and philosophical use of the term αἰών, Keizer (1999) and (2000).
53 Von Leyden (1964, 39–42) points out that Plato's is the first definition in which time is explicitly linked to number. According to von Leyden, the Pythagorean Archita of Tarentum may have provided such a definition even earlier, although the evidence we have in this regard is limited to fragments that are mostly considered spurious.

seen from *Opif.* 34–35, for Philo 'measure' is synonymous with 'idea,' and 'day one' appears as a measure of time in the sense that perpetuity represents its imperishable model:

Philo, *Opif.* 34–35

οὗτοι δ' εἰσὶν ἑσπέρα τε καὶ πρωΐα, ὧν ἡ μὲν προευαγγελίζεται μέλλοντα ἥλιον ἀνίσχειν ἠρέμα τὸ σκότος ἀνείργουσα, ἡ δ' ἑσπέρα καταδύντι ἐπιγίνεται ἡλίῳ τὴν ἀθρόαν τοῦ σκότους φορὰν πρᾴως ἐκδεχομένη. καὶ ταῦτα μέντοι, πρωΐαν λέγω καὶ ἑσπέραν, ἐν τῇ τάξει τῶν ἀσωμάτων καὶ νοητῶν θετέον· ὅλως γὰρ οὐδὲν αἰσθητὸν ἐν τούτοις, ἀλλὰ πάντα ἰδέαι καὶ μέτρα καὶ τύποι καὶ σφραγῖδες, εἰς γένεσιν ἄλλων ἀσώματα σωμάτων. ἐπεὶ δὲ φῶς μὲν ἐγένετο, σκότος δ' ὑπεξέστη καὶ ἀνεχώρησεν, ὅροι δ' ἐν τοῖς μεταξὺ διαστήμασιν ἐπάγησαν ἑσπέρα καὶ πρωΐα, κατὰ τἀναγκαῖον τοῦ χρόνου μέτρον ἀπετελεῖτο εὐθύς, ὃ καὶ ἡμέραν ὁ ποιῶν ἐκάλεσε, καὶ ἡμέραν οὐχὶ πρώτην, ἀλλὰ μίαν, ἣ λέλεκται διὰ τὴν τοῦ νοητοῦ κόσμου μόνωσιν μοναδικὴν ἔχοντος φύσιν.

These (boundaries) are evening and morning, of which the latter announces in advance that the sun is about to rise and gradually forces back the darkness, while the evening follows on the setting sun and gently admits the massive onset of the darkness. Mark well, however, that these two, I mean morning and evening, must be placed in the order of incorporeal and intelligible reality. For in that realm there is ideas and measures and marks and seals, incorporeal entities required for the genesis of the other bodily realm. So when light came into being, darkness retired and withdrew, while evening and morning were fixed as boundaries in the extended space in between, this necessarily entailed that a measure of time was produced forthwith. The maker called this measure day, and not the first day, but day one. It was named in this way because of the aloneness of the intelligible cosmos which has the nature of the unit.[54]

As Philo himself states, 'day one' corresponds to the first alternation of the intelligible evening and morning, which shows the first dawn of the intelligible cosmos. It is here that the τοῦ χρόνου μέτρον known as 'day one' takes place because of the uniqueness of the noetic cosmos, whose monadic nature is emphasized by the Philonian use of the adjective ἐξαίρετος (extraordinary) and the verb ὑπεξαιρέω (I 'except').[55] Incidentally, the same kind of lexicon will be found later in Philoponus, who, as we have seen, has described the excellence of 'day one' by using the participle ἐξῃρημένον. Another aspect that also emerges from these paragraphs, is Philo's use of the term διάστημα, employed here in an intelligible context. This noetic use of διάστημα may explain Philo's recourse to the Stoic def-

54 Transl. from Runia (2001, 54).

55 The exceptionality of the intelligible world is also emphasized by the fact that it is impossible (ἀμήχανον) to say everything that is contained in day one, because it contains the ideas of all things that are created. This impossibility underlines the narrowness of human language in describing all that God thinks and then creates.

inition of time in *Opif.* 26–28, which he, as usual, reinterprets and thus transforms by integrating it into his cosmology. As can be seen in *Opif.* 34–35, Philo speaks of the μεταξὺ διαστήματα, i. e. the 'middle intervals' in which the boundaries of the intelligible evening and morning are set: thus the boundaries of 'day one.' Διάστημα, therefore, appears as an 'interval' between evening and morning and between morning and evening. Transposed to a cosmic level, this term, as the expression of an 'interval in the movement of the world,' could indicate precisely the rotation of the stars that, between morning and evening—we could say, between an earlier νῦν and a later νῦν—determines the day, and hence that time which, even for Philo, is nothing but number.

Similarly to Philoponus, Philo has already presented a helical time, which in his view begins to flow on the second day, but which is made up of καιροί, of cyclically recurring 'opportune moments:'

Philo, *Opif.* 41–44

νυνὶ μὲν γὰρ ἐν μέρει γίγνεται τὰ γιγνόμενα χρόνοις διαφέρουσιν, ἀλλ' οὐκ ἀθρόα καιρῷ ἑνί· τίς γὰρ οὐκ οἶδεν ὅτι πρῶτον μέν ἐστι σπορὰ καὶ φυτεία, δεύτερον δὲ τῶν σπαρέντων καὶ φυτευθέντων αὔξησις, ἡ μὲν εἰς τὸ κάτω ῥίζας ἀποτείνουσα οἱονεὶ θεμελίους, ἡ δ' εἰς τὸ ἄνω πρὸς ὕψος αἰρομένων καὶ στελεχουμένων; ἔπειτα βλαστοὶ καὶ πετάλων ἐκφύσεις, εἶτ' ἐπὶ πᾶσι καρποῦ φορά· καὶ πάλιν καρπὸς οὐ τέλειος, ἀλλ' ἔχων παντοίας μεταβολὰς κατά τε τὴν ἐν μεγέθει ποσότητα καὶ τὰς ἐν πολυμόρφοις ἰδέαις ποιότητας· [...] ἐν δὲ τῇ πρώτῃ γενέσει τῶν ὅλων, καθάπερ ἔφην, ὁ θεὸς ἅπασαν τὴν τῶν φυτῶν ὕλην ἐκ γῆς ἀνεδίδου τελείαν καρποὺς ἔχουσαν οὐκ ἀτελεῖς ἀλλ' ἀκμάζοντας, εἰς ἑτοιμοτάτην καὶ ἀνυπέρθετον χρῆσιν καὶ ἀπόλαυσιν ζῴων τῶν αὐτίκα γενησομένων. ὁ μὲν δὴ προστάττει τῇ γῇ ταῦτα γεννῆσαι· ἡ δ' ὥσπερ ἐκ πολλοῦ κυοφοροῦσα καὶ ὠδίνουσα τίκτει πάσας μὲν τὰς σπαρτῶν, πάσας δὲ τὰς δένδρων, ἔτι δὲ καρπῶν ἀμυθήτους ἰδέας. ἀλλ' οὐ μόνον ἦσαν οἱ καρποὶ τροφαὶ ζῴοις, ἀλλὰ καὶ παρασκευαὶ πρὸς τὴν τῶν ὁμοίων ἀεὶ γένεσιν, τὰς σπερματικὰς οὐσίας περιέχοντες, ἐν αἷς ἄδηλοι καὶ ἀφανεῖς οἱ λόγοι τῶν ὅλων εἰσί, δῆλοι καὶ φανεροὶ γινόμενοι καιρῶν περιόδοις. ἐβουλήθη γὰρ ὁ θεὸς δολιχεύειν τὴν φύσιν ἀπαθανατίζων τὰ γένη καὶ μεταδιδοὺς αὐτοῖς ἀιδιότητος· οὗ χάριν καὶ ἀρχὴν πρὸς τέλος ἦγε καὶ ἐπέσπευδε καὶ τέλος ἐπ' ἀρχὴν ἀνακάμπτειν ἐποίει· ἔκ τε γὰρ φυτῶν ὁ καρπός, ὡς ἂν ἐξ ἀρχῆς τέλος, καὶ ἐκ καρποῦ τὸ σπέρμα περιέχοντος ἐν ἑαυτῷ πάλιν τὸ φυτόν, ὡς ἂν ἐκ τέλους ἀρχή.

For now plants develop in succession at different times, and not all together at a single opportune time. Everyone knows that first sowing and planting occur, and second the growth of what has been sown and planted. This growth partly extends downwards, establishing roots like foundations and partly extends upwards, whereby the plants lift themselves to a height and develop stems. Next come shoots and the growth of leaves, and finally the production of fruit takes place. [...] But in the case of the first genesis of the universe, as I just said, God causes all the timber of plants to rise from the earth complete with fruit which was not imperfect but as its peak, fully ready for the immediate use and enjoyment of the living beings that were very soon to come into existence. He thus gives orders to the earth to generate all these things. The earth, like a woman who has been pregnant for a long time and is now in travail, gives birth to every kind of sown plant, every kind of tree, and also countless

> kinds of fruit. But the fruit was not only ready to serve as food for living beings. It was also equipped for the perpetual genesis of what is similar in kind, containing as it does spermatic substances in which the indistinct and invisible patterns of the entire organisms are found. These patterns become distinct and visible as the cycles of the seasons proceed. For God had decided that nature should run a cyclical race, thereby immortalizing the kinds and giving them a share of eternity. On this account he not only guided and urged the beginning on towards the end, but also caused the end to turn back towards the beginning. Out of the plants emerges the fruit, as an end out of a beginning, while out of the fruit that encloses the seed within itself the plant emerges again, as a beginning out of an end.[56]

The recurrence of the καιροί, guaranteed by the presence of the Stoic 'seminal reasons,' shows the presence of a repetitive time that describes the 'dolichos race' of nature. This race, emphasized by Philo's neologism δολιχεύω, is characterized by an elliptical rather than circular course, in which nature repeatedly runs around the two fires of the 'stadium of the cosmos,' represented by the ἀρχή and the τέλος, which appear as the manifestation of each sunrise and sunset.[57]

6 Conclusion

To conclude and return to where our analysis began, namely *De op.* 2.23, we might ask whether Philoponus knew and had access to Philo's monumental work on the creation of *Genesis*, if not directly, then at least through thc Christian authors he mentions, such as Basil, Origen, but also Theodore of Mopsuestia (although he is mainly referred to critically).[58] The paragraphs of the *De opificio* in which Philo uses arithmology to justify the beginning of cosmogony in 'day one' and the origin of time seem to have been a point of reference for those Christian authors who often engaged with his thought.[59] It cannot be ruled out that the Christian Philoponus, like other authors, drew on the cosmological thought of Philo: the latter may have inspired some exegetical questions, such as why in Genesis the day is

---

56 Transl. from Runia (2001, 55–56).

57 On Philo's use of δολιχεύω, see Runia (2001, 184–185) and De Luca (2021b, 192–194).

58 For Theodore's criticism of Philo and his use of allegory and arithmology, see Runia (1999, or ed. 1993, 274–276) and De Luca (2025a). On the School of Antioch, see Schäublin (1974) and on Theodore's literalism and anti-allegorist polemic, see esp. Simonetti (1985, 167–180) and Devreesse (1948, 51; 53–55). In particular, on Theodore's rationalistic hermeneutics see Kofsky-Ruzer (2019).

59 Consider, for example, the case of Basil, who, as Runia (2001, 130) notes, in relation to the connection between the number 6 and the creation of the cosmos refers to specialists in arithmology whose exegesis, however, is considered too speculative for the needs of the Church.

spoken of as 'one' and not as 'first,' for which Philoponus also feels called upon to find a philosophical explanation.

Despite the differences, some points of contact can be found in the exegeses of Philo and Philoponus. Philoponus may have recognised in Philo's *De opificio* a relevant Jewish precedent for the presentation—through recourse to similar philosophical sources, such as Plato's *Timaeus*—of a created time that, once it has begun to flow, proceeds in its spirals: elliptical and imperishable for Philo, circular and continuing to the end of the cosmos for Philoponus. Their conceptions of time are both based on faith in a God who, in both works on creation, is implicitly presented as a watchmaker who not only builds the clock of the world but also operates it, making the ticking of the passage of time resound.

Both Philo and Philoponus take 'day one' to be the unit of time, although for Philo in 'day one' we are in the context of intelligible time, i. e. the perpetuity that characterizes the model, whereas for Philoponus we are in the context of sense-perceptible time, which for him is the only existing form of temporality. Both authors, in treating time as a number, draw more or less extensively on arithmological traditions of Neopythagorean origin in order to justify the significance of certain numbers in relation to the days of creation in *Genesis* and to emphasize their 'generative' character. Philo focuses above all on the generative character that defines the six days and thus the sense-perceptible world as 'generated,' while Philoponus emphasizes the poietic and generative properties of 'day one,' from which all time derives.

The philosophical sources on which Philo and Philoponus draw have a different weight in their works: one thinks of the marked recourse to Aristotelianism by Philoponus compared to the more implicit debt owed to Philo only in relation to certain issues, such as the correlation between time and number. But both authors show that they interpret Scripture philosophically, not merely by making philosophy an instrument at the service of faith (in the Jewish or Christian tradition), but also by 'doing philosophy:' both give philosophical answers to the exegetical questions raised by Scripture, such as that of 'day one' and the dawn of the world. For this reason, in their hexamerons (i. e. cosmologies) the cosmos can be seen as a clock whose mechanism is rationally justified and in which time is set in motion by God the watchmaker.

Bibliography

Alesso, M. 2004. "La génesis del tiempo en Filón de Alejandría." *Circe* 9: 17–32.
Annas, J. 1975. "Aristotle, Number and Time." *The Philosophical Quarterly* 25, no. 99: 97–113.
Aristote. 1965. *Du ciel. Texte établi et traduit*, edited by P. Moraux. Paris: Les Belles Lettres.

Aristotelis. 1951. *Physica*, edited by W. D. Ross. Oxford: Clarendon Press.
Aristotelis. 1957. *Metaphysica*, edited by W. Jaeger. Oxford: Clarendon Press.
Aristotelis. 1966. *Categoriae et Liber de interpretatione*, edited by L. Minio-Paluello. Oxford: Clarendon Press.
Basile de Césarée. 1968. *Homélies sur l'Hexaéméron*, edited and translated by S. Giet. Paris: Éditions du Cerf.
Broadie, S. 2014. *Philoponus: On Aristotle Physics 4.10–14.* Preface by R. Sorabji. London: Bloomsbury Academic.
Cavagnaro, E. 2002. *Aristotele e il tempo: Analisi di Physica, IV 10–14.* Naples: Liguori Editore.
Centrone, B. 2015. "L'esegesi del *Timeo* nell'Accademia antica." In *Il Timeo: Esegesi greche, arabe, latine*, edited by F. Clelia and A. Ulacco, 57–80. Pisa: Edizioni ETS.
Cicero. 1955–1958. *De natura deorum*, edited by A. S. Pease. 2 vols. Cambridge, MA: Harvard University Press.
Coope, U. 2005. *Time for Aristotle.* Oxford: Oxford University Press.
Crepaldi, M. G. 1985. *La concezione del tempo tra pensiero biblico e filosofia greca: Saggio su Filone di Alessandria.* Padua: Editrice Antenore.
De Bianchi, S. 2022. "Eternity, Instantaneity, and Temporality: Tackling the Problem of Time in Plato's Cosmology." In *Time and Cosmology in Plato and the Platonic Tradition*, edited by D. Vázquez and A. Ross, 156–178. Leiden/Boston: Brill.
De Luca, L. 2021a. *Il Dio architetto di Filone di Alessandria (De opificio mundi 17–20).* Preface by D. T. Runia. Milan: Mimesis Edizioni.
De Luca, L. 2021b. "Appendice. Mappatura delle metafore, similitudini, allegorie ed esempi nel *De opificio mundi* di Filone di Alessandria." In *Similitudini, metafore e allegoria nel De opificio mundi di Filone di Alessandria*, edited by L. De Luca, preface by A. Longo, 169–200. Rome: Edizioni di Storia e Letteratura.
De Luca, L. 2022. "Esegesi e astronomia ad Alessandria: un confronto tra Filone e Giovanni Filopono." *Adamantius* 28: 111–126.
De Luca, L. 2023a. "'Come un buon demiurgo' (οἷα δημιουργὸς ἀγαθός): un'esegesi ebraica di *Tim.* 29a3." In *Paradigmi della demiurgia. Studi sul lessico demiurgico nel pensiero antico e tardoantico*, edited by E. Maffi, preface by A. Longo, 149–173. Naples: Bibliopolis.
De Luca, L. 2023b. "Il linguaggio creazionistico dell'aristotelismo cristiano: la demiurgia divina nel *De opificio mundi* di Giovanni Filopono a confronto con i suoi *Commentari ad Aristotele.*" In *L'esegesi aristotelica alla prova dell'esegesi biblica. Il De opificio mundi di Giovanni Filopono*, edited by A. Longo and T. F. Ottobrini, 67–95. Rome: Edizioni di Storia e Letteratura.
De Luca, L. 2024a. "The Epistemological Impact of the Argument from Design in Philo of Alexandria." In *Design Discourse in Abrahamic Traditions. History, Metaphysics, and Science*, edited by E. R. V. Kojonen and S. A. Malik, 17–31. London/New York: Routledge.
De Luca, L. 2024b. "Echi filoniani nel *De opificio mundi* di Giovanni Filopono." *Materia Giudaica* 27: 11–23.
De Luca, L. 2025a. "The Urban Imagery in the Cosmologies of Philo of Alexandria and John Philoponus." In *The World as a City. History of a Philosophical Image between the Ancient World and the Three Monotheisms*, edited by L. De Luca and S. Mecci, 308–333. Leiden/Boston: Brill.
De Luca, L. 2025b. "Tempo e creazione in Filone di Alessandria. Una sintesi barbara." In *La saggezza dei barbari. Grecia, tradizione ebraica e Persia*, edited by F. Casella, 205–249. Naples: Istituto Italiano per gli Studi Filosofici Press.

Devreesse, R. 1948. *Essai sur Théodore de Mopsueste.* Città del Vaticano: Biblioteca Apostolica Vaticana.

Ferrari, F. 2001. "Struttura e funzione dell'esegesi testuale nel medioplatonismo: il caso del *Timeo.*" *Athenaeum* 89: 525–574.

Giardina, G. 1999. *Giovanni Filopono matematico tra neopitagorismo e neoplatonismo. Commentario alla Introduzione aritmetica di Nicomaco di Gerasa. Introduzione, testo, traduzione e note.* Catania: CUECM.

Giardina, G. 2011. "Philopon (Jean)." In *Dictionnaire des Philosophes Antiques, De Paccius à Plotin*, edited by R. Goulet. Vol. V/A, 455–502. Paris: Éditions du CNRS.

Giardina, G. 2015. "Providence in John Philoponus' Commentary on Aristotle's *Physics.*" *CHORA* 13: 149–172.

Giardina, G. 2023. "Il principio della creazione nel *De opificio mundi* di Giovanni Filopono." In *L'esegesi aristotelica alla prova dell'esegesi biblica. Il De opificio mundi di Giovanni Filopono*, edited by A. Longo and T. F. Ottobrini, 21–40. Rome: Edizioni di Storia e Letteratura.

Greene, B. A. 2018. *The Imperfect Present: Stoic Physics of Time.* PhD diss., San Diego.

Iosephus. 1955. *Flavii Iosephi opera*, edited by B. Niese. Vol. 1–4. Berlin: Weidmannsche Verlagsbuchhandlung.

Justin Martyr. 2009. *Justin, Philosopher and Martyr: Apologies*, edited with an Introduction, Translation, and Commentary on the Text by D. Minns and P. Parvis. Oxford/New York: Oxford University Press.

Keizer, H. M. 1999. *Life Time Entirety. A Study of AION in Greek Literature and Philosophy, the Septuagint and Philo.* PhD diss., Amsterdam.

Keizer, H. M. 2000. "'Eternity' Revisited. A Study of the Greek Word αἰών." *Philosophia Reformata* 65: 53–71.

Köckert, C. 2009. *Christliche Kosmologie und kaiserzeitliche Philosophie. Die Auslegung des Schöpfungsberichtes bei Origenes, Basilius und Gregor von Nyssa vor dem Hintergrund kaiserzeitlicher Timaeus-Interpretationen.* Tübingen: Mohr Siebeck.

Lauer, S. 1958. "Philo's Concept of Time." *Journal of Jewish Studies* 9: 39–46.

Lévy, C. 2011. "L'Aristotelisme, parent pauvre de la pensée philonienne?" In *Plato, Aristotle, or Both? Dialogues between Platonism and Aristotelianism in Antiquity*, edited by T. Bénatouïl, E. Maffi, and F. Trabattoni, 17–33. Hildesheim et al.: Olms.

Long, A. A. 2006. "The Stoics on world-conflagration and everlasting recurrence." In *From Epicurus to Epictetus: Studies in Hellenistic and Roman Philosophy*, edited by A. A. Long, 256–282. Oxford/New York: Oxford University Press.

MacCoull, L. S. B. 1989. "Philoponus and the London sundial: some calendrical aspects of the *De opificio mundi.*" *Byzantinische Zeitschrift* 82: 19–21.

Niehoff, M. R. 2007. "Did the *Timaeus* Create a Textual Community?" *Greek, Roman, and Byzantine Studies* 47: 161–191.

Niehoff, M. R. 2018. *Philo of Alexandria: An Intellectual Biography.* New Haven: Yale University Press.

Ottobrini, T. F. 2019. "Intorno al tempo nella cosmoktisi aristotelica del *De opificio mundi* di Giovanni Filopono." In *Tempo di Dio, tempo dell'uomo: XLVI Incontro di studiosi dell'antichità cristiana*, edited by M. Ghilardi, 295–310. Lugano: Nerbini International.

Ottobrini, T. F. 2023a. *Giovanni Filopono e l'esegesi biblica di matrice aristotelica: il De opificio mundi.* Milan: Vita e Pensiero.

Ottobrini, T. F. 2023b. "Lo sfruttamento di Aristotele in Filopono, *De op.* I.3: Tra l'auctoritas di Basilio Magno e una forma di manifesto esegetico-speculativo." In *L'esegesi aristotelica alla*

prova dell'esegesi biblica. Il De opificio mundi di Giovanni Filopono, edited by A. Longo and T. F. Ottobrini, 41–62. Rome: Edizioni di Storia e Letteratura.
Petrucci, F. M. 2015. "L'esegesi e il commento di Platone (a partire dall'esegesi della cosmogonia del *Timeo*)." *Rivista di Storia della Filosofia* 70, no. 2: 295–320.
Petrucci, F. M. 2018. *Taurus of Beirut. The Other Side of Middle Platonism.* London/New York: Routledge.
Petrucci, F. M. 2019. "'Il principio didascalías charin' nel medioplatonismo: breve storia di un dibattito filosofico." In *Studi sul medioplatonismo e il neoplatonismo*, edited by C. Natali, E. Cattanei, and R. Medda, 15–41. Rome: Edizioni di Storia e Letteratura.
Philo. 1962–1963. *Philonis Alexandrini opera quae supersunt*, edited by L. Cohn and P. Wendland. Vol. 1–7. Berlin: Reimer.
Philoponus. 1897. *Joannis Philoponi De opificio mundi libri VII*, edited by W. Reichardt. Leipzig: Teubner.
Philoponus. 1997. *De opificio mundi. Über die Erschaffung der Welt*, translated and introduced by C. Scholten. Vol. 1–3. Freiburg i. Br. et al.: Herder.
Philoponus. 1887–1898. *Ioannis Philoponi in Aristotelis Physicorum Libros Tres Priores Commentaria*, edited by H. Vitelli. Berlin: Reimer.
Plato. 1968. *Platonis opera*, edited by J. Burnet. Vol. 1–4. Oxford: Clarendon Press.
Plotinus. 1951–1973. *Plotini opera*, edited by P. Henry and H.-R. Schwyzer. Vol. 1–3. Leiden: Brill.
Ptolemaeus. 1930. *Die Harmonielehre des Klaudios Ptolemaios*, edited by I. Düring. Göteborg: Elanders.
Runia, D. T. 1986. *Philo of Alexandria and the Timaeus of Plato.* Leiden: Brill.
Runia, D. T. 1999. *Filone di Alessandria nella prima letteratura cristiana*, edited by R. Radice. Milan: Jaca Book.
Runia, D. T. 2000. "Philo's Longest Arithmological Passage: *De opificio mundi* 89–128." In *De Jérusalem à Rome: Mélanges J. Riaud*, edited by L.-J. Bord and D. Hamidovic, 155–174. Paris: Éditions du Cerf.
Runia, D. T. 2001. *On the Creation of the Cosmos according to Moses.* Leiden/Boston: Brill.
Runia, D. T. 2007. "The Rehabilitation of the Jackdaw: Philo of Alexandria and Ancient Philosophy." In *Greek and Roman Philosophy 100 BC–200 AD*, edited by R. Sorabji and R. W. Sharples. Vol. 2, 483–500. London: Routledge.
Sambursky, S. 1959. *Physics of the Stoics.* Westport, CT: Greenwood Press.
Sharples, R. W. 2008. "Philo and Post-Aristotelian Peripatetics." In *Philo of Alexandria and Post-Aristotelian Philosophy*, edited by F. Alesse, 55–74. Leiden/Boston: Brill.
Schäublin, C. 1974. *Untersuchungen zu Methode und Herkunft der antiochenischen Exegese.* Cologne/Bonn: Peter Hanstein.
Simonetti, M. 1985. *Lettera e/o allegoria: un contributo alla storia dell'esegesi patristica.* Rome: Istituto Patristico Augustinianum.
Sorabji, R. 2006. *Time, Creation and the Continuum: Theories in Antiquity and the Early Middle Ages.* Chicago: University of Chicago Press.
Sorabji, R. 2010. *Philoponus and the Rejection of Aristotelian Science.* London: Duckworth.
Stobaeus. 1884–1912. *Ioannis Stobaei Anthologium*, edited by C. Wachsmuth and O. Hense. Vol. 1–5. Berlin: Weidmannsche Verlagsbuchhandlung.
Strauss, Z. 2022. "God, the Grandfather of Time: Time and the Absolute in the Thought of Philo of Alexandria." In *Temporality and Eternity: Nine Perspectives on God and Time*, edited by M. Schmücker, M. T. Williams, and F. Fischer, 71–87. Berlin: De Gruyter.

Thein, K. 2020. "Planets and Time: A Timaean Puzzle." In *Plato's Timaeus: Proceedings of the Tenth Symposium Platonicum Pragense*, edited by C. Jorgenson, F. Karfík, and Š. Špinka, 92–111. Leiden/Boston: Brill.

Trotta, A. 1981. "Interpretazione e critica di Plotino della concezione del tempo dei suoi predecessori." *Rivista di Filosofia Neo-Scolastica* 31: 340–368.

von Leyden, W. 1964. "Time, Number, and Eternity in Plato and Aristotle." *Philosophical Quarterly* 54: 35–52.

Wildberg, C. 1988. *John Philoponus' Criticism of Aristotle's Theory of Aether.* Berlin/New York: De Gruyter.

Wolfson, H. A. 1966. "Plato's Pre-Existent Matter in Patristic Philosophy." In *The Classical Tradition: Literary and Historical Studies in Honor of Harry Chaplan*, edited by L. Wallach, 409–420. Ithaca, NY: Cornell University Press.

Maren R. Niehoff

The Conflagration of the World in Philo, Josephus and Rabbi Abbahu

Responses to a Circular Model of Time Advocated by the Stoics

The total conflagration of the world, or ἐκπύρωσις, was a prominent and unique aspect of Stoic cosmology, which prompted lively debates throughout the history of the school.[1] Diogenes Laertius introduces the idea as part of the Stoic distinction between an active and a passive principle in the universe. While the latter is substance without quality, the active principle is the divine reason permeating matter. God is eternal and the artificer of each thing, whereas "the elements are destroyed at the time of the conflagration" (τὰ δὲ στοιχεῖα κατὰ τὴν ἐκπύρωσιν φθείρεσθαι, *Lives* 7.134). Laertius lists a large number of treatises expounding this Stoic theory, ranging from Zeno's *On Existence* and *On the Whole* to Cleanthes' *On Atoms*, Chrysippus' *Physics* and Posidonius' *Physical Exposition* and *On the Cosmos.* Contrary to Aristotle, the Stoics deduced the destruction of the world from the observable fact that its parts perish and explained its mechanism by pointing to various qualities of the consuming fire and its relation to the demiurge.[2] Laertius concludes his report of the Stoic doctrine by noting the exceptional position of Panaetius, who insisted that the cosmos is "indestructible" (ἄφθαρτον, *Lives* 7.142).

The Stoic theory of the conflagration has also prompted lively debates in modern scholarship, which revolve around the question of Divine providence. In an

Note: A first draft of this article was presented at a Sapere conference in Göttingen (2022) and benefitted from a productive discussion. Moreover, the Israel Science Foundation (1346/21) and the European Research Council (advanced grant no. 101141400) generously supported the research on which this paper is based. The Einstein Center Chronoi in Berlin generously supported an *Exploration* on "Creationism and the Calculation of Time in Late Antiquity: Between Alexandria and the Land of Israel", which provided a congenial environment for the research on this paper and benefitted from the discussion at the workshop in Berlin (2023). Thanks also to Arnon Atzmon, Warren Z. Harvey, Jaap Mansfeld, Gretchen Reydams-Schils, Yakir Paz, David T. Runia and Sharon Weisser for their careful comments on a draft of this article. The translations are my own, unless otherwise stated.

1 Plutarch's remark that "Cleanthes contended for the conflagration", i.e. defended it (ἐπαγωνιζόμενος ὁ Κλεάνθης τῇ ἐκπυρώσει, *Mor.* 1075d) suggests that Stoic debates started at a very early stage, perhaps even at the time of Zeno.

2 Diogenes Laertius, *Lives* 7.141; see also Alexander of Lycopolis 19.2–4 quoted in Long and Sedley (1987, 1.276; 2.275).

 https://doi.org/10.1515/9783112225981-004

influential article, Jaap Mansfeld identified the prospect of the world's destruction as a "grim event" and dismantled Chrysippus' affirmation of Zeus' wholly positive role in it as a "sort of trick, which converts evil into good in a purely stipulative way."[3] Mansfeld furthermore looked for signs that the Stoics themselves perceived of a tension between the good demiurge and his part in the destruction, highlighting the dissatisfaction of later Stoics with the doctrine.[4] Anthony A. Long, by contrast, insisted that the conflagration "instantiates providence" and results from Zeus' benevolent and rational decision rather than from mechanical necessity to which even the demiurge has to submit.[5] In his view, the Stoics generally conceived the conflagration as part of a recurrent cosmic cycle supervised by a benevolent and providential god, namely Zeus, who is involved in the contrary, but complementary processes of expansion and withdrawal.

This stalemate in modern scholarship can be resolved by looking at Jewish interpretations of the Stoic conflagration. Jewish contributions are of special interest, because we possess the views of three authors respectively from the first and the third century CE, namely Philo, Josephus and Rabbi Abbahu. They span the period of important developments in the Stoic doctrine, when other sources are sparse. Moreover, these Jewish figures approach the topic from a religious perspective based on a commitment to the idea of a benevolent demiurge. Their historical and philosophical backgrounds, however, differ considerably and thus shed important light on the evolvement of the various debates concerning the conflagration. Philo and Josephus indicate the importance of Rome as a philosophical platform and even a turning point, while Abbahu engages an updated version of the doctrine which also became popular among Christian authors.

Let me briefly introduce the three Jewish authors, who are analyzed in this article. The Jewish philosopher Philo (ca. 20 BCE–50 CE) started his career as a Bible exegete in the Jewish community of Alexandria, but later spent several years in Rome as the head of the Jewish embassy to Gaius Caligula.[6] According to my analysis in the *Intellectual Biography*, Philo came into intensive contact with Roman Stoicism during his time in Rome and his works from this period throw light on the development of philosophical debates between Cicero and Seneca. The Jewish historian Josephus (ca. 37–100 CE) grew up in Jerusalem, but settled in Rome after the defeat of the Jewish revolt. He, too, participated in intellectual circles in the capital of the empire and addressed broader Greco-Roman

3 Mansfeld (1979, 137; 183); see also Mansfeld (2017, 114–118; 124–125); Ildefonse (2004); Salles (2005); Forschner (2018, 136–143).

4 Mansfeld (1979, 148–159), with ample references to Philo as a source of dissatisfied Stoics.

5 Long (1985, 270); see also Long and Sedley (1987, 1.277–279).

6 For details, see Niehoff (2018).

audiences.[7] Finally, Rabbi Abbahu, was a prominent leader of the Jewish community in third century Caesarea, who was well-versed in the Greek language and Greco-Roman culture.[8]

These three authors reacted to the Stoic notion of the world conflagration in complex and even surprising ways. Josephus is closest to the Stoics in terms of his philosophical affiliation. He declares himself a Pharisee and explicitly associates this school with the Stoics (*Vita* 12). Instead of embracing the conflagration, however, he is the only one of the three authors discussed here, who does not mention the Stoic concept. His reasons for doing so and carefully cleansing certain Biblical stories from elements that could suggest similarities with the conflagration will be analyzed in the context of first century Rome. Josephus suggests that in Rome the notion of a benevolent and providential demiurge surveying the world in an uninterrupted manner is of central importance. Philo, by contrast, is an author with a strong Platonic background, who dedicates one of his later Roman works to the indestructibility of the world and offers a detailed critique of the conflagration. Keen to dissuade his readers from the Classical Stoic doctrine, Philo highlights the diversity of views within the Stoic school and provides unique evidence of philosophical debates in first century CE Rome. He thus illuminates the transition to later Stoic perspectives and renders Seneca understandable.[9] Abbahu's contribution to philosophical debates in Late Antiquity is usually overlooked because he regularly expressed himself in Hebrew or Aramaic. Notwithstanding such linguistic distinctions, however, he was not only familiar with the updated concept of the conflagration, but wholeheartedly accepted it. His position remarkably differs from that of Philo in the first century CE, but resonates with that of the Church Father Origen, with whom he probably overlapped for several years in Caesarea.

7 For details, see Mason (2003, 559–589); Mason (2016, 89–107); Niehoff (2019, 83–103); Niehoff (2016, 135–146).

8 For details, see Levine (1975, 56–76); Niehoff (2019); Niehoff (2020); Niehoff (2025).

9 Philo's testimony to Stoic notions of the conflagration is more illuminating than that of Plutarch, who became too exasperated by what he called their "absurdities" (ἄτοπα, Levine 1975) to look for more congenial voices among them. For the complexity of Plutarch's attitude toward Stoicism, see Opsomer (2014, 88–103); Opsomer (2017, 296–321).

1 Josephus: a Benchmark in Late First Century Rome

We start our comparison of the three Jewish authors with Josephus, who explicitly associates himself with the Stoic school. His autobiography tells the story of his childhood in Jerusalem and his early diplomatic visit to Rome, which convinced him of the Romans' superiority and fortune (*Vita* 7–23). After testing the different Jewish philosophies, Josephus joins the "school of the Pharisees, which is similar to that called Stoic by the Greeks."[10] Adopting a Pharisaic approach primarily means for Josephus to take seriously the notion of Divine providence, which combines free will and moral choice with the "help" of fate (βοηθεῖν).[11] The Sadducees, by contrast, rejected providence altogether, while the Essenes attributed everything to it. Josephus' scheme of three Jewish schools with different interpretations of providence corresponds to Cicero's exposition of three schools of theology, which also differ on the issue of fate and providence. In his report, the Stoics stress beneficial providence taking care both of the universe and the individual, notions denied respectively by the Platonists and the Epicureans.[12] Josephus' interpretation of the Pharisees not only resonates with Cicero's presentation of Stoicism in Rome, but also has political implications. When transferring to the Roman side, he stresses Divine guidance and fashions himself as a prophet of Vespasian's ascension to power.[13] The Pharisees, too, recognized Rome's fortune and advised against rebellion.[14]

As a Roman author affiliated with Stoicism, Josephus mentions the term *ekpurosis* only once, namely as a description of the eruption of Mount Vesuvius.[15] His use of the term is remarkably mundane and lacks any philosophical connotation, but parallels that of the Roman historian Suetonius, who applies the Latin noun *conflagratio* to the same volcanic eruption (*Tit.* 8.3). This nomenclature implies a focus on limited natural catastrophes, with no expectation that the whole cosmos may be destroyed. Josephus' disregard for the Classical Stoic notion of the world conflagration resonates with Cicero's marginalization of it in *On the Nature*

10 Josephus, *Vita* 12: τῇ Φαρισαίων αἱρέσει κατακολουθῶν, ἣ παραπλήσιός ἐστι τῇ παρ' Ἕλλησιν Στωικῇ λεγομένῃ; see also Feldman (1998, 192–194); Niehoff (2017, 203–224).

11 Josephus, *B.J.* 2.162. The translations of Josephus' texts are based on the Loeb edition.

12 Cicero, *Nat. d.* 2.73–92, 164–167. The similarity between Josephus and Cicero raises questions concerning their historical dependence, which deserve further study.

13 Josephus, *B.J.* 3.350–354, 400–402.

14 Josephus, *Vita* 17–23.

15 Josephus, *A.J.* 20.144: Κατὰ τὴν ἐκπύρωσιν τοῦ Βεσβίου.

of the Gods. His Stoic spokesman Balbus pays hardly any attention to the conflagration. Initially, he explains that his school addresses the topic of the immortal gods with special attention to the existence of the gods, their benevolent nature and rule over the world as well as their care for humanity (*Nat. d.* 2.3). Balbus introduces Cleanthes, Chrysippus and Zeno with statements about the qualities of the world which prompt men to recognize the divine demiurge behind the natural elements. Cleanthes points to factors alerting men to the demiurge's activity, namely the efficacy of prophecy, benefits of a benign climate, unusual weather conditions and comets as well as the uniform motion of the heavenly bodies (*Nat. d.* 2.13–15). Cicero connects these, and especially the first and third, to Roman examples. He thus indicates their popularity in contemporary discussions and hints at the criteria which guided him in selecting ideas from Cleanthes' philosophy. Chrysippus is similarly quoted for arguments congenial to Roman sensibilities, uncovering the superhuman nature of the cosmos (*Nat. d.* 2.16). Zeno in turn provides short syllogisms which prove the world's divine qualities (*Nat. d.* 2.20–22).

Cicero introduces the conflagration only in *Nat. d.* 2.118 and immediately adds the qualification that Panaetius "doubted" it. Balbus then briefly states the doctrine: "ultimately the whole world will burn."[16] The emphasis on the temporal distance of the process ensures that no conflagration is to be expected in the readers' lifetime. Moreover, the aspect of destruction hardly receives any attention. Cicero's Balbus instead highlights that when nothing but fire is left, "the renewal of the world may occur and indeed the same cosmic order be restored."[17] Cicero's report highlights the return of the same cosmos (*Nat. d.* 2.118) and echoes Chrysippus' doctrine.[18] His language is remarkably tentative and avoids any reference to the controversial idea that human lives are repeated in each new installment of the cosmos, a prospect later attacked by various Christian authors. Cicero's report rather stresses the harmonious coordination of Nature, which aims at the "preservation of the world" (*mundi incolumitatem*, *Nat. d.* 2.119). We may thus conclude that while Cicero's Stoic spokesman Balbus mentions the conflagration as part of the school's theology, he does so in a minimal fashion. Little space is assigned

---

16 Cicero, *Nat. d.* 2.118: *ad extremum omnis mundus ignesceret.*

17 Cicero, *Nat. d.* 2.118: *renovatio mundi fieret atque idem ornatus oreretur.*

18 For other attestations of this Classical Stoic idea, see Nemesius 309.5–311.2; Simplicius, *Arist. Phys.* 886.12–16; Alexander of Aphrodisias, *In Arist. APo.* 180.33–36; 181.25–31, quoted and discussed in Long and Sedley (1987, 1.309–313; 2.306–308); see also Sedley (2007, 208–209); Forschner (2018, 138–141). Lactantius, *Inst.* 7.23 attributes a softer version to Chrysippus, who says that it is "evidently not impossible that we too after death will return again to the shape we now are, after certain periods of time have elapsed" (translation from Long and Sedley 1987, 1.308).

to it and the preservation of the world is stressed to the extent that queries about theodicy are pre-emptively solved. In first century BCE Rome, the conflagration no longer played the same role as in Cleanthes' and Chrysippus' thought. As an admirer of Panaetius, Cicero marginalized this aspect of Stoic cosmology and thus rendered it more palatable for Roman tastes.[19] Josephus follows in his footsteps and altogether refrains from mentioning the Stoic idea of the conflagration.

Josephus' oblivion may of course result from sheer ignorance. However, his careful interpretations of Biblical stories with similarities to the Stoic doctrine teach us otherwise and indicate that his avoidance of the conflagration is a conscious choice. His reaction to the Biblical story of the deluge, for example, is revealing. In Gen 6:5–13, God resolves to destroy humanity together with the earth, seeing that the latter "has been filled with evil on account of them."[20] Josephus' paraphrase focuses exclusively on humanity, while ignoring the destruction of the earth. He asserts that God loved Noah for his righteousness and condemned the sinners to the extent that he wished "to destroy all mankind existing then and to create another race pure of vice" (*A.J.* 1.75). In Josephus' paraphrase, the destruction of most of humanity is justified by the prospect of moral improvement. Josephus moreover adds that God "converted the dry land into a sea" in order to punish the wicked and provide a safe ark for the righteous (*A.J.* 1.76). Here, too, the force of the destruction is attenuated by stressing Divine providence protecting the singular righteous.

The Biblical story concludes with Noah's sacrifice and God's smelling of its pleasing odor, which prompts Him to promise: "I will never again curse the earth because of man [...] neither will I ever again destroy every living creature as I have done."[21] Josephus avoids such anthropomorphic images, especially God's repentance and enjoyment of material goods. He instead imagines Noah's prayer, which addresses the theological problems he himself had with a massive destruction initiated by God. His Noah fears that God may want to destroy mankind and continuously inflict calamities on the world (*A.J.* 1.96). The righteous, who have been saved, now deserve to be absolutely secure that no further deluge will flood the earth so that they can peacefully apply themselves to its cultivation. God

---

19 For Cicero's admiration of Panaetius, see esp. Cicero, *Off.* 3.7: "Panaetius then has without a doubt discussed moral duties in the most meticulous manner (*accuratissime*) and we have followed him above all others, with the addition of some correction"; on Cicero's free rather than "slavish" use of his work see Cicero, *Off.* 2.60.

20 Gen 6:13, the Hebrew and the LXX, both of which were available to Josephus, closely correspond to each other (כי מלאה הארץ חמס מפניהם והנני משחיתם את הארץ; against ὅτι ἐπλήσθη ἡ γῆ ἀδικίας ἀπ' αὐτῶν καὶ ἰδοὺ ἐγὼ καταφθείρω αὐτοὺς καὶ τὴν γῆν).

21 Gen 8:21; the LXX corresponds to the Hebrew.

in turn explains that "those who were destroyed did not perish by Him, but through their own wickedness" (*A.J.* 1.99). Had God planned to annihilate humanity, He "would not have introduced them to life, seeing that it is reasonable not to grant them life in the first place rather than to grant it and then destroy it" (*A.J.* 1.100). This exchange between Noah and God shows that the deluge is theologically problematic in Josephus' eyes, since it implies the notion of a changing and unpredictable God, who destroys innocent people in His wrath. The difficulty is solved by God's promise to ensure the regular course of Nature from now on. Any sign of His regret or change of mind is eliminated, including the introductory remark about God's remorse in Gen 6:6, which is already softened in LXX.

Another example is Josephus' interpretation of the story of Sodom and Gomorrah. The Biblical story mentions the "fire from the Lord", which destroys the city following the continued wickedness of its inhabitants.[22] Josephus uses the Greek verb καταπίμπρημι ("to burn down completely") in connection with the city and then adds a comparison to the land: "annihilating the earth in a similar burning" (τὴν γῆν ὁμοίᾳ πυρώσει ἀφανίζων, *A.J.* 1.203). The term *purosis* (πύρωσις), fire or burning, is introduced here without a *Vorlage* in the LXX. It is very close to the Stoic technical term *ekpurosis* but avoids its philosophical ballast. Whether or not Josephus consciously uses it to distinguish Biblical from Stoic fire, he speaks once more about a limited destruction, not a conflagration of the entire world.

Josephus' affiliation with the Stoic school thus turns out to be peculiarly Roman, namely focused on Divine providence in a perfect world. He marginalizes the conflagration even more than Cicero's Stoic spokesman Balbus and ignores it altogether. However, the theological concerns connected with the Stoic doctrine resurface in Josephus' interpretations of Biblical stories which have clear affinities with the Stoic narrative. His affirmation of a benevolent and providential demiurge and his insistence on the indestructibility of the world point beyond his personal sensibilities to broader queries that the Stoic doctrine would raise in an intellectual environment prioritizing Divine providence in a world-wide empire.

---

22 Gen 19:24; ואש מאת יהוה; against πῦρ παρὰ κυρίου.

2 Philo: A Unique Window on Debates about the Conflagration

Writing a generation before Josephus, Philo of Alexandria mentions the conflagration nineteen times throughout his oeuvre, but only once in the numerous treatises of his *Allegorical Commentary* from his earlier career within the Jewish community of Alexandria.[23] In *Her.* 228, he briefly dismisses the conflagration as a "mythological wonder account" (μυθευομένην τερατολογίαν) and asserts that Moses excludes the implied (Stoic) notion of a void surrounding the world into which the fire could extend. The other eighteen references to the conflagration come in Philo's later Roman writings, sixteen of them in his treatise *On the Indestructibility of the Cosmos.*[24] David T. Runia has drawn attention to the structure and importance of this treatise, which consists to a large extent of quotations from other authors, supplemented by Philo's detailed introduction, running comments and his own exposition in another, no longer extant treatise.[25] In my own analysis of Philo's oeuvre in its historical context, the treatise has emerged as one of the philosophical works from his later Roman period, written in the context of the embassy to Gaius Caligula.[26] Philo's philosophical treatises address broader Greco-Roman rather than Jewish audiences and engage themes animating Roman rather than Alexandrian discourses.[27] Not surprisingly, the topic of providence receives a special treatise during this period, some of its Greek fragments depicting God as a providential father and creator of the world.[28]

---

23 For details on the chronology of Philo's works and the respective place of the *Allegorical Commentary*, see Niehoff (2018, 1–22, 173–241).

24 In the Greek-English Loeb edition of Philo's works the treatise is misleadingly called "On the Eternity of the World", which refers to a world without beginning and end. This nomenclature has been highly influential in modern scholarship, even in Hebrew, despite the German translator's more faithful rendering "Über die Unvergänglichkeit der Welt" and the French translator's clarification that *De l'incurruptibilité du monde* is a more exact title. Philo's additional two references to the conflagration are to be found in *Spec.* 1.208, where he casually mentions the conflagration and the reconstruction as concepts held by others.

25 Runia (1981, 105–151); see also Arnaldez (1969, 11–70), with a review of scholarship; Morris (1987, Vol. 3.2, 858–859); Niehoff (2007, 35–55); Royse (2009, 56); Karshon (2015, 407–421).

26 For details, see Niehoff (2018, 69–90).

27 The distinctiveness of Roman philosophy has often been overlooked by scholars, who generally assume that Roman thinkers merely imitated the Greeks and can therefore serve only as a source for the latter. For different views, with emphasis on the role of Rome as an intellectual center in its own right, see Barnes and Griffin (1997); Griffin (1976); Griffin (2013); Long (2003, 184–210); Bartsch (2006); Bartsch and Schiesaro (2015).

28 For details, see Royse (2009, 57–58).

The treatise *On the Indestructibility of the Cosmos* clearly addresses a broader non-Jewish audience since Philo introduces Moses as the "lawgiver of the Jews" rather than self-evidently quoting Scriptural verses as he does in the *Allegorical Commentary* (*Aet.* 19). He moreover explains that the first of the five books of Moses is called "Genesis" and treats the creation of the world (*Aet.* 19). Parallel to Greek philosophers, such as Plato and Hesiod, Moses is said to advocate the indestructibility of the cosmos (*Aet.* 19). Philo's appeal to non-Jewish readers, who lack even the most basic knowledge about Moses and the Bible, has significant philosophical implications. His arguments must have been articulated with a view to Greek-speaking readers in Rome and probably reflect their interests and topical concerns. The very subject of the treatise is noteworthy in this context, because Philo considered it of little concern in his earlier Alexandrian period. We must thus ask why he has chosen to treat the indestructibility of the world at such length while active in Rome. Which debates does he hope to engage in? To what extent does he reflect the state of the discussion with which Seneca would also have been familiar?

The treatise opens with a review of various definitions of the term cosmos. The Stoics, Philo reports, define the cosmos as "extending through the conflagration, some substance which is either in an orderly or a disorderly state, and the measure of its movement, they say, is time."[29] The English translator Francis Henry Colson has rightly argued that the expression ἄχρι τῆς ἐκπυρώσεως cannot mean here "until the conflagration", but must refer to the extension of the world "continuously to and through the general conflagration", since Philo includes also the disorderly state which undoubtedly pertains to the time of the conflagration.[30] Colson's conclusion can be further substantiated by looking at Philo's inclusive use of ἄχρι in *Aet.* 60 and 96, in the latter passage in the sense of "as long as the stem is sound" (ἄχρι μὲν ὑγιαίνει τὸ στέλεχος). In *Aet.* 8 he moreover stresses that the Stoics recognize only one world, which continues throughout the conflagration. Philo has thus chosen a Stoic definition, which highlights the continuity of the world and is congenial to his own, Platonically inspired commitment to the

---

29 Philo, *Aet.* 4: διῆκων ἄχρι τῆς ἐκπυρώσεως, οὐσία τις ἢ διακεκοσμημένη ἢ ἀδιακόσμητος, οὗ τῆς κινήσεώς φασιν εἶναι τὸν χρόνον διάστημα. The Greek text is that of Cohn and Reiter (1925). Note that the vulgate text has διήκουσα, applying the participle to the feminine noun οὐσία, an option which creates an odd syntax. Colson (1985, 187) adopts Jessen's emendation δῆκον, even though he admits: "I do not see why [ὁ] διῆκων (sc. κόσμος) should not be possible." On the Stoic notion of time here and elsewhere in Philo's work, see Runia (1986, 216); Niehoff (2024, 59–76).

30 Colson (1985, 187). See the German, the French, and the Hebrew translators, who render "until the conflagration:" Bormann (1964, 79) "bis zum Weltenbrand;" Arnaldez (1969, 77) "jusqu'à la conflagration;" Karshon (2015, 424) עד הבערה הגדולה.

indestructibility of the world. He may have unconsciously used the ambivalent term ἄχρι, with its more common connotation of "until," because the two meanings reflect the different interpretations of the conflagration among the Stoics, which will occupy him throughout his treatise.

Philo's selection of this particular Stoic definition of the cosmos is conspicuous. It assumes that the cosmos is not destroyed at any point in the recurrent cycles of changes, but maintains its identifiable character so that the same name applies. It resonates with Diogenes Laertius' first definition of cosmos as god, the artificer of the orderly arrangement, "who at certain periods of time assimilates to himself all substance and generates it again from within himself."[31] Associated with God, the "indestructible and uncreated" (ἄφθαρτος καὶ ἀγένητος, *Lives* 7.137), the term cosmos pertains to the world's unchanging rational essence. While Philo himself does not accept such a material view of the demiurge and insists on the literal creation of the world, he quotes a Stoic definition of the cosmos, which is at once uniquely Stoic and involves the conflagration, but also implies the indestructibility of the cosmos advocated in a different manner by Plato and Aristotle.[32] The conflagration thus amounts to cosmic change under God's providential guidance. This Stoic definition is also close to the view of Balbus, Cicero's Stoic spokesman, who, as we saw, says in the context of the conflagration that Nature aims at the "preservation of the world" (*Nat. d.* 2.119).

Philo exposes further Stoic complexities in *Aet.* 8–9:

> (8) The Stoics, however, say that the world is one, that God is the cause of its creation, but that He is no longer the cause of its destruction (γενέσεως δ' αὐτοῦ θεὸν αἴτιον, φθορᾶς δὲ μηκέτι θεόν). They instead say that the power of the ever-fervent fire, which exists in all things (τὴν ὑπάρχουσαν ἐν τοῖς οὖσι πυρὸς ἀκαμάτου δύναμιν), resolves everything into itself in long intervals of time and from it again emerges the regeneration of the cosmos through the foresight of the architect (ἐξ ἧς πάλιν ἀναγέννησιν κόσμου συνίστασθαι προμηθείᾳ τοῦ τεχνίτου). (9) It is possible then, according to these, that the cosmos is in one sense said to be eternal, but perishable in another (δύναται δὲ κατὰ τούτους ὁ μέν τις κόσμος ἀίδιος, ὁ δέ τις φθαρτὸς λέγεσθαι). Perishable is the cosmos in terms of its disintegration, but eternal in terms of the conflagration, achieving immortality through the never-ceasing regenerations and cycles (ἀίδιος δὲ ὁ κατὰ τὴν ἐκπύρωσιν παλιγγενεσίαις καὶ περιόδοις ἀθανατιζόμενος οὐδέποτε ληγούσαις).

31 Diogenes Laertius, *Lives* 7.137: κατὰ χρόνων ποιὰς περιόδους ἀναλίσκων εἰς ἑαυτὸν τὴν ἅπασαν οὐσίαν καὶ πάλιν ἐξ ἑαυτοῦ γεννῶν.

32 Arnaldez (1969, 42) rightly emphasizes that the Stoic definition quoted by Philo resonates with Plato, Aristotle, Scripture and Ocellus, but then dismisses it as "un usage tout à l'opposé du stoicisme." The latter remark overlooks the variety of Stoic views. On Plato's and Aristotle's notion of the world's indestructibility, see Runia (2001, 113).

This description provides unique glimpses into Stoic concerns about the conflagration. Some Stoics evidently disconnected Zeus from the element of the destructive fire in order to absolve him from the responsibility for the damage inflicted on the world and humanity. He is reintroduced at the stage of the regeneration, overseeing as the providential architect the new installment of the cosmos. Philo's testimony is precious, because it offers the first extant formulation of the problem of theodicy among Stoics.[33] His report leaves no doubt that some of them wished to extract the demiurge from the element of destruction.

This interpretation of the conflagration undermines the Classical Stoic assumption of an inseparable connection between Zeus and the fire. In three passages of Philo's treatise *On the Indestructibility of the Cosmos*, which have thus far not been given sufficient attention, Chrysippus' doctrine is explained. While his predecessor Cleanthes thought that the world at the conflagration is consumed into fire, Chrysippus held that it resolves into light (αὐγή, *Aet.* 90). Moreover, the very fire, which resolved the world "is the seed of the cosmos which is about to be produced."[34] Indeed, "generation comes from seed and the resolution passes into seed" (*Aet.* 94). According to Chrysippus, the same element, namely fire, is responsible for both the destruction and the regeneration. The image of the light indicates that both aspects are perceived in positive terms. Philo supplements these insights in another passage by a quotation from Chrysippus' treatise *On Increase*, which discusses the conflagration in connection with the World Soul and providence (*Aet.* 45–51). Philo's polemics against the "atrocity" of destroying Divine providence is so strong at this point that Chrysippus' argument is not as clear as one would have hoped. The context, however, is the suspicion that the Stoic destruction also pertains to the gods.[35] Chrysippus seems to argue from the analogy of Dion and Theon that the substance of the world, which is resolved in the conflagration, is subsumed in the demiurge without losing its soul. A clear connection, if not identity, between god and the fire seems to be assumed.[36] While

33 Cf. Cleanthes' isolated sentence preserved by Plutarch, namely the "sun assimilates to itself the moon and the rest of the stars and changes them into itself" (*Mor.* 1075d), which Salles (2005) has reconstructed as a solution to the problem of theodicy, based on the fire as a necessary concomitant in a Platonic sense.

34 τὸ […] πῦρ τοῦ μέλλοντος ἀποτελεῖσθαι κόσμου σπέρμα, *Aet.* 94.

35 ἀφθαρσίαν δὲ θέους ἀποβαλεῖν ἀδύνατον, *Aet.* 46.

36 Philo's explanations are supplemented by the more general statements of Aetius and Stobaeus. According to the former, "the Stoics declare that God is intelligent, a designing fire which proceeds methodically to the generation of the cosmos," while according to Stobaeus Zeus, the sun, the moon, and the stars are "intelligent and prudent and have the fieriness of the designing fire" (Aet., *Plac.* 1.7.24; see also Mansfeld and Runia (2020, 4.2077–2078)); Stob. 1.213.15–21, see also Long and Sedley (1987, 1.274–275).

Chrysippus' doctrines are obviously relevant in first century Rome, where Philo may even have read his treatise *On Increase*, other Stoics seem to have reacted against him and proposed to disconnect Zeus from the destructive fire.

The theological background of these inner-Stoic debates emerges in a subsequent passage of Philo's treatise, where he offers a proof against the conflagration, which he expects to be approved by "thousands," who ask "for what reason will God destroy the cosmos?" (τίνος ἕνεκα τὸν κόσμον φθερεῖ ὁ θεός, *Aet.* 39). Philo suggests two alternatives: either God wishes to cease from world-making, which would be inconsistent with His nature, or He intended to prepare another world. The first alternative is easily dismissed and obviously enjoys no popularity, not even among the Stoics (*Aet.* 40). The second alternative, on the other hand, draws Philo's attention and seems to have resonated with his readers. He indeed presents the first extant account of the three possibilities, namely that the new world is either identical with the previous world or either better or worse (*Aet.* 41). As a Platonist, Philo associates the nature of the cosmos with its maker and consequently dismisses all three versions of a new world as reflecting negatively on the transcendental God.

Philo's arguments deserve attention, as they throw new light on later developments of the Stoic doctrine, most immediately on the views of Seneca and Rabbi Abbahu. Initially, Philo dismisses the assumption of an inferior world emerging from the conflagration by suggesting that it would imply a defect in the demiurge (*Aet.* 41). The support for this critique comes from an anonymous saying, suggesting that even a woman would prefer higher to lower quality. Philo's casual style indicates that he does not expect serious philosophical interest in the option of an inferior world. The prospect of an identical world, which goes back to Chrysippus, is similarly rejected on the grounds that it resembles the play of children on the beach willfully erecting and destroying mounds.[37] The third option, however, namely that of an improved world, is given serious philosophical consideration:

> Yet if the demiurge will create a better world, then also he himself will become better (γενήσεται τότε κρείττων καὶ ὁ δημιουργός), implying that when He prepared the previous one, He was less accomplished in skill and conception (τὴν τέχνην καὶ τὴν διάνοιαν ἦν ἀτελέστερος). To speculate thus is not lawful since God is equal to Himself and like Himself; He admits neither relaxation for the worse nor tension for the better. Human beings, by contrast, have made room for such irregularities, being naturally disposed to change in both directions, for the better and the worse, and being used to submit to increases and progressions and improvements as well as all their contraries" (*Aet.* 43).

37 Philo, *Aet.* 42; Plutarch significantly uses the same argument, based on the same Homeric image, in *Mor.* 393e, discussed by Hirsch-Luipold (2017, 31–32). This similarity suggests that Philo may also illuminate Plutarch's intellectual background and deserves further study.

Philo invests considerable energies in refuting the option of an improved world, most likely because it began to gain popularity in the Roman circles he addresses in his treatise. Platonic arguments are offered to refute it. Philo insists on God's perfect and transcendental nature, which excludes the need for improvement or even the very possibility of improvement.[38] Change of character belongs to the human, not to the divine realm.

Philo's detailed attention to the question of why the demiurge would destroy the world is conspicuous and points to broader debates in first century Rome. His unique discussion opens a window onto the intellectual climate in which Seneca formulated his own views on the conflagration. In comparison to Cicero, it is initially remarkable that he pays new attention to the topic, without, however, rendering it the center of his cosmology as the Classical Stoics had done. Seneca's renewed interest resonates with the lively debates among the Stoics to which Philo points. Already in his earliest treatise, the *Consolation to Marcia*, which was written during Gaius Caligula's reign, Seneca refers to the conflagration.[39] He encourages Marcia concerning the loss of her son by invoking the time when the world will be destroyed "in order to be regenerated" (*renovaturus, Marc.* 26.6). In the spirit of Chrysippus he asserts that human beings, too, will be changed again into their former elements (*in antiqua elementa, Marc.* 26.7).

In other treatises, however, Seneca offers additional perspectives on the conflagration, as Mansfeld already pointed out.[40] In *Ben.* 6.22, he highlights the disorder of the universe involved in the conflagration and in *Ep.* 9.16 he compares Zeus' role in the conflagration to the philosopher's contemplative withdrawal from society. The most interesting passage, however, comes in the treatise *Natural Questions*, which was written at the end of Seneca's career, long after Philo's death.[41] Following Cleanthes, the fire is identified here as the principal element from which everything grows, after it has seized control over the world and turned everything into itself (*Nat. d.* 3.13.1). More importantly, Seneca insists on a better world emerging from the total destruction involved in both the deluge and the conflagration:

> [...] in the same principle in which the conflagration will occur (*conflagratio futura est*). Both will occur when it seems best to god for the old things to be ended and better things to begin (*Utrumque fit, cum deo visum ordiri meliora, vetera finiri*). Water and fire dominate earthly

38 For details on the inspiration of Plato's Timaeus, see Runia (1986, 433–446).

39 For the early date of the *Consolation to Marcia*, see Griffin (1976, 396).

40 Mansfeld (2017, 124–125).

41 For details on the chronology and historical context of Seneca's work and the place of the *Natural Questions*, see Griffin (1976, 396).

> things. From them is the origin, from them death (*ex his ortus, ex his interitus est*). Therefore whenever a renewal for the universe is decided, the sea is sent against us from above, like raging fire, when another form of destruction is decided upon.[42]

While this passage has often been cited, it has to the best of my knowledge thus far been overlooked that Seneca advocates a notion first attested by Philo.[43] In contrast to Cicero's Stoic spokesman Balbus, Seneca describes a total destruction and envisions a clear end as well as a totally new beginning. The word *interitus* even implies a "violent end" or "premature death." Seneca moreover implies moral progress, not the return of the same world. His demiurge is intent on creating better things, *meliora*, and putting an end to the bad old stuff. While Seneca remains frustratingly reticent, he seems to imply that theodicy can be maintained by assuming that even destruction is ultimately beneficial to humanity and ushers in progress.

The diversity of Seneca's views and especially his notion of an improved world after the conflagration resonate with Philo's reports of Stoic views and his discussion of the three possible scenarios of a renewed world. Given the similarity of their philosophical concerns in the same location and at the same time, we have to ask about the possibility of a historical dependence between Seneca and Philo. Did they react to each other and, if so, who reacted to whom? Alternatively, can we explain the similarities between Philo and Seneca by assuming that they engaged in similar intellectual debates in Rome to which they individually responded? The chronology of their respective works also has to be taken into consideration. While the *Consolation* was roughly written at the same time as Philo's *Indestructibility of the Cosmos*, the *Natural Questions* belong to a later stage, even after Philo's death. The question of their historical dependence must thus be addressed with special attention to the different works. We must also consider the possibility that Seneca may earlier have expressed his ideas in oral ways that can no longer be reconstructed today, thus giving Philo an opportunity to react to them during his visit to Rome.

The prospect of Philo reacting to Seneca is supported by the fact that the latter was the most prominent Roman philosopher in Philo's lifetime.[44] Nobody else is known to have expressed the radical interpretation of the conflagration in the mid-first century CE. On the contrary, we have seen the earlier Roman tradition,

42 Cicero, *Nat. d.* 3.28.7, translated by E. H. Warmington with slight modifications.

43 Cf. Inwood (2009, 172), who interprets Seneca's statement as a mere reference to the mechanisms of natural phenomena.

44 On other Roman philosophers, partly teachers of Seneca, in contemporary Rome, see Morford (2002); Reydams-Schils (2005).

represented by Cicero's Balbus, who marginalizes the conflagration and softens the effect of the destruction. Seneca thus looks like an excellent candidate to have advocated the view of the complete destruction reported by Philo. His views moreover play a role in other passages of Philo's work. Most visibly, Philo reacts to Seneca's novel and particularly Roman prejudice against the Sabbath as a day of Jewish laziness.[45] Without mentioning his Roman colleague's name, Philo counters emphatically: "on this day we are commanded to abstain from all work, not because the law is a promoter of idleness" (*Spec.* 2.60). The remarkable fit between Seneca's view of the conflagration and Philo's critique of certain Stoic interpretations may thus indicate that he responds to Seneca, perhaps specifically to his views expressed in the *Consolation*. His position, with characteristic emphasis on death, would have alarmed Philo and perhaps even prompted him to write a treatise on the topic. Seneca's view of an improved world, on the other hand, is more difficult to explain. If Philo indeed reacted to it, we have to assume that Seneca orally expressed it much earlier.

Assuming Seneca as an implied target of Philo may furthermore explain his emphasis on alternative Stoics, who "inspired by God, abandoned the conflagrations and regenerations and deserted to a holier doctrine, namely that of the indestructibility of the whole cosmos" (*Aet.* 76). Panaetius, who was famous in Rome thanks to Cicero's praise and paraphrase of his work on moral duties, is mentioned by Philo next to Boethus of Sidon as one of the "men strong in Stoic doctrines" (ἄνδρες ἐν τοῖς Στωικοῖς δόγμασιν ἰσχυκότες, *Aet.* 76).[46] Philo associates himself with that philosophical tradition in Rome, which resonates with Cicero's Balbus, and attempts to move the debates in Rome in that direction. By highlighting Boethus and Panaetius he would have hoped to eclipse Seneca's influence in Stoic circles in Rome.

Alternatively, Philo and Seneca may more generally share the same intellectual environment in Rome. Upon arrival in the imperial capital, Philo became aware of debates concerning the conflagration to which Seneca also reacted. Philo's explanation of the prospect of an improved world could thus point to Seneca's sources of inspiration. Given the chronology of Seneca's and Philo's works, it is methodologically safer to assume that Philo's reports of a view which subsequently resurfaces in the *Natural Questions* reflects debates in Rome with which Seneca was also familiar. Reading Seneca in view of Philo's Roman treatises, we thus gain insights into the intellectual context which probably inspired Seneca to formulate

45 Seneca's views are preserved in a fragment from *De Superstitione* in Aug., *Civ.* 6.11, ed. and tr. by Stern (1974, 1.431); see also Schäfer (1997, 86–87), who highlights Seneca's innovative role in Roman debates about the Sabbath and his influence on Tacitus, Juvenal and Rutilius Namatianus.
46 See Cicero, *Off.* 3.7.

his own position during the different stages in his career. Philo emerges as the missing link between Cicero and Seneca, which explains a significant development in Roman philosophy.

To conclude, Philo's treatise *On the Indestructibility of the Cosmos* offers precious insights into the state of philosophical debates in first century Rome. The very choice of the topic during his Roman period indicates its renewed interest in the imperial capital. Moreover, Philo's reports of different Stoic views and his exposition of the different scenarios of a new world provide unique insights into the content of such Roman debates. Questions of theodicy seem to have become more pressing in an environment which prioritized Divine providence in a well-functioning world. The solution of a destruction, which is ushered in by the demiurge to purge the world of its old shortcomings and to facilitate a better world, would prove to be the most convincing in the long run. It was not only chosen by Seneca in one of his latest treatises, but also subsequently advocated by Rabbi Abbahu and Origen, who probably considered it more congenial to the Scriptures.

3 Abbahu: A Rabbi with an Updated Stoic View

Rabbi Abbahu was active in the second half of the third century CE in Caesarea Maritima, the seat of the Roman administration and a modest law school as well as a thriving center of Greco-Roman culture.[47] Rabbi Hoshaya, his predecessor in the city, had set up a Beit Midrash there next to Origen's Christian school, which drew Greek-speaking students from abroad.[48] The city boasted of an important library, which had become a center of scholarship under Origen, possibly even with access for non-Christians.[49] Origen wrote most of his works in Caesarea and eagerly engaged in conversations with Greek-speaking Jews.[50] Caesarea also became an important center of rabbinic scholarship, the "rabbis of Caesarea" being mentioned as a distinct group in the Jerusalem Talmud and *Genesis Rab-*

47 For details, see Isaac (2011, 2.17–35); Cotton and Eck (2002, 375–391); Cotton and Eck (2006, 31–52); Eck (2014); Geiger (1994, 3–21); Geiger (2012); Stemberger (1987).

48 On Origen's school, see Pietzner (2013, 273–383); Dorival (2004, 9–26); Rizzi (2007, 73–85).

49 Grafton and Williams (2006, 179–183); Kofsky (2006, 53–62); for a more minimalist approach, see Inowlocki 2004.

50 For details, see Nautin (1977, 371–412); Niehoff (2020); Niehoff (2018, 113–129); Niehoff (2022, 195–210).

bah.[51] Yet the views of Abbahu and other rabbis have only indirectly come down to us, because rabbinic works are compilations, which have been collected over time.[52] The profile of individual rabbis emerges only through layers of redaction, which need to be critically analyzed. Rabbi Abbahu's image, for example, is preserved more faithfully in *Genesis Rabbah* than in later collections, such as *Lamentations Rabbah* and the Babylonian Talmud.[53]

Genesis Rabbah preserves two unique passages in which Abbahu speaks of the destruction of the world.[54] No precise Hebrew transliteration or equivalent of the Greek term *ekpurosis* is used, even though Abbahu occasionally mentions Greek words in his Biblical interpretations.[55] Abbahu instead uses the Biblical verb חרב, to destroy, which resonates with Philo's and Diogenes Laertius' wording (*Aet.* 5, 39; *Lives* 7.134). Overall Abbahu expresses himself in this context in a mixture of Hebrew and Aramaic. While his argument is identical in both passages, the Biblical prooftexts adduced for it differ. In the first passage the following tradition is preserved:

> "And it was evening" (Gen 1:5). R. Yehuda b. R. Simon said: "Let there be evening" is not written here, but "and it was evening," hence we know that a time-order existed before this. Rabbi Abbahu said: hence we know that the Holy-One-Blessed-Be-He went on creating and destroying worlds until he created this one. He said "this one pleases me, those did not please me." R. Pinehas said: this is R. Abbahu's reason: "And God saw everything that He had made and, behold, it was very good" (Gen 1:31); this pleases me, but those did not please me.[56]

---

51 While Levine (1975, 96), following Lieberman (1930), identified the rabbinic references to the rabbis of Caesarea as evidence of a continuous school there, Niehoff (forthcoming) suggests that it reflects later layers of redaction, especially in the Jerusalem Talmud, and constructs Tiberian identity; on the history of scholarship, see also Stemberger (2011, 192–194).

52 For details, see Stemberger (2011, 59–70).

53 For details on the unreliability of Abbahu's image in later rabbinic sources, see Herman (2018, 112–115); Niehoff (2025); on the nature of *Gen. R.* and its modern study, see Stemberger (2011, 306–304); Morgenstern (2022, 1–8).

54 These traditions appear for the first time in rabbinic literature in *Gen. R.* but are later also preserved in *Eccl. R.* 3.5 and anonymously in *Yalk. Shim.* 16.5.

55 E. g. *Gen. R.* 14.2.

56 *Gen. R.* 3.7: [ויהי ערב ויהי בקר וגו'] אמר ר' יהודה בר' סימון יהי ערב אין כתוב כאן אלא ויהי ערב מיכן שהיה סדר זמנים קודם לכאן, אמר ר' אבהו מיכן שהיה הקדוש ברוך הוא בורא עולמות ומחריבן עד שברא את אילו אמר דין הניין לי יתהון לא הניין לי, אמר ר' פינחס טעמיה דר' אבהו וירא אלהים את כל אשר עשה והנה טוב מאד (בראש' א לא) דין הניין לי יתהון לא הניין לי Translated by Freedman (1939), with slight modifications. The Hebrew text is that of Theodor and Albeck (1965).

Rabbi Abbahu's view of the conflagration is placed by the redactor of *Genesis Rabbah* between R. Yehuda's initial analysis of Gen 1:5 and R. Pinehas' reflection regarding his prooftext. This arrangement draws attention since R. Yehuda belongs to the fourth generation of Amoraic teachers and was thus active after Abbahu, who belongs to the third generation.[57] Historically, Yehuda's analysis can hardly have served Abbahu as a starting point for his own view. The redactor apparently placed Yehuda's analysis, which is not attested elsewhere in rabbinic literature, before Abbahu's statement in order to explain the latter. The expression "hence" (מיכן) is used for both Yehuda and Abbahu,[58] and also reflects the hands of the redactor, who not only placed the two interpretations together, but also harmonized their style. In the present form of the tradition, it is no longer clear whether the "hence" in the mouth of Abbahu refers to the Biblical prooftext or supposedly to Yehuda's preceding analysis.

Pinehas' reflection on the Biblical impetus for Abbahu's position raises the question whether this fifth generation Amoraic teacher was familiar with the suggestion of Gen 1:5 as a prooftext, which would have rendered his own proposition superfluous.[59] Moreover, his prooftext does not quite fit Abbahu's statement, according to which God was content only with part, but not with all of His creation(s). Pinehas' reaction to Abbahu may thus entail a theological revision, which subordinates the idea of imperfect creations to the Biblical affirmation that one unique creation fulfilled all Divine expectations.

Given these traces of redactional activity, it seems that Abbahu originally made an independent statement about the conflagration, which parallels other scientific insights transmitted in his name.[60] His view was subsequently contextualized in Biblical exegesis, Pinehas initially suggesting Gen 1:31 as a prooftext, while the redactor subsequently placed it after Yehuda's analysis of Gen 1:5. In the parallel passage in *Gen. R.* 9.2 Abbahu's view, with the same wording and R. Pinehas' reflection, is placed after R. Tanhuma's analysis of Eccl 3:11.[61] Here,

57 On the dates of these two rabbis, see Stemberger (2011, 105, 109).

58 This terminology was later adapted to the style of the Halachic Midrashim, *Yalk. Shim.* reading מגי׳ and the Venice print of *Gen. R.* reading מלמד (ed. Theodor-Albeck 1.23).

59 On the dates of R. Pinehas b. Chama, see Stemberger (2011, 111).

60 See, for example, his views of the Ocean and the survival of early born babies in *Gen. R.* 14.2; 23.7; cf. Goshen-Gottstein (1996, 71–72), who argues that Abbahu derived his idea from Gen 1:2 and identified the *Tohu Wawohu* with carefully designed, previous worlds.

61 *Gen. R.* 9.2: "R. Tanhuma opened (his sermon): "He has made everything beautiful in its time" (*Koh.* 3.11). Said R. Tanhuma: the world was created in its due season and the world was not fit to be created earlier (אמר ר' תנחומא בעונתו נברא העולם, לא היה העולם ראוי לבראות קודם לכן). Said R. Abbahu: hence we know that the Holy-One-Blessed-Be-He went on creating and destroying worlds until he created this one. He said "this one pleases me, those did not please me" (אמר ר' אבהו מיכן

too, Abbahu's view does not exactly fit the context into which it has been placed, as Tanhuma, another fifth generation Amora, asserts that no prior world to this one was fitted to be created.[62] Considerable hermeneutic efforts were thus invested into accommodating Abbahu's view and attenuating its implications, which seem to have been rather more shocking to later generations of rabbis. Respect for the towering figure of Rabbi Abbahu, however, ensured the inclusion of his view in *Genesis Rabbah.*

Regarding the content of Abbahu's view, the initial editor Yehuda Theodor noted in the apparatus that "an interpretation like this is already found in the books of Philo."[63] He surely meant that the conflagration of the world is mentioned by Philo, a fact amply confirmed in the preceding section of this article. We may moreover add that both Philo and Abbahu, according to the redactor's reconstruction, share the Stoic notion of time as the measure of the heavenly bodies' movement. As we saw above, Philo briefly mentions this Stoic definition in *Aet.* 4. In *Opif.* 26 he stresses that "time is the measure of the world's movement" so that there was no time before the world came into being. A similar notion underlies the above-quoted rabbinic passage. Yehuda b. R. Simon deduced from the Biblical expression "and it was evening," most likely from the *Wav-haHippuh*, that "a time-order existed before this" (סדר זמנים קודם לכאן). He also assumes that the distinction between day and night requires instruments of measuring time, which must have existed beforehand. Placed into this context, Rabbi Abbahu is presented by the redactor as suggesting that heavenly bodies must have existed in a prior world to measure time.

Despite these similarities, however, Abbahu's and Philo's views differ remarkably.[64] In fact, the rabbi advocates precisely one of the Stoic interpretations of the conflagration which Philo rejected. Abbahu entertains the idea of God trying out different creations until He reaches a degree of perfection that satisfies him. Unlike the Platonically inspired Philo, Abbahu has no qualms about imaging God as creating and destroying worlds. He is not disturbed by anthropomorphic images of God. If the issue of theodicy crossed his mind, he must have assumed, like Sene-

---

שהקב"ה בורא עולמות ומחריבן עד שברא את אלו אמר דן הניין לי יתהון לא הניין לי). R. Pinehas said: this is R. Abbahu's reason: "And God saw everything that He had made and, behold, it was very good" (Gen 1:31); this pleases me, but those did not please me." Translated by Freedman (1939), with slight modifications.

62 On Tanhuma's dates, see Stemberger (2011, 112).

63 ודרש זה נמצא כדוגמתו בספרי פילון (ed. Theodor-Albeck 1.23); on the importance of Theodor's contribution in comparison to Albeck, who completed the edition after his death, see Kadari (2017, 30–38).

64 This difference has already been noted by Harvey (1992, 96–100).

ca, that overall progress justifies momentary destruction. Unlike Seneca, however, Abbahu confines the process of the different conflagrations to the primordial realm, insisting that the present world is the final one, which pleases God.

Abbahu's contribution to the debates concerning the conflagration is significant in third-century CE Caesarea. It not only bears witness to the presence of the updated Stoic view of the conflagration in this region of the Mediterranean, but also resonates with contemporary Christian approaches. Origen expresses a similar interpretation in one of his earlier Alexandrian works:

> But as there will be another world after the destruction of this one, thus we believe that other worlds had come into being before this one existed. Both are confirmed by the authority of the Divine Scripture. [...] But that there already existed other worlds before this one, Koheleth shows by saying "What is that which has become? That, which will be. And what is that which was created? That, which will be created; and nothing is new under the sun. If there is a thing[65] of which it is said 'see, this is new', it has been already in the ages before us" (Eccl 1:9–10; ed. H. Görgemanns and H. Karpp, 1976, 626–628).[66]

Origen interprets the conflagration as a total destruction and draws his prooftext from the book of Ecclesiastes which is also used by the redactor of *Gen. R.* 9.2, who associates Abbahu's view via R. Tanhuma with Eccl 3:11 ("He has made everything beautiful in its time"). Unlike Abbahu, however, Origen is neither interested in the quality of the prior worlds nor in the reasons for their successive creation, but in the symmetry of future and past worlds. The expectation of future worlds, which may well derive from New Testament apocalypses, is absent from the rabbi's world view. Indeed, Abbahu seems to have developed his view independently of Origen and in closer dialogue with the broader philosophical debates about the conflagration.

Origen, however, returns to the topic of the conflagration in *Contra Celsum*, one of his latest books written in Caesarea.[67] In his reply to the critique of the Pagan Platonist Celsus, Origen treats Pagan traditions in much greater detail

---

65 "Thing" translates the Hebrew Vorlage דבר in the expression יש דבר שיאמר. The Latin translation quoted in Rufinus' translation of Origen's text, misinterprets the noun דבר as "speech" and constructs the verb *loquor*, which hardly fits the present context.

66 Origen, *Princ.* 3.5.3: *Sed sicut post corruptionem huius erit alius mundus, ita et antequam hic esset, fuisse alios credimus. Quod utrumque divinae scripturae auctoritate firmabitur* [...] *Quod autem ante hunc mundum fuerint etiam alii, Ecclesiastes ostendit dicens: "Quid est quod factum est? Ipsum quod futurum est. Et quid est quod creatum est? Hoc ipsum quod creandum est; et nihil est omnino recens sub sole. Si qui loquetur et dicet: Ecce hoc novum est, iam fuit id in saeculis, quae fuerunt ante nos"* (Eccl 1 :9–10). Note that the Latin translation of the Biblical text is not identical with the Vulgate.

67 On the late date of *Contra Celsum*, see Chadwick (1953, XIV–XV); Nautin (1977, 375–376).

than he does in works addressing only Christian audiences.[68] Celsus prompts Origen's renewed discussion of the conflagration by arguing that the Christians amateurishly applied a Stoic idea, which is ridiculous on its own terms and contradicts the Platonic notion of God's unchanging nature.[69] One bone of contention between the two is the idea of a return of the same world. Origen mocks the Stoic idea of successive, identical worlds and compares them to superior Christian notions. In his view, it is silly to imagine that the same Socrates will be born again and live the same life, marrying, for example, the same wife. The Stoics themselves realized the problem and "tried to heal the dissonance" by claiming that "all men in any cycle will be indistinguishable (ἀπαραλλάκτους), I do not know how, from those in previous cycles, so that Socrates will not live again, but someone indistinguishable from Socrates" (Origen, *Cels.* 4.68). According to Origen, God does not recreate the same or indistinguishable worlds or people, but rather better ones. The conflagration is an instrument to purge the world of the wicked and make it better (*Cels.* 4.69; 5.15). While this view was previously discussed in Rome, it is now coopted as a distinctly Christian belief, which differs from Stoic doctrine.[70] Rabbi Abbahu stands on the same side of this debate as Origen, without, however, explaining as much in the short fragment preserved in *Genesis Rabbah.*

4 Conclusion

The three Jewish authors discussed in this article shed light on vivid debates about the Stoic notion of the conflagration in different cultural and historical contexts. Josephus, who declares himself a Pharisee and associates with the Stoic school, avoids the philosophical notion of a conflagration in first century Rome. He never mentions it, probably because it does not fit his views of the Biblical demiurge and Divine providence. However, his discussion of theological problems arising from similar Biblical stories of destruction indicates wider concerns about the indestructibility of the world and the unchangeability of God. As an ambassador to Gaius Caligula, Philo in turn addresses Roman readers with remarkable openness to Stoicism. His treatise *On the Indestructibility of the Cosmos* provides a hith-

---

68 Cf. Edwards (2022, 284), who points to Origen's misconceptions of Stoic notions of the conflagration in *Contra Celsum*, but then rightly concludes that he "differentiates the Stoic cosmogony from his own conjecture, loosely grounded in one biblical text, that God has created worlds before the present one;" for additional examples of Origen discussing Pagan traditions in greater detail in *Contra Celsum* than elsewhere, see Niehoff (2020).

69 Origen, *Cels.* 1.19–20; 4.11; 5.14.

70 For a similar rhetorical strategy in Justin Martyr, see Thorsteinsson (2012, 558–564).

erto overlooked window into lively debates in first century Rome. Rather than simply dismissing Stoic notions, Philo points to the variety of views within the Stoic school and endeavors to promote the one which amounts to the indestructibility of the cosmos. His reports represent the missing link between Cicero and Seneca, providing crucial background information for the shift from an attenuated to a radical interpretation of the conflagration. In particular, Philo illuminates the emerging assumption of improved worlds, which inspired Seneca and later Jewish and Christian authors.

Rabbi Abbahu, even though a native Hebrew or Aramaic speaker and thus seemingly distanced from Greco-Roman debates, expressed the updated Stoic view of a conflagration initiated to improve the world. It is perhaps somewhat paradoxical that this third century rabbi was a keener adept of the Stoic idea than Philo of Alexandria, who was immersed all his life in Greco-Roman culture and expressed himself in Greek. Abbahu's views are preserved in *Genesis Rabbah* even though later rabbis and the redactor of the Midrash seem to have become rather more ambivalent about them and tried to subordinate them to Biblical verses, which actually convey contrary assumptions about the world. This reception is of special interest in view of Origen, who shared Abbahu's basic interpretation of the conflagration in the context of Christian theology.

Bibliography

Aetius. 1879. *Placita philosophorum.* In *Doxographi Graeci*, edited by H. Diels, 267–444. Berlin: Reimer.

Alexander of Aphrodisias. 1883. *In Aristotelis analyticorum priorum librum I commentarium*, edited by M. Wallies. Commentaria in Aristotelem Graeca 2.1. Berlin: Reimer.

Alexander of Lycopolis. 1974. *Critique of the Doctrines of Manichaeus.* Translated by P. W. van der Horst and J. Mansfeld. Leiden: Brill.

Arnaldez, R. 1969. *De Aeternitate Mundi: Traduction, Introduction et Notes.* Paris: Éditions du Cerf.

Barnes, J., and M. T. Griffin, eds. 1997. *Philosophia Togata II: Plato and Aristotle at Rome.* Oxford: Clarendon Press.

Bartsch, S. 2006. *The Mirror of the Self: Sexuality, Self-Knowledge, and the Gaze in the Early Roman Empire.* Chicago: University of Chicago Press.

Bartsch, S., and A. Schiesaro, eds. 2015. *The Cambridge Companion to Seneca.* Cambridge: Cambridge University Press.

Bormann, K. 1964. "Über die Unvergänglichkeit der Welt." In *Philo von Alexandria. Die Werke in deutscher Übersetzung*, edited by L. Cohn et al., 71–121. Berlin: De Gruyter.

Cicero, Marcus Tullius. 1915–1966. *De Natura Deorum*, edited by C. F. W. Müller. Leipzig: Teubner.

Cicero, Marcus Tullius. 1915–1966. *De Officiis*, edited by C. Atzert. Leipzig: Teubner.

Chadwick, H., trans. 1953. *Origen: Contra Celsum.* Cambridge: Cambridge University Press.

Cohn, L., and S. Reiter, eds. 1925. *Philonis Alexandrini Opera Quae Supersunt.* Vol. 6. Berlin: Reimer.

Colson, H. H. 1985. *Philo. In Ten Volumes.* Vol. 9. Cambridge, MA: Harvard University Press/Heinemann.

Cotton, H., and W. Eck. 2002. "A New Inscription from Caesarea Maritima and the Local Elite of Caesarea Maritima." In *What Athens Has to Do with Jerusalem: Essays on Classical, Jewish, and Early Christian Art and Archaeology in Honor of Gideon Foerster*, edited by L. V. Rutgers, 375–391. Leuven: Peeters.

Cotton, H. M., and W. Eck. 2006. "Governors and Their Personnel on Latin Inscriptions from Caesarea Maritima." *Cathedra: For the History of Eretz Israel and Its Yishuv* 122: 31–52. [Hebrew]

Diogenes Laertius. 1964. *Lives of Eminent Philosophers*, edited by H. S. Long. Oxford Classical Texts. Oxford: Clarendon Press.

Dorival, G. 2004. "Est-il légitime d'éclairer le Discours de remerciement par la Lettre à Grégoire et réciproquement? Ou la tentation de Pasolini." In *La Biografia di Origene fra storia a agiografia*, edited by A. Monaci Castagno, 9–26. Turin: Pazzini.

Eck, W. 2014. *Judäa – Syria Palästina.* Tübingen: Mohr Siebeck.

Edwards, M. 2022. "Origen, Celsus, and the Philosophers." In *The Oxford Handbook of Origen*, edited by R. E. Heine and K. J. Torjesen, 287–292. Oxford: Oxford University Press.

Feldman, L. H. 1998. *Josephus's Interpretation of the Bible.* Berkeley: University of California Press.

Forschner, M. 2018. *Die Philosophie der Stoa: Logik, Physik und Ethik.* Darmstadt: Wissenschaftliche Buchgesellschaft.

Freedman, H., and M. Simon, eds. 1939. *Genesis Rabbah.* Vol. 1–2 of *Midrash Rabbah.* London: Soncino Press.

Geiger, J. 1994. "Latin in Roman Palestine." *Cathedra* 74: 3–21. [Hebrew]

Geiger, J. 2012. *The Tents of Japhet: Greek Intellectuals in Ancient Palestine.* Jerusalem: Yad Ben Zvi. [Hebrew]

Origen. 1976. *Vier Bücher von den Prinzipien*, edited by H. Görgemanns and H. Karpp. Darmstadt: Wissenschaftliche Buchgesellschaft.

Goshen-Gottstein, A. 1996. "The Myth of 'The Works of Creation' in Amoraic Literature." In *Myth in Judaism*, edited by H. Pedayah, 58–77. Beer Sheva: Ben-Gurion University Press. [Hebrew]

Grafton, A., and M. H. Williams. 2006. *Christianity and the Transformation of the Book: Origen, Eusebius, and the Library of Caesarea.* Cambridge, MA: Belknap Press of Harvard University Press.

Griffin, M. T. 1976. *Seneca: A Philosopher in Politics.* Oxford: Oxford University Press.

Griffin, M. T. 2013. *Seneca on Society: A Guide to the De Beneficiis.* Oxford: Oxford University Press.

Harvey, W. Z. 1992. "Rabbinic Attitudes toward Philosophy." In *Open Thou Mine Eyes: Essays on Aggadah and Judaica Presented to Rabbi William G. Braude on His Eightieth Birthday and Dedicated to His Memory*, edited by H. J. Blumberg, 83–101. Hoboken, NJ: Ktav Publishing House.

Heine, R. E., and K. J. Torjesen, eds. 2022. *The Oxford Handbook of Origen.* Oxford: Oxford University Press.

Hirsch-Luipold, R. 2017. "The Dividing Line: Theological/Religious Arguments in Plutarch's Anti-Stoic Polemics." In *A Versatile Gentleman: Consistency in Plutarch's Writing*, edited by J. Opsomer, G. Roskam, and F. B. Titchener, 17–36. Leuven: Peeters.

Ildefonse, F. 2004. *Les Stoïciens: Zénon, Cléanthe, Chrysippe.* Paris: Les Belles Lettres.

Inowlocki, S. 2004. "What Caesarea has to Do with Alexandria? The Christian Library between Myth and Reality." *Scriptura Classica Israelica* 43: 1–19.

Inwood, B. 2009. *Reading Seneca: Stoic Philosophy at Rome.* Oxford: Oxford University Press.

Isaac, B. 2011. “Caesarea.” In *Corpus Inscriptionum Iudaeae/Palaestinae.* Vol. 2, edited by W. Ameling and H. Cotton, 17–35. Berlin: De Gruyter.

Josephus, Flavius. 1885–1895. *Antiquitates Iudaicae,* edited by B. Niese. Berlin: Weidmann. Corrected reprint, 1955.

Josephus, Flavius. 1959–1969. *De Bello Iudaico,* edited by O. Bauernfeind and O. Michel. Munich/Darmstadt: Kösel-Verlag / Wissenschaftliche Buchgesellschaft.

Josephus, Flavius. 1959. *Vita,* edited by A. Pelletier. Paris: Les Belles Lettres.

Kadari, T. 2017. *Minkhah L'Yehudah: Julius Theodor and the Redaction of the Aggadic Midrashim of the Land of Israel.* Jerusalem: Schechter Institute of Jewish Studies/Leo Baeck Institute.

Karshon, N. 2015. “Philo: *De Aeternitate Mundi.*” In *Philo of Alexandria. Writings,* edited by M. R. Niehoff, 405–463. Jerusalem: The Israeli Academy of Sciences and Humanities/The Bialik Institute. [Hebrew]

Kofsky, A. 2006. “Pamphilus and the Christian Library of Caesarea.” *Cathedra: For the History of Eretz Israel and Its Yishuv* 122: 53–62. [Hebrew]

Lactantius, Caecilius. 1890–1897. *Divinae Institutiones*, edited by S. Brandt and G. Laubmann. Vienna: Tempsky.

Levine, L. I. 1975. *Caesarea under Roman Rule.* Leiden: Brill.

Lieberman, S. 1930. “The Talmud of Caesarea: Yerushalmi Nezikin.” *Tarbitz* 2: 1–108.

Long, A. A. 1985. “The Stoics on World-Conflagration and Everlasting Recurrence.” In *Recovering the Stoics. Spindel Conference 1984,* edited by R. H. Epp. Supplement to *The Southern Journal of Philosophy* 23: 13–37.

Long, A. A. 2003. “Roman Philosophy.” In *Cambridge Companion to Greek and Roman Philosophy,* edited by D. Sedley, 184–210. Cambridge: Cambridge University Press.

Long, A. A., and D. Sedley, eds. 1987. *The Hellenistic Philosophers.* 2 vols. Cambridge: Cambridge University Press.

Mansfeld, J. 1979. “Providence and the Destruction of the Universe in Early Stoic Thought. With Some Remarks on the ‘Mysteries of Philosophy.’” In *Studies in Hellenistic Religions*, edited by M. J. Vermaseren, 129–188. Leiden: Brill.

Mansfeld, J. 2017. “The End of the World in Ancient Philosophy.” *Eranos* 18: 91–140.

Mansfeld, J., and D. T. Runia. 2020. *Aetiana V: An Edition of the Reconstructed Text of the Placita with a Commentary and Collection of Related Texts.* 4 vols. Leiden: Brill.

Mason, S. 2003. “Flavius Josephus in Flavian Rome: Reading On and Between the Lines.” In *Flavian Rome: Culture, Image, Text,* edited by A. J. Boyle and W. J. Dominik, 559–589. Leiden: Brill.

Mason, S. 2016. “Josephus as a Roman Historian.” In *A Companion to Josephus*, edited by H. H. Chapman and Z. Rodgers, 13–35. Oxford: Wiley-Blackwell.

Midrash Rabbah: Ecclesiastes (Qohelet Rabbah). 1885–1887. Vilna: Romm.

Morford, M. 2002. *The Roman Philosophers.* New York: Routledge.

Morris, J. 1987. “The Jewish Philosopher Philo.” In *The History of the Jewish People in the Age of Jesus Christ by Emil Schürer.* Vol. 3.2, edited by G. Vermes, F. Millar, and M. Goodman, 809–889. Edinburgh: T & T Clark.

Nautin, P. 1977. *Origène: Sa Vie et son Œuvre.* Paris: Beauchesne.

Nemesius. 1802. *De natura hominis*, edited by F. Matthäi. Halle: Gebauer. Reprint, Hildesheim: Olms, 1967.

Niehoff, M. R. 2007. “Philo's Contribution to Contemporary Alexandrian Metaphysics.” In *Beyond Reception: Judaism, Christianity and Antiquity,* edited by A. Jacobsen, J. Ullrich, and D. Brakke, 35–55. Bern: Peter Lang.

Niehoff, M. R. 2016. "Josephus and Philo in Rome." In *A Companion to Josephus in His World*, edited by H. Chapman and Z. Rodgers, 135–146. Oxford: Wiley-Blackwell.

Niehoff, M. R. 2017. "Parodies of Educational Journeys in Josephus, Justin Martyr and Lucian." In *Journeys in the Roman East: Imagined and Real*, edited by M. R. Niehoff, 203–224. Tübingen: Mohr Siebeck.

Niehoff, M. R. 2018. *Philo of Alexandria: An Intellectual Biography*. New Haven: Yale University Press.

Niehoff, M. R. 2019. "A Hybrid Self: Rabbi Abbahu in Legal Debates in Caesarea." In *Self, Self-Fashioning, and Individuality in Late Antiquity*, edited by M. R. Niehoff and J. Levinson, 291–329. Tübingen: Mohr Siebeck.

Niehoff, M. R. 2020. "Homer between Celsus, Origen and the Jews of Late Antique Palaestina." In *Text and Intertext in Greek Epic and Drama: Essays in Honor of Margalit Finkelberg*, edited by J. Price and R. Zelnick-Abramovitz, 185–209. London: Routledge.

Niehoff, M. R. 2024. "Philons und Origenes' Interpretation von Platons Zeitvorstellung in *Timaeus 38b–d*." In *Platon und die Zeit*, edited by I. Männlein and K. Corcilius, 59–76. Tübingen: Mohr Siebeck.

Niehoff, M. R. 2025. "Sermons as Platforms for Textualizing Secondary Orality. Origen and Rabbi Abbahu in 3rd Century Caesarea." *Mnemosyne* 78: 384–407.

Niehoff, M. R. forthcoming. "The Rabbis of Caesarea: The Formation of a Group Image as Key to the Redaction of Genesis Rabbah and the Jerusalem Talmud." *Te'uda*. [Hebrew]

Opsomer, J. 2014. "Plutarch and the Stoics." In *A Companion to Plutarch*, edited by M. Beck, 88–103. Oxford: Wiley Blackwell.

Opsomer, J. 2017. "Is Plutarch Really Hostile to the Stoics?" In *From Stoicism to Platonism? The Development of Philosophy, 100 BCE–100 CE*, edited by T. Engberg-Pedersen, 296–321. Cambridge: Cambridge University Press.

Origen. 1967–1976. *Contra Celsum*, edited by M. Borret. Sources Chrétiennes 132, 136, 147, 150, 227. Paris: Éditions du Cerf.

Origen. 1978–1984. *De principiis*, edited by H. Crouzel and M. Simonetti. Sources Chrétiennes 252, 253, 268, 269, 312. Paris: Éditions du Cerf.

Pietzner, K. 2013. *Bildung, Elite und Konkurrenz. Heiden und Christen vor der Zeit Constantins.* Tübingen: Mohr Siebeck.

Plutarch. 1925–1960. *Moralia*, edited by W. R. Paton et al. Leipzig: Teubner.

Reydams-Schils, G. 2005. *The Roman Stoics: Self, Responsibility, and Affection.* Chicago: University of Chicago Press.

Rizzi, M. 2007. "Ancora sulla paternita dell'Encomio di Origene. Spunti geographici e storicosoziali." In *Il Giusto che Fiorisce come Palma. Gregoria il taumaturgo fra Storia a Agiographia*, edited by B. Claus and V. Milazzo, 73–85. Rome: Institutum Patristicum.

Royse, J. 2009. "The Works of Philo." In *The Cambridge Companion to Philo*, edited by A. Kamesar, 32–64. Cambridge: Cambridge University Press.

Runia, D. T. 1981. "Philo's De Aeternitate Mundi: The Problem of Interpretation." *Vigiliae Christianae* 35: 105–151.

Runia, D. T. 1986. *Philo of Alexandria and the Timaeus of Plato.* Leiden: Brill.

Runia, D. T. 2001. *Philo of Alexandria: On the Cosmos according to Moses. Introduction, Translation and Commentary.* Leiden: Brill.

Salles, R. 2005. "Ekpyrosis and the Goodness of God in Cleanthes." *Phronesis* 50: 56–78.

Schäfer, P. 1997. *Judeophobia: Attitudes toward the Jews in the Ancient World.* Cambridge, MA: Harvard University Press.

Sedley, D. 2007. *Creationism and Its Critics in Antiquity.* Berkeley: University of California Press.
Seneca, Lucius Annaeus. 1917. *Epistulae Morales,* translated by R. M. Gummere. Vol. 1. Cambridge, MA: Harvard University Press.
Seneca, Lucius Annaeus. 1920. *Epistulae Morales,* translated by R. M. Gummere. Vol. 2. Cambridge, MA: Harvard University Press.
Simplicius. 1882–1895. *In Aristotelis Physica Commentaria,* edited by H. Diels. *Commentaria in Aristotelem Graeca* 9–10. Berlin: Reimer.
Stemberger, G. 1987. *Juden und Christen im Heiligen Land. Palästina unter Konstantin und Theodosius.* Munich: C. H. Beck.
Stemberger, G. 2011. *Einleitung in Talmud und Midrasch.* 9th rev. ed. Munich: C. H. Beck.
Stern, M. 1974. *Greek and Latin Authors on Jews and Judaism.* 2 vols. Jerusalem: The Israel Academy of Sciences and Humanities.
Stobaeus, J. 1884–1912. *Eclogae physicae et ethicae*, edited by K. W. Wachsmuth. 2 vols. Berlin: Weidmann.
Theodor, J., and C. Albeck. 1965. *Midrash Bereshit Rabba: Critical Edition with Notes and Commentary.* Jerusalem: Wahrmann Books.
Thorsteinsson, R. M. 2012. "Justin and Stoic Cosmo-Theology." *Journal of Theological Studies* 63.2: 533–571.
Yalkut Shimoni. 1864. Vilna: Romm.

Christoph Markschies

The Concept of Time in Origen

The longer I study the works and thought of Origen (and I have been doing so for quite a while), the more I pay attention to the importance of the different literary genres and the different original historical contexts in which Origen formulated his thoughts in oral discourse or exegetical reflection.[1] First of all, most of his works deal with the interpretation of Holy Scripture and are not thematic monographs on philosophical and theological concepts or problems. It is correspondingly problematic to simply ask for a "concept of time in Origen" across genres and contexts. *The Concept of Time in Origen* is the title of an extraordinarily comprehensive but not unproblematic monograph by Panayiotis Tzamalikos, who teaches in Thessaloniki, from 1991 (it was also supplemented by other publications, including two monographs and various essays).[2] Adele Monaci Castagno also provided a kind of brief overview of Origen's concepts in her article "Tempo" in the Origen dictionary of Italian Origen research that she edited.[3] Tzamalikos divides his study according to systematic aspects into five chapters—"God. World and Time," "The Conception of Time," "The Character of Time," "Time and the Notion of Eternal" and "The End of Time." Monaci Castagno divides the article into three sections: "God and Time," "Αἰών as a Homonym" and "The Definition of Time." The excellent article "God, World, Time and Eternity in Origen" by Charlotte Köckert (which contains important critical comments on the work of Tzamalikos) also follows a complex systematic structure.[4] One will search in vain for a presentation based on the genres or chronology of Origen's works, a desideratum addressed in this article, in which I wish to offer some initial considerations and programmatic reflections rather than an exhaustive study.

Far be it from me to bring up the old question about whether Origen is more of an interpreter of the Bible or a systematic thinker, whether there is a "system"

---

1 On the role of Origen's scribes and team of helpers, see Markschies (2004, 33–50) [= 2007, 223–238].

2 Tzamalikos (1991a); first published as PhD thesis, University of Glasgow, 1986; Tzamalikos (2006); Tzamalikos (2007); Tzamalikos (1987/1988, 396–418); Tzamalikos (1991b, 535–561). Cf. the review by Ramelli (2008, 453) and Ramelli and Konstan (2007). Less well known is to my point of view: Kassomenakis (1967). Cf. also the discussion at https://www.reddit.com/r/ChristianUniversalism/comments/zkc52 m/megathread_on_ilaria_ramellis_translation_work (last accessed November 20, 2024).

3 Monaci Castagno (2000, 457–459).

4 Köckert (2009a, 253–297). On the criticism of Tzamalikos, see in particular Köckert (2009a, 261–262, n. 27).

 https://doi.org/10.1515/9783112225981-005

of thought behind his biblical exegesis or whether his tentative style and his cautious thinking do not rather expose him as the opposite of a systematic thinker. Hermann Josef Vogt has rightly emphasized, in my opinion, that Origen repeatedly leaves questions open at central points and does not answer them against the background of a system with concepts on central philosophical or theological topoi.[5] I spoke about these connections in 2022 at the "Origeniana Tertia Decima" in Münster in a lecture soon to be published.[6] In contrast to the aforementioned accounts based on concepts within a system, we assume here that certain basic assumptions about "time" and "eternity" formed the coordinate system of Origen's interpretation of the Bible or—to use a description by Ekkehard Mühlenberg—the grammar of content which allowed him to construct his texts.[7] But what he wrote was oriented towards the endeavor to understand concrete biblical passages in their context according to the rules of the contemporary philological method, with a view to the solution of certain related problems. Therefore, we take the starting point for our remarks in the commentary on the biblical days of creation in the fragments of the original thirteen-volume Genesis commentary and the Genesis Homilies of Origen, which are usually dated to the years 231–234 and 340 CE.[8] We then deal with two of Origen's New Testament commentaries, the commentaries on John and Matthew, and only then with the basic treatise Περὶ ἀρχῶν/*De principiis.* Some concluding remarks summarize our observations.

In view of the extensive secondary literature, it is important to emphasize that this is only an outline, based on a few key texts by Origen. A more complete treatment will be reserved for a monograph currently in progress on "God's Time," which I hope will become a companion piece to my book on God's body.[9]

1 Concepts of Time in the Interpretation of Genesis in Commentaries and Homilies

Remarkably, no detailed reflections on the topics of time and eternity and on the temporality of creation have survived from the great Genesis commentary; Origen is only interested in the topic with regard to inner-Trinitarian problems (if we may trust the double transmission of the piece in Markell of Ancyra and Pamphilus):

5 Vogt (1974) and Vogt (1999).
6 Markschies (2025, 563–571).
7 Mühlenberg (1994, 9–24).
8 Origenes (ed. Metzler, 2010, 4–5).
9 Markschies (2019).

> For God did not begin to be a Father after he had been somehow hindered from it, as men who become fathers are hindered by the fact that they could not somehow be fathers until then. For if God is always perfect, and the ability to be a father belongs to him, and if it is a good thing that he is the father of such a son, why should he postpone it and deprive himself of the good, and not become a father as soon as he can be a father, so to speak? [The same is to be said of the Holy Spirit in any case].[10]

οὐ γὰρ ὁ θεὸς πατὴρ εἶναι ἤρξατο κωλυόμενος—God did not begin to be something at some point. Why did Origen deal with such problems in his commentary on Genesis? Obviously, in interpreting the very first verse of the creation account in Genesis, he was concerned with the question of who exactly created what and thus with the question of whether the divine Trinity was itself a part of creation or its timeless precondition, irrespective of different tasks in different acts of creation. Since Origen interprets the biblical ἐν ἀρχῇ/*in principio* in relation to Christ (as the homilies in particular make clear), it made sense to deal with these connections right at the beginning of the commentary. In addition, we know from a report in the commentary on Timaeus by the late antique philosopher Calcidius that Origen's commentary on Genesis states that "beginning is hardly said in the temporal sense, for there was no time before the formation of the world, nor before the alternation of day and night, by which the periods of time are measured."[11]

This formulation οὐ γὰρ ὁ θεὸς πατὴρ εἶναι ἤρξατο κωλυόμενος, interspersed in the text of the biblical interpretation, apparently alludes to a debate, whose prominent echo can be heard around a hundred years later in the great Trinitarian theological debate surrounding the Alexandrian presbyter Arius. It led to the famous formulation in an anathema of the creed of the First Imperial Council of

10 Or., *in Gen. frg.* D 4 (66.21–26 Metzler): οὐ γὰρ ὁ θεὸς πατὴρ εἶναι ἤρξατο κωλυόμενος, ὡς οἱ γινόμενοι πατέρες ἄνθρωποι, ὑπὸ τοῦ μὴ δύνασθαί πω πατέρες εἶναι. εἰ γὰρ ἀεὶ τέλειος ὁ θεός, καὶ πάρεστιν αὐτῷ δύναμις τοῦ πατέρα αὐτὸν εἶναι, καὶ καλὸν αὐτὸν εἶναι πατέρα τοιούτου υἱοῦ, <τί> ἀναβάλλεται καὶ τοῦ καλοῦ ἑαυτὸν στερίσκει καί, ὡς ἔστιν εἰπεῖν, ἐξ οὗ δύναται πατὴρ εἶναι, οὐ <γίνεται πατήρ>; τὸ αὐτὸ μέντοιγε καὶ περὶ τοῦ ἁγίου πνεύματος λεκτέον = Marcellus Ancyranus, frg. 21 Vinzent = 39 Klostermann/Hansen.

11 Or., *in Gen test.* C II 1 (48.3–12 Metzler) = Calcidius, *Tim.* 2.276 (280.12–281.5): *Omnia tamen haec in unum aiunt concurrere, ut et generata sit ea quae subiecta est uniuerso corpori silua sermonesque ipsos sic interpretantur: 'initium' minime temporarium dici—neque enim tempus ullum fuisse ante mundi exornationem dieique et nocturnas uices quibus temporis spatia dimensa sunt—, tum initii multas esse significationes, ut* initium sapientiae timorem domini *fore Salomon ait, item:* Initium sapientiae cultus dei *nihiloque minus:* Initium uiae optimae iustus actus*; atque etiam in praeconio sapientiae caelestis auctor* Initium uitae panis et aqua et tunica, *inquit,* et domus idonea uelandis pudendis, *quippe in his non una initii sed diuersa et multiplex habetur significatio.* Cf. also Tzamalikos (1991a, 179–271).

Nicaea, which, as is well known, reads Τοὺς δὲ λέγοντας· ἦν ποτε ὅτε οὐκ ἦν, καὶ πρὶν γεννηθῆναι οὐκ ἦν, καὶ ὅτι ἐξ οὐκ ὄντων ἐγένετο, […] τούτους ἀναθεματίζει ἡ καθολικὴ καὶ ἀποστολικὴ ἐκκλησία, in translation: "But those who say 'there was a time when he was not' and 'he was not before he was begotten', and that he became from the non-existent, […] the Catholic and Apostolic Church imposes the anathema on them."[12] Our formulation shows (like some others) that the dispute of the fourth century had its prehistory in disputes of the third century. We can therefore also leave open the question of whether—as Tzamalikos assumes—Origen, when he said ἦν ποτε ὅτε οὐκ ἦν of the Logos and Christ, presupposed the distinction between a πρῶτος νοῦς and a ὁ ἐνεργείᾳ νοῦς, as found in Alexander of Aphrodisias.[13]

Let us proceed to Origen's interpretation of Genesis and to a fragment from the third book of his commentary that has been handed down many times: because there can be no beginning in God after time, he also knows the future beforehand without causing it—as a longer passage from the Genesis commentary, which has been handed down both in Eusebius and the *Philokalia* and the *Genesis Catechesis*, makes clear, in which Origen proves "that God foreknows the future."[14] It is interesting, however, how this idea is explained, namely both through detailed scriptural evidence from the Old and New Testaments, as well as through a precise recourse to a (seemingly) philosophical theorem (ἀξίωμα δυνάμεως νοῦ θεοῦ) in order to argue for divine foreknowledge (πρόγνωσις): "That therefore God knows long beforehand of every single future event that it will happen, this is clear by itself, even without Scripture, from the general idea of God, to him who knows the principle of the power of the mind of God."[15] Of course, one can provide all kinds of evidence from contemporary philosophers for the idea

12 Brennecke et al., eds. (2007, 109), Urk. 24 = Dok. 26: "But those who say 'it was once that he was not' or 'he was not before he was begotten' or 'out of nothing he became' or who claim that he is from another hypostasis or another being, or who say that the Son of God is created, changeable or mutable, these the Catholic and Apostolic Church condemns." Cf. also Markschies (2022, 11–40) with Ramelli (2014, 237–290 [= 2025, 237–284]). I recently dealt with this formulation of the fourth century in more detail in an article dedicated to Barbara Aland.

13 Tzamalikos (2016, 991 with n. 754): Alexander Phil., *Comm. Metaph.* Λ 7 ad 1072b23 (698.34–699.25 Hayduck; these passages have not yet been critically re-edited by Pantelis Golitsis in the series "Commentaria in Aristotelem Graeca et Byzantina").

14 Or., *in Gen. frg.* D 7.6 (80.12–13 Metzler): Ἀποδεδειγμένου τοίνυν ἡμῖν περὶ τοῦ προγνώστην εἶναι τὸν θεὸν οὐκ ἀκαίρως […]

15 Or., *in Gen. frg.* D 7.4 (76.15–17 Metzler): Ὅτι μὲν οὖν ἕκαστον τῶν ἐσομένων πρὸ πολλοῦ οἶδεν ὁ θεὸς γενησόμενον, καὶ χωρὶς μὲν γραφῆς αὐτόθεν ἐκ τῆς ἐννοίας τῆς περὶ θεοῦ δῆλον τῷ συνιέντι ἀξίωμα δυνάμεως νοῦ θεοῦ.

of God's foreknowledge not determining world events,[16] but the ἀξίωμα δυνάμεως νοῦ θεοῦ is not a common phrase; in the *Corpus Hermeticum* it says: ὁ οὖν λόγος ἐστὶν εἰκὼν καὶ νοῦς τοῦ θεοῦ;[17] what is presented here as such is certainly not common contemporary philosophical terminology, and such incongruities are covered up when Origen is presented as a Platonist without further ado. Incidentally, there is also no direct terminological reference to the aforementioned distinction between πρῶτος νοῦς and ὁ ἐνεργείᾳ νοῦς, as found in Alexander of Aphrodisias.

In one of the later volumes of the Genesis commentary, Origen evidently also dealt with the mention of the days of creation in the Bible and their counting, as a fragment preserved in the Catena tradition makes clear:

> Some, however, have already thought it improper to suppose that God, after the manner of a master builder, who is able to build a house only in several days, completed the world in several days, and they say that everything came into being in a moment, and from there they establish this; and for the sake of order, they believe, the enumeration of the days and what came into being in them is mentioned. Plausibly they might also make use for this purpose of a word from the bible which may be supposed to establish this doctrine, namely, 'He spoke, and they came into being; he commanded, and they were created.'[18]

At this point, Origen adopts Philo's solution and understands the expression "in a moment" (ὑφ' ἕν) as a timeless moment, thus distinguishing categorical timelessness from the duality of time and eternity, both of which presuppose the creation of time by God.[19] This view distinguishes him fundamentally from the thinking of contemporary Platonists. God brings the world into being all at once through the power of his will; since he is not subject to time, the will, the decision to act, and the accomplishment of the same coincide.[20]

Unfortunately, no further reflections on time have survived from the thirteen volumes of the Genesis commentary, but there are further reflections in the much later homilies preserved in Rufin's translation. They help to better understand

---

16 See Or., *Philoc.* 21–27 (ed. Junod, 1976, 142–143, n. 1).
17 CH XII 14 (179.17 Nock/Festugière).
18 Or., *in Gen. frg.* D 13 (166.12–18 Metzler) = frg. 193 Petit: Ἤδη δέ τινες ἄτοπον εἶναι νομίζοντες τό ὑπολαμβάνειν τὸν θεόν, δίκην οἰκοδόμου μὴ διαρκέσαντος χωρὶς ἡμερῶν πλειόνων πληρῶσαι τὴν οἰκοδομήν, ἐν πλείοσιν ἡμέραις τετελεκέναι τὸν κόσμον, φασὶν ὑφ' ἓν πάντα γεγονέναι καὶ ἐντεῦθεν τοῦτο κατασκευάζουσιν, ἕνεκεν δὲ τάξεως οἴονται τὸν κατάλογον τῶν ἡμερῶν εἰρῆσθαι καὶ τῶν ἐν αὐταῖς γινομένων. πιθανῶς δ' ἂν πρὸς τοῦτο κατασκευάζειν νομιζομένῳ χρήσαιντο ῥητῷ τῷ *αὐτὸς εἶπε καὶ ἐγενήθησαν, αὐτὸς ἐνετείλατο καὶ ἐκτίσθησαν.*
19 Köckert (2009a, 257–258); cf. Köckert (2009b, 238–240).
20 See Or., *in Gen. frg.* D 3 (62.20–64.5 Metzler) = Eus., *Praep. ev.* 7.20.1–2 (402.7–16 Mras).

what has only been handed down in fragments from the commentary. Already in the first homily, Origen points out that it does not say "first day" (*dies prima*) but "one day" (*dies una*) (in Genesis 1:5): "Because time did not exist before the world existed. But time begins to exist where days follow one another; for the second and third and fourth day and all the rest of the days begin to signify time."[21] Even in the extended moment of creation, it is not yet possible to speak of time, as Charlotte Köckert summarizes; time only comes into being with a succession of days, i. e. a measurable and countable temporal extension. The alternation of day and night does not constitute time, but makes it possible to measure time.[22] This is a variation of the Aristotelian concept, according to which time is a number that must be measured with the help of something—for the Aristotelians with the help of the movement of the heavens or the striving of the souls of the heavenly bodies, for Origen with the help of the alternation of day and night and the sequence of days that God has set.[23] However, the extent to which it is really changed (after all, the celestial bodies imagined by Origen to be animated indicate the alternation of day and night) certainly depends on one's point of view. One could certainly assume that the variation is due to Origen taking the biblical text seriously.

We now turn to two much shorter sections devoted to the Commentary on John and then *De principiis.*

2 Concepts of Time in the Commentaries on John and Matthew

The commentary on John is chronologically close to the Genesis commentary. I will begin with two fragments from the catenae, which actually deserve a more detailed discussion due to their place of transmission: in a Munich catena (Monac. Graec. 208), an interpretation by Origen of the beginning of the Gospel

21 Or./Ruf., *Hom. Gen.* 1.1 (3.8–4.2 Habermehl): *Secundum spiritalem vero intellegentiam videamus, quid sit, quod, cum Deus in initio illo, quo superius diximus, 'fecerit coelum et terram', dixerit quoque, ut 'lux fieret', et 'diviserit inter medium lucis et tenebrarum, et vocaverit lucem diem, et tenebras noctem', et dixerit, quia "factum est vespere, et factum est mane", non dixit: dies prima, sed dixit: "dies una." Quia tempus nondum erat, antequam esset mundus. Tempus autem esse incipit ex consequentibus diebus. Secunda namque dies et tertia et quarta et reliquae omnes tempus incipiunt designare.*

22 Köckert (2009a, 260).

23 Arist., *Phys.* 4.11, 219b2–5.7–9; 4.12, 220b8,32–221a9 and Alexander of Aphrodisias, *De tempore* (ed. Sharples 1982, 61–62).

of John has come down to us, which possibly originates from his commentary and could be dated to the early thirties. There Origen says:

> One must know that the main temporal meaning of the verbs, namely 'was', 'is' and 'will be', may not be used with timeless things. For God's Logos, Son of the Father, is also timeless God and therefore the verbs referring to him must not be used with the implication of time. For he is not under time (ὑπὸ χρόνον). But a verb is that which denotes time, as Aristotle says.

Remarkably, Aristotle is apparently cited here as an authority in his *De interpretatione*,[24] but in reality, the quotation (or more precisely: the allusion to a quotation) does not substantiate what is being argued, but provides additional, somewhat superfluous information. Similarly, in a fragment that has survived in various catena types, which also comes from an interpretation of the beginning of the fourth Gospel, it is stated with reference to Plato (*Timaeus* 37a) that the use of the two different tenses at the beginning of the biblical text is appropriate, i. e. ἐγένετο (John 1:6) and ἦν (John 1:1), since the first form ἐγένετο is better suited to describe the incarnation in time, while the second ἦν describes the divinity, even if it would be better to designate it with ἐστίν:

> However, since we are dealing with eternal realities (αἰδίων), the meanings of the verbs should not be applied to them in the strict sense, since the realities they denote have an existence (ὑπάρξις) corresponding to time. But the Logos of God, who is God, is eternal, and therefore the verbs, as far as he is concerned, are not to be understood in the sense that they imply the idea of time, because he whom they denote is not subject to time.[25]

In his commentary on John, of which we only have a few books, Origen apparently often insisted on this idea of the categorical timelessness of God and constantly repeated it because, in his view, it was of central importance for all theological

---

24 Arist., *Int.* 1.3, 16b6: Ῥῆμα δέ ἐστι τὸ προσσημαῖνον χρόνον, οὗ μέρος οὐδὲν σημαίνει χωρίς, καὶ ἔστιν ἀεὶ τῶν καθ' ἑτέρου λεγομένων σημεῖον. "The time word is a word which also denotes time and whose parts mean nothing in particular and which always denotes what is said by another."
25 Or., *Comm. Jo.* frg. 1 (483.13–484.3 Preuschen): ὀρθότατα πρὸς τοὺς τοιούτους ὁ θεολόγος γράφει τὸ "Ἐν ἀρχῇ ἦν ὁ λόγος" καὶ καταλλήλως τοῖς ῥήμασι χρησάμενος, τῷ μὲν "Ἐγένετο" ἐπὶ τῆς σαρκὸς, τῷ δὲ "Ἦν" ἐπὶ τῆς θεότητος [αὐτοῦ σημαίνει]. καὶ ἦν μὲν κυριώτερον ἐπὶ τοῦ θεοῦ λόγου τὸ "Ἔστιν" εἰπεῖν· ἀλλ' ἐπεὶ πρὸς διαφορὰν τῆς ἐνανθρωπήσεως γενομένης ἔν τινι καιρῷ ἐδήλου τὴν ὕπαρξιν τοῦ λόγου, ἀντὶ τοῦ "Ἔστιν" τῷ "Ἦν" ὁ εὐαγγελιστὴς κέχρηται. τῶν δὲ ῥημάτων τὰς κυρίας σημασίας ἐκλαμβάνειν οὐ δεῖ ἐπὶ τῶν ἀϊδίων· ὅτε μὲν γὰρ τὰ σημαινόμενα ὑπὸ τούτων χρόνῳ συμμετρουμένην ἔχει τὴν ὕπαρξιν, <ὡς> τὸ "Ἦν" <τὸ> μηκέτ' ὄν, ἀλλά ποτε ὕπαρξιν σημαίνει· ὁμοίως τὸ "Ἔστι" δηλοῖ τὸ νῦν ὑπάρχον, […] (The given English translation of this passage is abridged.)

(and philosophical) knowledge. A passage at the beginning of the commentary in the first book states:

> The words 'You are my son, today I have begotten you' (Psalm 2:7) [...] are the words of God the Father, who always has 'today' in himself (ἀεί), as for God there is neither evening nor morning; on the contrary, time (if I may say so) extends over the whole duration of his uncreated life (ἀλλὰ ὁ συμπαρεκτείνων τῇ ἀγενήτῳ καὶ ἀϊδίῳ αὐτοῦ ζωῇ) and is for him this very 'today', in which he created the Son, without which we could find the beginning of the creation and also the 'today.'[26]

At this point, our chronologically and genre-differentiated approach does not result in a fundamental change—Origen certainly emphasizes the principle timelessness of God more strongly in his commentary on John than in his interpretations of Genesis, but it may well be due to certain conversational constellations that he felt challenged to make corresponding statements.

We must furthermore consider Origen's commentary on the Gospel of Matthew, which is not covered in Charlotte Köckert's excellent analysis.[27] The commentary was written in Caesarea about ten years after the Commentary on John, that is, between 244 and 248 CE.[28] Origen provides here an overview of the New Testament parables that mention a vineyard and asks the question "whether we can call the whole of the present world a day, which, though long from our perspective, is short and brief in comparison to the life of God and Christ and the Holy Spirit."[29] Origen answers this question in the affirmative with a characteristic consideration, which he presents as a conjecture:

> For perhaps it is the same for some of the blessed powers, [...] in relation to their life, the whole of the present world time, as the one day is in relation to the whole time that a human being can live. But whether or not such a mystery is revealed in Deuteronomy in the hymn

---

26 Or., *Comm. Jo.* 1.29.204 (37.6–12 Preuschen): Ἀλλὰ διὰ τούτων πάντων οὐ σαφῶς ἡ εὐγένεια παρίσταται τοῦ υἱοῦ, ὅτε δὲ τὸ "Υἱός μου εἶ σύ, ἐγὼ σήμερον γεγέννηκά σε" λέγεται πρὸς αὐτὸν ὑπὸ τοῦ θεοῦ, ᾧ ἀεί ἐστι τὸ "σήμερον",—οὐκ ἔνι γὰρ ἑσπέρα θεοῦ, ἐγὼ δὲ ἡγοῦμαι, ὅτι οὐδὲ πρωΐα, ἀλλὰ ὁ συμπαρεκτείνων τῇ ἀγενήτῳ καὶ ἀϊδίῳ αὐτοῦ ζωῇ, ἵν' οὕτως εἴπω, χρόνος ἡμέρα ἐστὶν αὐτῷ σήμερον, ἐν ᾗ γεγέννηται ὁ υἱός, ἀρχῆς γενέσεως αὐτοῦ οὕτως οὐχ εὑρισκομένης ὡς οὐδὲ τῆς ἡμέρας. (The given English translation of this passage is abridged.)

27 Köckert 2009a. The commentary is discussed in Tzamalikos (1991a), esp. p. 249.

28 Vogt (1983, 49–54, 314).

29 Or., *Comm. Matt.* 15.31 (442.24–30 Klostermann): καὶ ὅρα εἰ δυνάμεθα τὸν ὅλον ἐνεστῶτα αἰῶνα ἡμέραν τινὰ εἰπεῖν, μεγάλην μὲν ὡς πρὸς ἡμᾶς, μικρὰν δέ τινα καὶ ὀλιγοχρόνιον ὡς πρὸς τὴν τοῦ θεοῦ καὶ τοῦ Χριστοῦ καὶ τοῦ ἁγίου πνεύματος ζωήν.

> where it says (Deut 32:7), 'Remember the day of judgment,' is a question for someone who is able to investigate.[30]

This passage and others, which we cannot discuss in detail here, show that Origen did not really change his position on how to deal with concepts of time in biblical texts in the course of his life. In the commentary on Matthew, however, it is noticeable at various points (such as the one quoted) that the interpreter repeatedly emphasizes his lack of knowledge and the complexity of the subject.[31] This can be interpreted either as a form of exegetical wisdom of age or as a consequence of the fundamentally scrupulous character of Origen.

It remains for us to briefly address *De principiis*.

3 Concepts of Time in *De principiis*

Origen's *De principiis* obviously dealt with fundamental problems that arose in his school in Caesarea in the scholarly study and interpretation of the Holy Scriptures.[32] It is therefore all the more surprising that the theme of time, which is so central to the commentaries on Genesis and John, hardly plays a prominent role in this work. In contrast to contemporary Platonic thinkers, "time" was certainly *not* a "mega-topic" for Origen. In contrast to Alexander of Aphrodisias and Plotinus, he did not publish a treatise on time or even an excursus-like section in one of his commentaries, such as Simplicius in his commentary on Aristotle's Physics.[33] Only in one place is time dealt with very briefly and summarily in a short section of its own and again, as in the Genesis commentary, in the context of a discussion of the second person of the Christian Trinity. Origen writes:

> But even our sentence: 'Never was, since he was not,' must be taken with a grain of salt. For these words 'there' and 'never' are themselves temporal concepts; but what is said about the Father, Son and Holy Spirit is to be thought beyond all time and beyond all ages and beyond all eternity. It is this Trinity alone that transcends all comprehension, not only in the sense

---

30 Or., *Comm. Matt.* 15.31 (442.33–443.18 Klostermann): τάχα γὰρ καί τινων τῶν μακαρίων δυνάμεων καὶ ἐπαναβεβηκυιῶν, συγκρίσει τῶν πολλῶν γένους τῶν ὑποκάτω τῆς ἀρχικῆς τριάδος. <τοῦτον γὰρ τὸν> λόγον ἔχει ὅλος ὁ ἐνεστὼς αἰὼν ὡς πρὸς τὴν ζωὴν αὐτῶν, ὃν λόγον ἔχει ἡ παρ' ἀνθρώποις ἡμέρα πρὸς ὅλον τὸν δυνατὸν ἀνθρώπῳ ζῆν χρόνον. εἰ δὲ τοιοῦτόν τι μυστήριον ἐν Δευτερονομίῳ δηλοῦται κατὰ τὴν ᾠδὴν ἐν ᾗ γέγραπται· "μνήσθητε ἡμέρας αἰῶνος" ἢ μή, ζητήσει ὁ δυνάμενος.

31 Cf. esp. Or., *Comm. Matt.* 14.12 (304.27–305.17 Klostermann).

32 For this topic see Markschies (2015, 71–91).

33 Simplicius (eds. Golitsis and Hoffmann, 2024).

> of the temporal, but also of the eternal. Everything else that lies outside the Trinity, on the other hand, can be measured in terms of world times and times.[34]

Origen could not have made the point more clearly to his students: *Cetera vero, quae sunt extra trinitatem, in saeculis et in temporibus metienda sunt.*[35] Everything else, however, that lies outside the Trinity can be measured in terms of world times and times.

Strikingly, as we have already seen, the genre-typical differences between commentaries, homilies and *De principiis* naturally determine the way in which Origen deals with time. Allusions to philosophical authorities, for example, can only be found in the scholarly commentaries, not, of course, in the homilies intended for a simple local congregation. But a chronological line of development of Origen's thought over time cannot be established between the earlier texts from Alexandria and the later texts from Palaestina. In other words, with regard to *De principiis*, Origen obviously did not change his thinking over time, or only changed it so slightly that it remains below the radar of our sometimes very superficial knowledge of his writings due to the fragmentary nature of the transmission.

4 Concluding Considerations

At the end of our reflections, we return to the questions raised at the beginning. As we have seen, Origen makes a strict distinction between the timelessness of God on the one hand and the duality of time and eternity on the other. This, for example, distinguishes him, as Mark Edwards or Charlotte Köckert have also noted,[36] from Plato and many thinkers of the Platonic tradition. Mark Edwards even gave his relevant monograph the title "Origen against Plato," thus clearly rejecting the approach, established in the German Protestant tradition since Harnack, according to which Origen was a philosophizing Christian Platon-

34 Or., *Princ.* 4.4.1 (932.8–17 Fernández): *Hoc autem ipsum quod dicimus, quia numquam fuit quando non fuit, cum venia audiendum est. Nam et haec ipsa nomina temporalis vocabuli significantiam gerunt, id est 'quando' vel 'numquam,' supra omne autem tempus et supra omnia saecula et supra omnem aeternitatem intellegenda sunt ea, quae de patre et filio et spiritu sancto dicuntur. Haec enim sola trinitas est, quae omnem sensum intellegentiae non solum temporalis, verum etiam aeternalis excedit. Cetera vero, quae sunt extra trinitatem, in saeculis et in temporibus metienda sunt.*

35 Or., *Princ.* 4.4.1 (932.16–17 Fernández).

36 See Köckert (2009a, 255–256, 265); cf. Sorabji (1983, 112–114, 123).

ist.[37] Eternity is not linked to God, but rather God is conceived (as if taking up a Platonic idea) as once again categorically beyond eternity. In her brief article "tempo" in the Italian Origen dictionary, Adele Monaci Castagno pointed out the homonymous use of the term αἰών as a term for both timeless eternity and the limited time created by God, which Origen adopts from the Old and New Testaments. In the commentary on Paul's letter to the Romans, the Greek original of which is dated shortly after the Genesis Homilies around 244 CE, Origen discusses the connections in detail because Paul's biblical text suggests the topic: "But now that you are free from sin and have become God's servants, you have your fruit in this, that you become holy; but the end is eternal life."[38] Origen comments on the expression ζωὴν αἰώνιον or *vitam aeternam:*

> We have often spoken about eternal life in other places, but we must also briefly mention it here. For 'eternity' in Scripture sometimes refers to that which knows no end, but at other times to that which has an end not in this time, but in the time to come. Sometimes a certain period of time or even the lifespan of an individual person is called 'eternity', as it is written in the law about a Hebrew slave: 'If he loves his wife and children and wants to remain a slave for their sake, you shall pierce his ear with an awl on a pole, and he shall be your slave forever' (Exod 21:5–6). 'Eternity' here undoubtedly means the duration of a human life. On the other hand, the Book of Kohelet says: 'One generation goes, another comes. The earth stands forever' (Eccl 1:4). Here 'eternity' refers to the present world time. But where eternal life is mentioned, we must consider the words of the Redeemer: 'This is eternal life: to know you, the only true God, and Jesus Christ whom you have sent' (John 17:3). And elsewhere: 'I am the way, the truth and the life' (John 14:6). The apostle says in another context: 'We will be caught up in the clouds to meet Christ. And so we will always be with the Lord' (1 Thess 4:17). But just as there is no end to abiding with the Lord, we must also believe that eternal life has no end.[39]

---

37 Edwards (2002, 64–65).

38 Rom 6:22: νυνὶ δὲ ἐλευθερωθέντες ἀπὸ τῆς ἁμαρτίας δουλωθέντες δὲ τῷ θεῷ ἔχετε τὸν καρπὸν ὑμῶν εἰς ἁγιασμόν, τὸ δὲ τέλος ζωὴν αἰώνιον resp. *Nunc vero liberati a peccato servi autem facti Deo habetis fructum vestrum in sanctificationem finem vero vitam aeternam.*

39 Or., *Comm. Rom.* 6.5 in Rom 6:20–22 (224.10–226.3 Heither): *De uita autem aeterna, quamuis et in aliis locis saepe a nobis dictum sit, tamen et in praesenti breuiter perstringendum est quod aeternitas in scripturis aliquando pro eo ponatur ut finem nesciat, aliquando uero, ut in praesenti quidem saeculo finem non habeat, habeat tamen in futuro. Aliquando temporis alicuius uel etiam uitae unius hominis spatium aeternitas appellatur, ut est illud in lege scriptum de seruo Hebraeo: "si dilexerit" inquit "uxorem suam et filios suos et permanere uoluerit in seruitute propter ipsos, subula" inquit "pertundes aurem eius in poste et erit tibi seruus in aeternum." Aeternum hic sine dubio tempus uitae hominis posuit. Et iterum in Ecclesiaste dicitur: "generatio uadit et generatio uenit, terra autem in aeternum stat;" hic "aeternum" praesentis saeculi tempus ostendit. Ubi uero dicit uitam aeternam, ad illud aspiciendum est quod ipse saluator dixit: "haec est autem uita aeterna, ut cognoscant te solum uerum Deum et quem misisti Iesum Christum;" et iterum: "ego sum uia et ueritas et uita." Et ipse apostolus in aliis dicit: quia "rapiemur in nubibus obuiam Christo in*

Monaci Castagno comments on this passage by remarking that Origen "ultimately [...] regards αἰών as a homonym, and this allows him to favor sometimes one meaning, sometimes another, in order to find in certain cases the confirmation of his most controversial doctrines in Scripture." Here, it seems to me, it is not really taken seriously that Origen does not approach biblical texts with a preconceived system, but at best with a system of coordinates or a grammar, as we said at the beginning. First of all, as a trained grammarian, he perceives a linguistic point in biblical texts—namely that of the homonymity of a term—and accordingly examines in all passages which of the possible meanings is meant in a particular passage. The accusation that the differentiation of meanings made it possible to use Scripture as an authority for arbitrary doctrines was already leveled at Origen in late antiquity. Whatever one thinks about this accusation and its appropriateness, it does not do justice to Origen's self-conception as a learned exegete and his strict methodological awareness as well as his prudent, thoroughly tentative and cautious way of working.

Bibliography

Brennecke, H. C., U. Heil, A. Stockhausen, and A. Wintjes, eds. 2007. *Dokumente zur Geschichte des arianischen Streits. Lieferung 3: Bis zur Ekthesis makrostichos.* Athanasius Werke Vol. 3.1. Berlin/Boston: De Gruyter.

Edwards, M. J. 2002. *Origen against Plato.* Aldershot: Ashgate.

Eusebius von Caesarea. 1972. *Gegen Marcell: Über die kirchliche Theologie. Die Fragmente Marcells*, edited by E. Klostermann and G. C. Hansen. GCS Eusebius Vol. 4. Berlin: Akademie Verlag.

Eusebius von Caesarea. 1982. *Praeparatio evangelica*, edited by K. Mras and É. des Places. Eusebius Werke. Vol. 8.1: Einleitung. Die Bücher I bis X. Berlin/Boston: De Gruyter.

Kassomenakis, J. S. 1967. *Zeit und Geschichte bei Origenes.* PhD thesis, Ludwig-Maximilians-Universität München.

Köckert, C. 2009a. "Gott, Welt, Zeit und Ewigkeit bei Origenes." In *Zeit und Ewigkeit als Raum göttlichen Handelns. Religionsgeschichtliche, theologische und philosophische Perspektiven*, edited by R. G. Kratz and H. Spieckermann, 253–297. Berlin/Boston: De Gruyter.

Köckert, C. 2009b. *Christliche Kosmologie und kaiserzeitliche Philosophie.* Tübingen: Mohr Siebeck.

Markell von Ankyra. 1997. *Die Fragmente. Der Brief an Julius von Rom*, edited, introduced and translated by M. Vinzent. Supplements to Vigiliae Christianae 39. Leiden et al.: Brill.

Markschies, C. 2004. "Eusebius als Schriftsteller. Beobachtungen zum sechsten Buch der Kirchengeschichte." In *La Biografia di Origene fra storia e agiografia. Atti di VI Convegno di Studi del Gruppo Italiano di Ricerca su Origene e la Tradizione Alessandrina*, Biblioteca di Adamantius

aera et ita semper cum Domino erimus." Sicut ergo semper cum Domino esse finem non habet, ita et uita aeterna nullum finem habere credenda est.

1, edited by A. di Monaci, 33–50. Villa Verucchio: Pazzini. Reprinted in Markschies, C. 2007. *Origenes und sein Erbe. Gesammelte Studien*, 223–238. Berlin/Boston: De Gruyter.

Markschies, C. 2015. *Christian Theology and Its Institutions in the Early Roman Empire. Prolegomena to a History of Early Christian Theology.* Waco, TX: Baylor University Press.

Markschies, C. 2019. *God's Body. Jewish, Christian, and Pagan Images of God*, translated by A. J. Edmonds. Waco, TX: Baylor University Press.

Markschies, C. 2022. "ἦν ποτε ὅτε οὐκ ἦν oder: Schwierigkeiten bei der Beschreibung dessen, was vor aller Zeit war." In *Platonismus und Christentum. Ihre Beziehung und ihre Grenzen* [Barbara Aland zum 85. Geburtstag], edited by E.-M. Becker and H. Strutwolf, 11–40. Tübingen: Mohr Siebeck.

Markschies, C. 2025. "Das tentative Element im intellektuellen Profil des Origenes – Erwägungen zu Passagen seines Matthäus-Kommentars." In *Origen and Philosophy. A Complex Relation. Proceedings of the 13th International Origen Congress, Münster, 15–19 August, 2022*, edited by A. Fürst, 563–571. Leuven: Peeters.

Monaci Castagno, A. 2000. *Origen. Dizionario. La cultura. Il pensiero. Le opere.* Rome: Città Nuova.

Mühlenberg, E. 1994. "Augustins Predigen." In *Predigt in der Alten Kirche*, edited by E. Mühlenberg and J. van Oort, 9–24. Kampen: Kok Pharos.

Nock, A. D., and A. J. Festugière, eds. 1945–1954. *Corpus Hermeticum I–IV.* Paris: Société d'Édition Les Belles Lettres.

Origenes. 1903. *Der Johanneskommentar*, edited by E. Preuschen. Leipzig: J. C. Hinrichs'sche Buchhandlung.

Origenes. 1935. *Matthäuserklärung I: Die griechisch erhaltenen Tomoi*, edited by E. Klostermann. GCS Origenes Vol. 10. Leipzig: J. C. Hinrichs'sche Buchhandlung.

Origène. 1976. *Philocalie 21–27. Sur le libre arbitre*, introduction, text, translation and notes by É. Junod. Paris: Les Éditions du Cerf.

Origenes. 1990–1999. Commentarii in Epistulam ad Romanos. Römerbriefkommentar, edited by T. Heither. Fontes Christiani 2, vol. 1–6. Freiburg i. Br. et al.: Herder.

Origenes. 2010. *Die Kommentierung des Buches Genesis*, edited, introduced and translated by K. Metzler. Origenes Werke mit deutscher Übersetzung 1/1. Berlin/Boston: De Gruyter; Freiburg i. Br. et al.: Herder.

Origenes. 2011. *Homilien zum Hexateuch in Rufins Übersetzung. Teil 1: Die Homilien zu Genesis (Homiliae in Genesin)*, edited, introduced and translated by P. Habermehl. GCS NF Vol. 17.1. Berlin/Boston: De Gruyter.

Orígenes. 2015. *Sobre los principios*, introduction, critical text, translation and notes by S. Fernández. Madrid: Ciudad Nueva.

Ramelli, I. 2008. "Tzamalikos, Origen: Philosophy of History & Eschatology." *Rivista di Filosofia Neo-Scolastica* 100: 453.

Ramelli, I. 2014. "Alexander of Aphrodisias: A Source of Origen's Philosophy?" *Philosophie Antique* 14: 237–290. Reprinted in Ramelli, I. L. E. 2025. *Origen, the Philosophical Theologian. Trinity, Christology, and Philosophy-Theology Relation. Selected Studies/Kleine Schriften*, 237–284. Berlin/Boston: De Gruyter.

Ramelli, I., and D. Konstan. 2007. *Terms for Eternity: aiônios and aïdios in Classical and Christian Texts.* Piscataway, NJ: Gorgias Press.

Sharples, R. W. 1982. "Alexander of Aphrodisias, On Time." *Phronesis* 27.1: 58–81.

Simplicius de Cilicie. 2024. *Commentaire à la ›Physique‹ d'Aristote: Digressions sur le lieu et sur le temps: Édition critique avec introduction et traduction*, edited by P. Golitsis and P. Hoffmann. Berlin/Boston: De Gruyter.

Sorabji, R. 1983. *Time, Creation and the Continuum. Theories in Antiquity and the Early Middle Ages.* Ithaca, NY: Cornell University Press.

Tzamalikos, P. 1987/1988. "Origen: The Source of Augustine's Theory of Time." *Philosophia. Yearbook of the Center for the Research of Greek Philosophy at the Academy of Athens* 17/18: 396–418.

Tzamalikos, P. 1991a. *The Concept of Time in Origen.* New York et al.: Peter Lang (Originally PhD thesis, University of Glasgow, 1986, https://theses.gla.ac.uk/76635/1/10948128.pdf, last accessed November 20, 2024).

Tzamalikos, P. 1991b. "Origen and the Stoic View of Time." *Journal of the History of Ideas* 52: 535–561.

Tzamalikos, P. 2006. *Origen: Cosmology and Ontology of Time.* Leiden et al.: Brill.

Tzamalikos, P. 2007. *Origen: Philosophy of History & Eschatology.* Leiden et al.: Brill.

Tzamalikos, P. 2016. *Anaxagoras, Origen, and Neoplatonism: The Legacy of Anaxagoras to Classical and Late Antiquity.* Berlin/Boston: De Gruyter.

Vogt, H. J. 1974. *Das Kirchenverständnis des Origenes.* Cologne/Vienna: Böhlau.

Vogt, H. J. 1983. *Origenes, Der Kommentar zum Evangelium nach Mattäus.* Vol. 1. Stuttgart: Anton Hiersemann.

Vogt, H. J. 1999. *Origenes als Exeget*, edited by W. Geerlings. Paderborn et al.: Schöningh.

Oz Tamir

The Time and Context of the Consolation Prophecies

Preliminary Insights into Historical Interpretations in Late Antique Judaism

Introduction

The importance of Jerome as a unique witness to late antique Jewish thought is well established.[1] His dual role as both an independent observer and a complex, multifaceted source provides not only valuable reflections on rabbinic literature but also preserves insights and traditions absent from surviving Jewish sources, making his writings a gold mine of exegetical and historical information about Jews and Judaism. During his residence in Rome, Antioch, and Constantinople, Jerome had many fruitful encounters with Jews, which allowed him to learn from them. His connections with Jews expanded and deepened when he was forced to leave Rome and move to Palestine. In Bethlehem, and possibly other locations in Palestine, Jerome studied with Jews, consulted them on difficulties in Hebrew, and listened to their interpretations of Scripture. These connections provided the basis for some 300 interpretive traditions explicitly attributed to Jews in Jerome's

Note: I would like to express my sincere gratitude to my advisors, Prof. Maren R. Niehoff and Prof. Yitzhak Hen, whose expertise, guidance, and continuous support have been indispensable in shaping this paper. I would also like to thank Dr. Yakir Paz for his helpful and kind feedback, as well as the anonymous reviewer for his valuable comments. I am grateful to the Einstein Center Chronoi in Berlin for their generous support, and to all the participants in the workshop "Creationism and the Calculation of Time in Late Antiquity: Between Alexandria and the Land of Israel" (Berlin, 2023) for their insightful feedback. I would also like to express my appreciation to my academic home, the Jack, Joseph, and Morton Mandel School for Advanced Studies in the Humanities, for their ongoing support, as well as the ROMANA project of the European Research Council (advanced grant no. 101141400, led by Prof. Maren R. Niehoff), for its support. This research is also supported by the Israeli Science Foundation (grant no. 1346/21; PI Prof. Maren R. Niehoff).

1 See, for instance, Rahmer (1861); Ginzberg (1900; 1933; 1935); Hayward (1989); Kamesar (1993); Kedar-Kopfstein (1994); Hayward (1995); Lössl (2002); Williams (2006); Graves (2007); Williams (2008); Hayward (2010); Salvesen (2013); Cameron (2016); Kraus (2017); Krewson (2017); Newman (2018). Particularly noteworthy is Hillel Newman's pioneering work, Newman (1997).

 https://doi.org/10.1515/9783112225981-006

writings, as well as numerous other exegetical allusions. While their Jewish roots are not explicitly mentioned, their clear alignment with rabbinic literature or Jewish Aramaic targum reveals their Jewish origin.

Jerome's preservation of Jewish traditions provides a unique window into the richness of Jewish exegetical thought, revealing parallels with rabbinic literature as well as numerous other traditions for which no other records have survived. One of the most important aspects of these traditions are the midrashim on the Prophets. While fragments of midrash have been preserved in various works of rabbinic literature, no comprehensive midrash on the Prophets has endured, unlike those on the Torah or parts of the Writings. Jerome's role as a crucial source becomes particularly evident when examining how Jews in Late Antiquity interpreted the prophetic scriptures.

This paper offers a preliminary study on unique Jewish interpretive traditions that adopt a historical approach to the consolation prophecies. While rabbinic thought presents a variety of perspectives on the Messiah, redemption,[2] and the *eschaton*, two fundamental beliefs remain unchallenged: the Messiah and redemption will eventually come, and the biblical prophets have already predicted it. Ephraim Elimelech Urbach's pioneering work demonstrates that despite the rabbis' diverse views on numerous messianic themes—ranging from allegorical interpretations of a future redemption to more immediate, national revival—there is one common thread: biblical prophecies, particularly the consolation prophecies, served as the primary source of messianic inspiration.[3] In rabbinic literature, the consolation prophecies of Isaiah, Jeremiah, Ezekiel, and some of the minor prophets were interpreted allegorically or typologically, arguing that they referred to the coming of the Messiah.[4] As Urbach has shown, this dominant view left little room for alternative interpretations within rabbinic texts. In the same way, critical re-evaluations of rabbinical messianism, such as Philip Alexander's,[5] Annette Yoshiko Reed's,[6] Adiel Schremer's,[7] and in a certain sense Michael Fishbane's,[8] do not deny these two fundamental elements of future coming and the "Biblicalization" of the messianic view.

2 I believe "redemption" better represents the Hebrew term "גאולה," which is closely related to the coming of the Messiah, the eschaton. See, for instance, Flusser (2007, 152).

3 Urbach (1982). See also Klausner (1958) and Herr (1985), who share, more or less, the same view. For a discussion on pre-rabbinic messianism in Judaism, see Schäfer (1998).

4 I should also mention the importance of Daniel as another source of this point of view.

5 Alexander (2007).

6 Reed (2014).

7 Schremer (2007).

8 Fishbane (1998).

This paper aims to explore a distinct Jewish interpretive tradition that offers a radically different approach to these prophecies—an approach that has left no trace in the rabbinic corpus but is preserved in Jerome's writings.[9] Around twenty Jewish interpretations in Jerome's commentaries preserve a unique approach to consolation prophecies, arguing that these prophecies refer to a historical event, that is, the return of Zerubbabel, Ezra, and Nehemiah to Jerusalem after the edict of Cyrus.[10] This approach merits further inquiry: what can we learn from these examples about the theological or political origin of these unknown Jewish interpretations? How does this approach comply with the rabbinic one? And how can these rare glimpses be used to improve our understanding of the cultural and exegetical map of late-antique Judaism? Although I will not answer all these questions in this paper, I would like to share my initial findings and stimulate further discussion and reflections.

To lay a solid ground for the discussion, I have chosen to focus on key passages, reserving the analysis of the other sources for another opportunity. The primary reason for selecting these passages is that they preserve both interpretations: one that understands the prophecies in their historical context, and another that connects the consolation prophecies to the coming of the Messiah, much like we find in rabbinic literature. This enables a clear comparative study between the unique sources in Jerome's writings and those found in rabbinic texts. Some of the additional passages preserved by Jerome contain only the historical interpretation, without the messianic one, while others contain both interpretations. However, there is no direct parallel in rabbinic literature that suggests the same prophecy was understood in the same way as the sources brought by Jerome. By focusing on the selected sources, I hope to demonstrate the existence of a systematic Jewish historical approach to the consolation prophecies, distinct from messianic interpretations, which, as noted, are also attested in rabbinic literature. The comparison with rabbinic literature will illustrate Jerome's importance in reconstructing the multifaceted and diverse landscape of Jewish interpretations in Late Antiquity, a diversity often obscured by the surviving edited rabbinic texts.

---

9 Theodore of Cyrus preserves several Jewish traditions with similar characteristics. I will address this issue in greater detail elsewhere. For now, see McCollough (1984, 126–137) However, as Newman (1997, 201) demonstrated, McCollough's proposal to interpret these traditions as referring to the future coming of the Messiah does not hold up under critical scrutiny.

10 Newman (1997, 201–202) has already remarked on the exceptional nature of these traditions.

1

Let us begin with Jerome's commentary on Zech 2:14–16. The biblical text states:

> Sing praise and rejoice, O daughter of Zion, for behold I come, and I will dwell in the midst of you, says the Lord. And many nations shall be joined to the Lord on that day, and they shall be My people, and I will dwell in the midst of you, and you shall know that the Lord of Hosts has sent me to you. And the Lord shall possess Judah as His portion in the sanctified land, and He will yet choose Jerusalem.[11]

In his commentary on these verses, after explaining the passage and connecting it to the first coming of Christ, Jerome quotes a Jewish interpretation of the passage:

> *Some of the Jews* think that this was fulfilled in part under Zerubbabel and Joshua, Ezra and Nehemiah, especially since Jerusalem is chosen and Judah is possessed; namely, the two tribes that returned from the Babylonian captivity and were called Judah and not Israel, who still lives to this day among the Medes. *But others* put it off to the future, because at that time nations shall believe in the one who is sent by the Lord, and Jerusalem is to be chosen, since with certainty now all nations have believed in the Lord and Savior, and she who has been utterly destroyed cannot be chosen.[12]

Jerome mentions two different Jewish interpretations. The first takes these verses as referring to the return to Jerusalem under Zerubbabel, Jesus the high priest, Ezra, and Nehemiah, while the second understands it as a future prophecy. Jerome's wording with reference to the Jewish interpretations—"some of the Jews think […] but others" (*iudaeorum alii putant* […] *alii uero* […])—gives the impression that the two options are equal in their logical argument, at least in Jerome's eyes, and that they both rely on the same idea that this prophecy is related to the

---

11 Cf. *BHS*, Zech 2:14–16: רָנִּי וְשִׂמְחִי בַּת־צִיּוֹן כִּי הִנְנִי־בָא וְשָׁכַנְתִּי בְתוֹכֵךְ נְאֻם־יְהוָה׃
וְנִלְווּ גוֹיִם רַבִּים אֶל־יְהוָה בַּיּוֹם הַהוּא וְהָיוּ לִי לְעָם וְשָׁכַנְתִּי בְתוֹכֵךְ וְיָדַעַתְּ כִּי־יְהוָה צְבָאוֹת שְׁלָחַנִי אֵלָיִךְ׃
וְנָחַל יְהוָה אֶת־יְהוּדָה חֶלְקוֹ עַל אַדְמַת הַקֹּדֶשׁ וּבָחַר עוֹד בִּירוּשָׁלִָם׃

12 Jerome, *Comm. Zach.* 2:14–16 (Scheck 2017, 17 [with some changes, emphasis mine]), see also Adriaen 1970, 768–769*): iudaeorum alii putant sub zorobabel et iesu, esdra et nehemia, haec ex parte completa, maxime quoniam hierusalem eligitur, et possidetur iudas; duae uidelicet tribus quae reuersae sunt de captiuitate babylonica, et appellatae sunt iudas, et non israel, qui apud medos huc usque uersantur. alii uero in futurum differunt, quod tunc crediturae sint gentes in eum qui mittatur a domino, et eligenda sit hierusalem, cum utique iam omnes gentes crediderunt in dominum saluatorem, nec possit eligi quae omnino destructa est.* Jerome's note that this prophecy "was fulfilled in part (*ex parte completa*)" could be understood either as his own observation or as part of the Jewish tradition, which held that the prophecy was not fully realized, perhaps because the prophet had promised that all nations would come to believe in God and His appointed one.

Jews and their redemption. The differences lie in the methods and ambitions. The first tradition reads these verses historically, whereas the second is quite literal but oriented to the future, with political and national visions. However, as far as Jerome is concerned, the historical interpretation comes first and seems to be the main approach. He gives much more attention to the historical reading, providing a detailed explanation of how the interpreters read Zechariah's prophecy, while the second interpretation is explained only in general, saying that some Jews "put it off to the future (*in futurum different*)" when "nations shall believe in the one who is sent by the Lord, and Jerusalem is to be chosen (*crediturae sint gentes in eum qui mittatur a domino, et eligenda sit hierusalem*)." The second interpretation does not address the specific details highlighted in the prophecy, such as the selection of Judah rather than Israel, as the first interpretation does. Instead, it merely refers to the prophecy as pertaining to an unspecified time in the future.

Therefore, the impression is that Jerome's comment is more in line with the historical interpretation. This fact could be related to his approach, mentioned before the two Jewish interpretations, in which he explained the prophecy as referring to Jesus' first coming. Furthermore, in his introduction to the commentary on Zechariah, while mentioning the works of Origen, Hippolytus, and Didymus on the book of Zechariah, Jerome specifically states that "their entire exegesis was allegorical, and they touched hardly a few things concerning the history,"[13]—which is exactly what he aims to address. His explicit historical approach could explain why he chose to emphasize the Jewish historical view and not the future messianic interpretation.

The second view, in which Zechariah's prophecy was interpreted as a future event, can be found in rabbinic literature. In *Song of Songs Rabbah*, a Palestinian midrash from the sixth or seventh century CE,[14] we read:

> A noblewoman whose husband the king, her sons, and her sons-in-law went to a country overseas. [Her servants] told her: "Your sons have come [home]." She said: "What do I care? Let my daughters-in-law rejoice." They said to her: "Your sons-in-law have come." She said: "What do I care? Let my daughters rejoice." They said to her: "Your husband, the king, has come." She said: "This is complete joy, joy compounded by joy." So too, in the future, the prophets will come and say to Jerusalem: "Your sons will come from afar," (Isa 60:4) and it will say to them: "What do I care? 'Your daughters shall be carried on

13 Jerome, *Comm. Zach.*, Introduction (Scheck 2017, 2) [with some changes], for the Latin text, see Adriaen (1970, 748): *tota eorum ἐξήγησις allegorica fuit, et historiae uix pauca tetigerunt.*

14 As mentioned, there are no extant classical midrashim on the Prophets, which means we lack a comprehensive view of the rabbinic approaches to these texts. This fact shall also explain why this is the first record of rabbinic exegesis on Zech 2:14–16.

> the hip,' (Isa 60:4)" and it will say to them: What do I care? When they say to it: "Behold, your king is coming to you, righteous and victorious," (Zech 9:9) it says: This is a complete joy, as it is written: "Rejoice greatly, daughter of Zion, [behold your king is coming to you]," (Zech 9:9) and it is written: "Sing and rejoice, daughter of Zion [for behold I am coming]," (Zech 2:14) [...][15]

The framing of this story as a parable of the future-to-come, and afterward, the use of Zech 2:14 as proof, indicates that this prophecy was understood as a future prophecy. However, Jerome's commentary also acknowledges another Jewish perspective that situates the consolation prophecies within their historical context. This perspective is particularly striking because it diverges from the dominant eschatological interpretations found in late-antique rabbinic literature. Instead, it reflects an interpretive approach that emphasizes the immediacy of the prophecies' relevance to historical realities. To better understand this unique viewpoint and its broader implications, let us examine another illustrative example.

2

Another example of this kind of combination—two different Jewish traditions and an opposing Christian interpretation—is found in Jerome's commentary on Isa 52:11–12. The biblical text reads:

> Depart, depart, go out from there; touch no unclean thing; go out from the midst of her; purify yourselves, you who bear the vessels of the Lord. For you shall not go out in hast, and you shall not go in flight, for the Lord will go before you, and the God of Israel will be your rear guard.[16]

In his commentary on these verses, Jerome says the following:

---

15 *Song. Rab.* 1.4 (Dunsky 1980, 28): "מטרונה שהלך המלך בעלה ובניה וחתניה למדינת הים, ובאו ואמרו לה באו בניך אמרה מה איכפת לי תשמחנה כלותי, כיון שבאו חתניה אמרו לה באו חתניך אמרה מה איכפת לי תשמחנה בנותי, אמרו לה בא המלך בעליך אמרה האי חדותא שלימה חדו על חדו, כך לעתיד לבא באין הנביאים ואומרים לירושלים בניך מרחוק יבואו (ישעיהו ס, ד) והיא אומרת להם מה איכפת לי, ובנותיך על צד תאמנה (שם) אמרה מה איכפת לי, כיון שאמרו לה הנה מלכך יבא לך צדיק ונושע (זכריה ט, ט) אמרה הא חדותא שלימה דכתיב גילי מאד בת ציון (שם) וכתיב רני ושמחי בת ציון (שם ב, יד) באותה שעה היא אומרת שוש אשיש בה' תגל נפשי באלהי (ישעיהו סא, י). The use of Zech 2:14 as a reference to the coming of the Messiah is also mentioned in *Tanna Devei Eliyahu*, 18 and *Pesiqta Rabbati*, 35.

16 Cf. *BHS*, Isa 52:11–12: סֻורוּ סֹורוּ צְאוּ מִשָּׁם טָמֵא אַל־תִּגָּעוּ צְאוּ מִתֹּוכָהּ הִבָּרוּ נֹשְׂאֵי כְּלֵי יְהוָה׃ כִּי לֹא בְחִפָּזֹון תֵּצֵאוּ וּבִמְנוּסָה לֹא תֵלֵכוּן כִּי־הֹלֵךְ לִפְנֵיכֶם יְהוָה וּמְאַסִּפְכֶם אֱלֹהֵי יִשְׂרָאֵל׃

> *The Jews* attempt to explain even this in the following manner. "Go out" from Babylon and forsake their idols. "Go out of the midst of her," and bring back to the temple the vessels that Nebuchadnezzar had taken when he captured Jerusalem, when Cyrus released the captives under Zerubbabel and Ezra. "Go forth" thus from Babylon, not as you fled before from Egypt "with a tumult" and fear, but with peace and by the will of the king of the Persians and Medes, unto whom the will of the Lord appeared, who protected and "gathered you together." *Others*[17] interpret what we have said about Babylon as referring to the Roman Empire because all these things are fulfilled at the advent of Christ,[18] who would come to liberate them.[19]

As in the previous passage, Jerome highlights two distinct Jewish interpretive approaches to this prophecy. The first approach interprets the prophecy as referring to the return from Babylon under Zerubbabel and Ezra. This historical interpretation, however, is inconsistent with the rabbinic approach, which closely aligns with the second Jewish interpretation quoted by Jerome. According to this second view, the prophecy is understood as a future promise for the Jewish people, envisioning the Messiah liberating them and bringing them back to the Land of Israel. This view is shared by the *Mekhilta of Rabbi Ishmael*, a Palestinian halakhic midrash from the third century CE. In Tractate *Pisha* chapter 7, we read:

17 Unlike the previous example, the structure here raises one important question about the origin of this second interpretation. While in his commentary on Zech 2:12–14, by using the correlative formula—*iudaeorum alii putant X, alii uero Y*—Jerome creates a clear comparative structure between two Jewish views, here, in his explanation, he attributes the first interpretation to the "Jews" (*Iudaei*), and the second one to "others" (*alii*); without any specific reference to their Jewishness. However, the continuation of his commentary, where he explains his own view, proves beyond any doubt that these are two Jewish interpretations. Jerome states that "we interpret this not as referring to the Jews, but as referring to the chorus of apostles and all the saints (*nos autem* [...] *nequaquam hoc de Iudaeis, sed de apostolorum omnium que sanctorum intellegimus choro*)," indicating that the two interpretations mentioned before are both related to the Jews and their reading of Isaiah's prophecy.

18 Jerome's use of the word *Christus* (Χριστός) to describe the Jewish Messiah deserves further attention, though this topic lies beyond the scope of the current paper.

19 Jerome, *Comm. Isa.* 14 (Scheck 2015) [with some changes]), for the Latin text, see Gryson and Deproost (1998, 1509): *'Et hoc Iudaei sic disserere conantur.' Exite de Babylone et idola eorum derelinquite. Exite de medio illius, et uasa quae Nabuchodonosor capta Hierusalem tulerat, Cyro laxante captiuos sub Zorobabel et Ezra referte in templum. Nec sicut prius de Aegypto cum tumultu et timore fugistis, ita egredimini de Babylone, sed cum pace et uoluntate regis Persarum atque Medorum, in quo domini uoluntas apparuit, qui protexit et congregauit uos. Alii quae de Babylone diximus, de romano regno interpretantur, quod in aduentu Christi, qui eos liberaturus sit, haec omnia compleantur.*

> "And you shall eat it [Paschal lamb] in haste." (Exod 12:11)[20] This refers to the bustle of the Egyptians. You interpret it so, but perhaps this is not so, but it refers to the bustle of the Israelites? [...] Abba Hanin in the name of R. Eliezer says: It refers to the haste of the Shekhinah. And though there is no proof for this, there is a hint of it: "Hark! My beloved! Behold He comes, etc. Behold He stands behind our wall." (Song 2:8–9) One might think that in the future-to-come also the deliverance will be in haste. But it says: "For you shall not go out in haste, neither shall you go by flight; for the Lord will go before you." (Isa 52:12)[21]

The midrash raises a question about the concept of haste, wondering whether it refers to the Israelites or the Egyptians. Abba Hanin, in the name of R. Eliezer, says, and this is the relevant part to our discussion, that the haste is the haste of Shekhinah, that is, the presence of God. Abba Hanin explains his position by stressing that although "there is no proof for this" in Scripture, "there is a hint of it." Two verses, Song 2:8–9, demonstrate the Shekhinah's haste; another verse, Isa 52:12, the verse under discussion, shows, according to Abba Hanin, that in the "future to come (לעתיד לבוא)," the Shekhinah will not hasten, as the verse reads: "For you shall not go out in haste, neither shall you go by flight; for the Lord will go before you." The use of this specific verse from Isaiah as a hint for the future emphasizes that this prophecy was interpreted not in its historical context, but as a prediction for future events.

Another midrash, *Pesiqta de-Rav Kahana* (5, 19), a Palestinian midrash from the fifth or sixth century CE, demonstrates the same understanding of this prophecy in Isaiah:

> "Eat not of it [Paschal lamb] raw" (Exod 12:9) [...] R. Samuel bar Nahman said: Seeing that in this world you had to eat the roasted flesh in haste, what is said of the manner of your deliverance in the world-to-come? "You shall not go out in haste, neither shall you go by flight; for the Lord will go before you, and the God of Israel will be your rearguard (Isa 52:12).[22]

20 Exod 12:11: ואכלתם אתו בחפזון

21 *Mek. of Rabbi Ishmael*, Tractate *Pisha*, 7 (Lauterbach 2004, 35–37 [with some changes]): "ואכלתם אותו בחפזון זה חפזון מצרים. אתה אומר כן או אינו אלא חפזון ישראל כשהוא אומר ולכל בני ישראל לא יחרץ כלב לשונו (שמות יא, ז) הרי חפזון ישראל אמור הא מה אני מקיים ואכלתם אותו בחפזון זה חפזון מצרים. רבי יהושע בן קרחה אומר ואכלתם אותו בחפזון זה חפזון ישראל. אתה אומר כן או אינו אלא חפזון מצרים כשהוא אומר כי גורשו ממצרים הרי חפזון מצרים אמור. ומה תלמוד לומר בחפזון זה חפזון ישראל. אבא חנן משום רבי אליעזר אומר זה חפזון שכינה אף על פי שאין ראיה לדבר זכר לדבר. קול דודי הנה זה בא מדלג על ההרים מקפץ על הגבעות (שיר השירים ב, ח) ואומר הנה זה עומד אחר כתלנו (שם ב, ט) יכול אף לעתיד לבא יהא בחפזון ת"ל כי לא בחפזון תצאו ובמנוסה לא תלכון כי הולך לפניכם יי' וגו' (ישעיהו נב, יב).

22 *Pesiq. Rab. Kah.* 5.9 (Braude and Kapstein 2002, 163 [with some changes]): "אל תאכלו ממנו נא (שמות יב, ט)... א"ר שמואל בר נחמן לפי שבעולם הזה ואכלתם אתו בחפזון (שם), אבל לעתיד לבא מה כת', כי לא בחפזון תצאו ובמנוסה לא תלכון כי הולך לפניכם י"י ומאספכם אלהי ישראל (ישעיהו נב, יב)"

Similar to the *Mekhilta*, the *Pesiqta* quotes Isa 52:12 as a source depicting the future. By using this verse to explain the differences between this world and the world-to-come, these interpreters reveal their perspective on the prophecy. In their view, the prophecy refers to the future and not to historical circumstances.

On the other hand, the first Jewish interpretation quoted by Jerome offers a different approach—Isaiah's prophecy is explained as referring to the return of Zerubbabel and his companions to Jerusalem after the Edict of Cyrus. This interpretation reads the prophecy in its historical context, aimed at explaining God's consolation as an accomplished mission. It is, as mentioned, inconsistent with the rabbinic approach. Furthermore, this interpretation, and not the second one, seems to be the main interpretation as far as Jerome is concerned: it is mentioned first and in far greater detail than the second, rabbinic one. While quoting the Jewish interpreters, Jerome provides a close reading of the biblical text, explaining it word by word, and showing how the Jews interpret the whole prophecy. The second Jewish interpretation quoted by Jerome, on the other hand, appears in his narrative in passing. There is no close reading of the biblical verses, nor explanation of how the Jews read the whole text; there is only a general statement that "*others* interpret [...] these things" on the future coming of the Messiah.

Once again, very much like the previous comment on Zechariah, Jerome's decision to emphasize the Jewish historical interpretation might be understood in light of his own ambitions to provide a historical reading of the biblical prophecy. I should briefly mention that the two Jewish interpretations presented by Jerome serve in his work as a starting point to present his own view on the prophecy which follows. While presenting his view, he asserts that Isaiah's words should be interpreted as referring to "the chorus of apostles and all the saints (*apostolorum omnium que sanctorum* [...] *choro*)," providing a detailed, verse-by-verse analysis of the prophecy.

Building on his earlier comment on Zech 2:12–14, it can be said that Jerome, by distinguishing between the two Jewish traditions and contrasting them with his Christian tradition, highlights three distinct approaches to interpreting consolation prophecies: a Jewish historical approach, a Jewish messianic approach, and a messianic–historical Christian approach. To further elaborate on this conclusion, I will present an additional source.

3

In Hos 3:4–5, we read:

> For the children of Israel shall dwell many days without king or prince, without sacrifice or pillar, without ephod or household gods. Afterward, the children of Israel shall return and seek the Lord their God, and David their king, and they shall come in fear to the Lord and to his goodness in the latter days.[23]

These two verses are part of a short, well-structured prophecy in Hos (chapter three). The prophecy begins with God's command to Hosea to take a "woman who is loved by another man and is an adulteress," (Hos 3:1) to illustrate the devotion of the people of Israel to sin and their worship of idols. The narrator states that Hosea followed God's command and took a wife. He told her, "You must dwell as mine for many days. You shall not play the whore, or belong to another man; so will I also be to you." (Hos 3:3) The two verses highlighted by Jerome explain this action: God separated the people of Israel from their kingdom, worship, and idols, creating a situation that will inspire them to "return and seek the Lord their God."

Jerome begins his comment on these verses by addressing the subtle differences between the Hebrew text and the Septuagint, using this as a springboard to introduce his Christian interpretation of the prophecy. He asserts that Hosea's words prophesy the second future coming of Jesus. He describes how, after "many days during which the unhappy synagogue, the adulterous woman, has been fed with barley and sat diminished, because she cannot stand with Christ (*infelix synagoga et mulier adultera hordeo pascitur, et sedit contracta, quia cum christo stare non potest*)," the Day of Judgment will arrive. At that time, the Jews "will return and seek the Lord their God and David their king," which Jerome interprets as referring to Jesus Christ. Unlike his interpretations of the earlier passages from Zech and Isa, which Jerome linked to the first, historical coming of Jesus, this prophecy is understood as pointing to Christ's second coming. Jerome's interpretation on these verses concludes with the following:

> *Some of the Jews* have interpreted the present chapter as being about the Jews' Babylonian captivity, when for seventy years the Temple was desolate and there was no altar, sacrifices, or priesthood, and afterward, under Zerubbabel, they returned to their former habitations. *Others,*[24] including us, apply it to the future time. Those [other interpreters] are unable to find any cause, apart from the execution of the Savior, that could have caused such great offense that despite [the Jews] not worshiping idols, they have been rejected for such a long time.[25]

---

23 Cf. *BHS*, Hos 3:4–5: כִּי יָמִים רַבִּים יֵשְׁבוּ בְּנֵי יִשְׂרָאֵל אֵין מֶלֶךְ וְאֵין שָׂר וְאֵין זֶבַח וְאֵין מַצֵּבָה וְאֵין אֵפוֹד וּתְרָפִים׃ | אַחַר יָשֻׁבוּ בְּנֵי יִשְׂרָאֵל וּבִקְשׁוּ אֶת־יְהוָה אֱלֹהֵיהֶם וְאֵת דָּוִד מַלְכָּם וּפָחֲדוּ אֶל־יְהוָה וְאֶל־טוּבוֹ בְּאַחֲרִית הַיָּמִים׃

24 Along with the content itself, the correlative structure—*alii iudaeorum* [...] *alii*—proves that the second interpretation is a Jewish one. See above, n. 17.

25 Jerome, *Comm. Os.* 3:4–5 (trans. Scheck 2017, 174 [with some changes]), for the Latin text, see Adriaen (1969, 37): *praesens capitulum, alii iudaeorum super babylonica captiuitate interpretantur,*

Jerome quotes two Jewish traditions about the prophecy. The first, attributed to "some of the Jews (*alii iudaeorum*)," interprets the prophecy as referring to a historical event—the return to the Land of Israel under Zerubbabel and the restoration of the Temple after seventy years of Babylonian captivity. The second Jewish tradition, attributed to "others (*alii*)," applies it "to the future time" without any specific explanation of the biblical text. Jerome connects the second interpretation with his own Christian view since they both interpret the prophecy as referring to a future time: Jerome, as mentioned, explains it as referring to Jesus' second coming, and the Jewish tradition reads it, apparently, as referring to the future coming of the Messiah. Jerome includes a polemical remark about the second Jewish tradition, asserting that the delay in the arrival of the Jewish Messiah can only be interpreted in light of Jesus' execution (*interfectio*), which he attributes to the culpability of the Jews. He argues that, although the Jews abandoned their physical idols, they did not attain salvation. Their subsequent forsaking by God, Jerome claims, can only be understood as a consequence of their ancient crime—the crucifixion of Jesus.

An examination of the two Jewish interpretations reveals that they offer distinct readings of Hosea's prophecy. The first interprets it historically, while the second applies it to the future. Moreover, as noted regarding the earlier sources, it appears that the first, "historical" tradition is considered the primary interpretation, at least from Jerome's perspective. This tradition is much more detailed and offers a close interpretation of the biblical text. The prophecy that "the children of Israel shall dwell many days without king or prince, without sacrifice or pillar, without ephod or household gods" is clarified by the lack of an altar, sacrifices, and priesthood during the Babylonian captivity. God's promise that afterward "they shall come in fear to the Lord and to His goodness in the latter days" is interpreted as referring to the return to Jerusalem under Zerubbabel. The second tradition, on the other hand, applies it to "the future time" without providing any explanation. Jerome focuses primarily on advocating the Christian view that the "execution of the Savior" is the cause of God's continuous abandonment of the Jews.

While the first Jewish tradition quoted by Jerome has no other written record, the second tradition can be confirmed, once again, by rabbinic literature. In the Jerusalem Talmud tractate *Berakhot*, we find a discussion about the order of the different parts of the Amidah prayer (also called the *Shemoneh Esreh* [שמנה

---

quando septuaginta annis desolatum est templum, et altare et uictimae ac sacerdotium non fuerunt, et postea sub zorobabel in sedes pristinas sunt reuersi. alii, ut nos, in futurum tempus differunt, et quae sit causa tam grandis offensae, ut tanto tempore relicti sint, maxime cum idola non colant, praeter interfectionem saluatoris, aliam non ualent inuenire.

עשרה]). One phrase, delivered by Rabbi Levi in the name of Rabbi Aha bar Hanina, quotes Hos 3:5 and reveals the rabbinic view on this prophecy:

> Rabbi Levi, in the name of Rabbi Aha bar Hanina: What did they see in placing "He Who blesses the years" adjacent to "ingatherer of the dispersed of Israel"? Because of "you, mountains of Israel, sprout your branches and carry your fruits for my people Israel," why? "Because they will soon come" (Ezek 36:8). When the dispersed are gathered in, justice will be done, the evildoers will succumb, and the just will be happy. It was stated: One includes the apostates and the wicked in "He Who subdues the evildoers," the converts and the elders in "refuge of the just," David in "Builder of Jerusalem." "Then the children of Israel will repent, seek the Eternal, their God, and their king David." (Hos 3:5)[26]

The Talmud opens with a question: Why is the prayer for blessing the years, the ninth prayer of Amidah, followed by the prayer for the gathering of Israel's dispersed? One verse, Ezek 36:8, explains this connection: "You, mountains of Israel, sprout your branches and carry your fruit for my people Israel." Why? "Because they will soon come." The mountains of the Land of Israel will sprout branches and carry fruit for the people of Israel, supposedly in anticipation of the return of the Israelites from captivity. This is why the prayer for blessing the years is followed by the prayer for the gathering of Israel's dispersed. The Talmud continues by explaining the subsequent order of the prayers, arguing that this sequence symbolizes the future redemption's order: "When the dispersed are gathered in (the tenth prayer), then justice will be done, the evildoers will succumb (the eleventh prayer), and the just will be happy (the twelfth prayer)." Although the meaning of this sentence may seem somewhat obscure, the framing is clear: the order of the prayers reflects the order of the future redemption.[27] The Talmud then in-

26 *y. Ber.* 2:4 (Guggenheimer 2000, 208–209 [with minor changes]): "ר' לוי בשם ר' אחא בר חנינא. מה ראו לסמוך מברך השנים למקבץ נדחי ישראל על שם "ואתם הרי ישראל ענפכם תתנו ופירייכם תשאו לעמי ישראל" למה "כי קרבו לבוא" [יחזקאל לו, ח]. נתקבצו הגליות והדין נעשה הזידים נכנעים והצדיקים שמיחים. ותני עלה כולל של מינים ושל רשעים במכניע זידים. ושל גרים ושל זקנים במבטח לצדיקים. ושל דוד בבונה ירושלים "אחר ישובו בני ישראל ובקשו את יי' אלהיהם ואת דוד מלכם" [הושע ג, ה]".

27 A much more detailed (and clear) version of this phrase is preserved in the Babylonian Talmud, *b. Meg.* 17b: "What was their reason for saying the gathering of the exiles after the blessing of the years? Because it is written, 'But you, O mountains of Israel, you shall shoot forth your branches and yield your fruit to your people Israel, for they are at hand to come.' (Ezek 36:8). And when the exiles are gathered, judgment will be visited on the wicked, as it says, 'And I will turn my hand upon you and purge away your dross as with lye' (Isa 1:25) and it is written further, 'And I will restore your judges as at the first' (Isa 1:26). And when judgment is visited on the wicked, apostates will cease, and presumptuous sinners are included with them, as it is written, 'But the destruction of the transgressors and of the sinners shall be together, and they that forsake the Lord shall be consumed' (Isa 1:28). And when the transgressors have disappeared, the horn of the righteous will be exalted, as it is written, 'All the horns of the wicked also will I cut

cludes a tannaitic quotation, presumably to reinforce this point, saying, "It was stated: One includes the apostates and the wicked in 'He Who subdues the evildoers,' the converts and the elders in 'refuge of the just,' David in 'Builder of Jerusalem.'" This enigmatic quotation is also preserved in the Tosefta,[28] as well as in two other places in the Jerusalem Talmud.[29] It refers to three prayers that were at some point separated into six but are now, according to the Palestinian tradition, unlike the Babylonian, meant to be delivered as three double prayers.[30] In what appears to be a reinforcement of the previous argument—and this is the most important point for our purpose—the Talmud continues by quoting Hos 3:5 to explain why the prayer for the future coming of David's son, the Messiah, is included in "Builder of Jerusalem."[31]

---

off, but the horns of the righteous shall be exalted' (Ps 95:11). And 'righteous converts' are included with the righteous, as it says, 'Before the hoary head rise up, and honor the face of the elder,' and the text goes on, 'And if a stranger sojourns with you' (Lev 19:32)." [=ומה ראו לומר קיבוץ גליות לאחר ברכת השנים – דכתיב ואתם הרי ישראל ענפכם תתנו ופריכם תשאו לעמי ישראל כי קרבו לבוא. וכיון שנתקבצו גליות – נעשה דין ברשעים, שנאמר: ואשיבה ידי עליך ואצרף כבר סיגיך, וכתיב ואשיבה שפטיך כבראשנה. וכיון שנעשה דין מן הרשעים – כלו המינים, וכולל זדים עמהם, שנאמר: ושבר פשעים וחטאים יחדו ועוזבי ייי יכלו. וכיון שכלו המינים – מתרוממת קרן צדיקים, דכתיב וכל קרני רשעים אגדע תרוממנה קרנות צדיק, וכולל גירי הצדק עם הצדיקים, שנאמר מפני שיבה תקום והדרת פני זקן, וסמיך ליה וכי יגור אתכם גר.]. The importance of this paragraph for understanding the development of rabbinic perspectives on messianism was convincedly demonstrated by Alexander (2007, 237–240).

28 *t. Ber.* 3:25 (Lieberman 1955, 17–18): שמונה עשרה ברכות שאמרו חכמים כנגד שמונה עשרה אזכרות שבהבו לה' בני אלים כולל של מינים בשל פרושין ושל גרים בשל זקנים ושל דוד בבונה ירושלם אם אמר אלו לעצמן ואילו לעצמן יצא.

29 *y. Ber.* 4:3 (Sussman 2001, 37); *y. Ta'an.* 2:2 (Sussman 2001, 713–714).

30 See Lieberman (2001, 53–55).

31 This explanation can be understood, once again, by the parallel discussion in the Babylonian Talmud, *b. Meg.* 17b–18a: "And where is the horn of the righteous exalted? In Jerusalem, as it says, 'Pray for the peace of Jerusalem, may they prosper that love you.' (Ps 122:6) And when Jerusalem is built, David will come, as it says, 'Afterwards the children of Israel shall return and seek the Lord their God, and David their king.' (Hos 3:5) And when David comes, prayer will come, as it says, 'Even then will I bring them to my holy mountain, and make them joyful in my house of prayer.' (Isa 56:7) And when prayer has come, the Temple service will come, as it says, 'Their burnt-offerings and their sacrifices shall be acceptable upon my altar.' (Isa 56:7) And when the Temple service comes, thanksgiving will come, as it says, 'Whoever offers the sacrifice of thanksgiving honors me.' (Ps 50:23)" [=והיכן מתרוממת קרנם – בירושלים, שנאמר שאלו שלום ירושלים ישליו אהביך. וכיון שנבנית ירושלים – בא דוד, שנאמר: אחר ישבו בני ישראל ובקשו את ה' אלהיהם ואת דוד מלכם. וכיון שבא דוד – באתה תפלה, שנאמר והביאותים אל הר קדשי ושמחתים בבית תפלתי. וכיון שבאת תפלה – באת עבודה שנאמר עולתיהם וזבחיהם לרצון על מזבחי. וכיון שבאת עבודה – באתה תודה, שנאמר זבח תודה יכבדנני.]. Unlike the Jerusalem Talmud, the Babylonian does not address the issue of combining the prayers for David and Jerusalem into one. According to the Babylonian tradition, these two prayers remain separate. The Babylonian Talmud focuses on explaining the order of the Amidah prayers and cites Hos 3:5 to reference the sequence. It emphasizes the word "אחר" (afterward) as an

It is clear, then, that Hos 3:5 was interpreted by the rabbis as referring to a future time, specifically to the coming of the Messiah. This understanding is further supported by the following discussion in the Talmud:

> The Rabbis say: this King Messiah, if he is from the living, his name is David. If he is from the dead, his name is David. Rabbi Tanhuma said: I am declaring the reason "He gives kindness to His anointed, to David (Ps 18:51)." Rabbi Joshua ben Levi said, his name is Zemah. Rabbi Yudan, the son of Rabbi Aivu, said his name is Menahem.[32]

The quotation from Hos 3:5 is followed by a discussion about the name of the Messiah, underscoring the rabbinic view that this prophecy is wholly future-oriented, with no historical reference, much like the second Jewish tradition quoted by Jerome.

4

In addition to the three examples adduced above, there are approximately twenty more comments in Jerome's work, in which he quotes Jewish traditions that share the same historical approach to the consolation prophecies. Some of them, like the three presented, contain the rabbinic-messianic perspective as well. The coexistence of the rabbinic and the historical interpretations in Jerome's commentaries is noteworthy. It emphasizes Jerome's credibility as a unique preserver of Jewish knowledge. Since we can find parallels between his Jewish quotations and rabbinic literature, there is no reason to doubt his non-rabbinic sources. And yet, the absence of written records for the historical approach is intriguing and raises crucial questions: How should we understand this unique interpretation? What could have been the historical and theological circumstances that allowed the development, preservation, and distribution of this kind of interpretation? And what insights can we gain as far as the Jewish society of late-antique Palestine and its eschatological expectations are concerned? In the following section, I would like to present preliminary insights and propose potential avenues for further inquiry, while also considering alternative explanations for the origins and motivations underpinning the historical Jewish perspective.

---

indication that the prayer for the coming of David's son should follow the prayer for the building of Jerusalem.

32 Guggenheimer (2000, 210): רבנן אמרי אהן מלכא משיחא אין מי חייא הוא דוד שמיה אין מי דמכייא הוא דוד שמיה. א"ר תנחומא אנא אמרית טעמא, ועושה חסד למשיחו לדוד (תהלים יח:נא). רבי יהושע בן לוי אמר צמח שמו. ר׳ יודן בריה דר׳ אייבו אמר מנחם שמו.

4.1

The primary insight drawn from these sources is the identification of a Jewish exegetical approach that situates the consolation prophecies within their historical context. The examples cited above reveal a consistent methodology characterized by several shared elements: the central roles of Zerubbabel, Ezra, Nehemiah, and Joshua the High Priest; a close and detailed reading of the biblical text; and an effort to interpret the events of *Shivat Tzion* as the fulfillment of earlier prophecies. Moreover, the comparative analysis presented here suggests, with reasonable confidence, that the rabbinic interpretation of these specific prophecies diverges from the historical approach preserved by Jerome. While the historical reading reflects a past-oriented perspective on the prophecies, rabbinic sources take an entirely different stance, viewing these passages as allusions to a messianic future.

However, this dichotomy should be regarded with caution for several reasons. First, it is important to acknowledge the absence of extant classical midrashim on the Prophets, which limits our ability to comprehensively assess rabbinic approaches to these texts. The comparative analysis offered here shows that, at least in the specific cases discussed, the historical reading quoted by Jerome contrasts with rabbinic interpretations, while the messianic reading aligns closely with rabbinic thought. Nevertheless, it is plausible that certain rabbis occasionally adopted a historical perspective, but these interpretations were excluded by the editors of the Midrashic compilations. Second, traces of historical readings can be found in rabbinic sources, suggesting that this approach was at least known, if not fully embraced, within rabbinic circles. This nuance underscores the complexity of exegetical traditions and cautions against drawing overly rigid distinctions between historical and messianic interpretations. Traces of rabbinic historical reading, can be found, for instance, in Song of Songs Rabbah 2.13:

> "The sound of the turtledove [*hator*] is heard in our land." (Song 2:12) Rabbi Yohanan said: The voice of a good explorer was heard in our land. Who is that? It is the voice of Cyrus. That is what is written: "So said Cyrus king of Persia [...] any of you from His entire people [...] [may go up]." (Ezra 1:2–3) "The sound of the turtledove is heard in our land." What is that? It is the voice of the messianic king who proclaims and says: "How pleasant are the footsteps of the herald on the mountains." (Isa 52:7)[33]

33 Dunsky (1980, pp. 70–71): ״וקול התור נשמע בארצנו״. א״ר יוחנן: קול תייר טב נשמע בארצנו. איזה זה. זה קולו של כורש. הה״ד: ״כה אמר כורש מלך פרס מי בכם מכל עמו״... ״וקול התור נשמע בארצנו״. איזה זה. זה קולו של מלך המשיח שמכריז ואומר ״מה נאוו על ההרים רגלי מבשר״. A partial parallel can be found in *Pesiq. Rab. Kah., Ba-ḥodesh* 9 (Mandelbaum 1987, 96-97): ״וקול התור נשמע בארצנו״. א״ר יוחנן: קול תייר טב נשמע בארצנו, זה כורש. ״כה אמר כורש מלך פרס כל ממלכות הארץ״ וגו׳... ״וקול התור נשמע בארצנו״. א"ר יוחנן

This example of R. Yohanan illustrates that even within rabbinic literature—and even in the name of the same rabbi—we find both "messianic" and "historical" interpretations. While this particular case may not directly qualify as a consolation prophecy, its historical orientation is nonetheless clear. This duality highlights the complexity of drawing a sharp distinction between historical and messianic interpretations, especially when examining rabbinic literature.[34] That said, it is undeniable that the historical motif occupies a marginal place in rabbinic thought. For various reasons, historical readings of the Bible are far from central to rabbinic exegesis. Instead, we observe the opposite trend: a "rabbinization of the past," in which biblical figures are imbued with rabbinic characteristics, such as engagement in Torah study and observance of commandments.[35] Consequently, there is no doubt that Jerome's comments preserve a distinctive perspective absent from rabbinic literature, offering a glimpse into an interpretive tradition that did not survive within the rabbinic corpus.

4.2

The historical reading preserved by Jerome should be understood in light of other Jewish and non-Jewish exegetical traditions as well. The practice of interpreting the bible according to its historical context was well-known in Hellenistic Judaism. Flavius Josephus, for instance, states at the very beginning of his eleventh book of *Antiquitates Iudaicae* that:

> In the first year of Cyrus' reign—this was the seventieth year from the time when our people were fated to migrate from their own land to Babylon—God took pity on the captive state and misfortune of those unhappy men and, as He had foretold to them through the prophet Jeremiah before the city was demolished [...].[36]

״מה נאוו על ההרים רגלי מבשר״ קול תייר טב נשמע בארצינו, זה מלך המשיח. I would like to thank Dr. Yakir Paz for these references.

34 See also *b. Sanh.* 94a, where the Talmud presents not only detailed messianic homilies but also a form of historical exegesis regarding King Hezekiah and his potential role as the Messiah. Similarly, *Seder Olam* offers a chronographic-oriented exegesis that shares significant similarities with a historical interpretation of the Bible. See especially, Milikowsky (2013, 125; 128–129).

35 Gafni (2007, 304–305).

36 Josephus, *Ant.* 11.1 (Marcus 1937, 314–315 [with minor changes]): Τῷ δὲ πρώτῳ τῆς Κύρου βασιλείας ἔτει (τοῦτο δ' ἦν ἐβδομηκοστὸν ἀφ' ἧς ἡμέρας μεταναστῆναι τὸν λαὸν ἡμῶν ἐκ τῆς οἰκείας εἰς Βαβυλῶνα συνέπεσεν) ἠλέησεν ὁ θεὸς τὴν αἰχμαλωσίαν καὶ τὴν συμφορὰν ἐκείνων τῶν ταλαιπώρων, καὶ καθὼς προεῖπεν αὐτοῖς διὰ Ἰερεμίου τοῦ προφήτου [...].

A few sentences later Josephus adds that Cyrus' decision to encourage the Jews to build up their destroyed temple was a result of his:

> [...] reading the book of prophecy, which Isaiah had left behind 210 years earlier. For this prophet had said that God told him in secret, "It is my will that Cyrus, whom I shall have appointed king of many great nations, shall send my people to their own land and build my temple." Isaiah prophesied these things 140 years before the Temple was destroyed.[37]

Josephus' interpretation reflects not just a historical reading of the biblical prophecy but also a historical reading of the specific issue of *Shivat Tzion*. In his interpretation, supposedly attributed to Cyrus, some consolation prophecies on the future redemption of the Jewish people were understood as referring to the time of Zerubbabel, Ezra, and Nehemiah, very much like the Jewish traditions quoted by Jerome.

A few decades later, in his polemic, apologetic tractate *Dialogue with Trypho*, Justin Martyr records some other echoes of a Jewish historical reading of the Bible, particularly in passages related to Jewish messianic views. Thus, for instance, he accuses the Jews of interpreting Ps 110:4—"The Lord has sworn and will not change his mind, 'You are a priest forever after the order of Melchizedek'"—as referring to King Hezekiah rather than Jesus.[38] Similarly, certain prophecies of Isaiah, especially Isa 7:14, are also interpreted by the Jews, according to Justin, as referring to Hezekiah or Solomon.[39] Jerome himself, in his commentary on Isa 7:14, cites a Jewish tradition that reads the prophecy on Hezekiah, and in some other instances, he also records Jewish historical readings of the Bible.[40]

Likewise, in his treatise *Contra Celsum*, Origen criticizes his contemporary Jews for interpreting Isa 7:14 as referring to Ahaz and Hezekiah.[41] On another oc-

---

37 Josephus, *Ant.* 11.2 (Marcus 1937, 314–317): ἀναγινώσκων τὸ βιβλίον ὃ τῆς αὑτοῦ προφητείας ὁ Ἠσαΐας κατέλιπεν πρὸ ἐτῶν διακοσίων καὶ δέκα· οὗτος γὰρ ἐν ἀπορρήτῳ εἶπε ταῦτα λέγειν τὸν θεόν, ὅτι "βούλομαι Κῦρον ἐγὼ πολλῶν ἐθνῶν καὶ μεγάλων ἀποδείξας βασιλέα πέμψαι μου τὸν λαὸν εἰς τὴν ἰδίαν γῆν καὶ οἰκοδομῆσαί μου τὸν ναόν." ταῦτα Ἠσαΐας προεφήτευσεν ἔμπροσθεν ἢ κατασκαφῆναι τὸν ναὸν ἔτεσιν ἑκατὸν καὶ τεσσαράκοντα.

38 Justin Martyr, *Dial.* 33.2; 83.1–4 (Marcovich 2005, 124–125; 213–214).

39 Justin Martyr, *Dial.* 43.3–8; 67.1; 68.7–8; 71.3; 77.1; 85.1 (Marcovich 2005, 140–141; 184–185; 188; 193; 203; 216. Justin also mentioned Ps 72 as a source that the Jews attributed to Solomon. See Justin Martyr, *Dial.* 36.1–2 (Marcovich 2005, 130). On King Hezekiah as a Jewish Messiah, see Newman (2006) and the many references provided there.

40 For preliminary research with some references, see Newman (1997, 204–206).

41 Origen, *Cels.* 1.35 (Borret 1967, 170). For the historical context of this record, see Niehoff (2021, 238–239).

casion, he argues against Celsus and the Jew quoted by Celsus for promoting an anti-Christian interpretation. Origen argues that "in the words attributed to the Jew when he (i. e., Celsus) is addressing believers from his own people, he says that *the prophecies that are applied to this man* (i. e., Jesus) *can be referred to other events as well* [...]"[42] Celsus raises the Jewish argument that the prophecies, which Christians explain as referring to Jesus, can fit many other historical scenarios. As Maren R. Niehoff has shown, the Jewish quotations in *Contra Celsum* should be attributed to an Alexandrian Jew who composed them as a scholarly anti-Christian critique in the mid-second century CE.[43] According to Niehoff, this "anonymous Jewish author shares the same cultural background as the Greek scholars,"[44] and represents the first known instance of a Jewish author directly engaging with Christianity.[45]

The evidence spanning from the late first century (Josephus) to the mid-third century CE (Origen) provides a plausible background for the Jewish historical exegetical approach quoted by Jerome. While it is not necessary to directly link Jerome's Jewish quotations to these earlier sources, it is clear that the historical approach is not entirely foreign to Jewish exegesis. When we also consider the hints of historical interpretation found in rabbinic literature, the context for such an approach becomes much clearer. The sources mentioned here are specific and may not fully capture the breadth of Jerome's Jewish traditions, but a connection remains plausible.

Additionally, the flourishing philological-historical approach to the Old Testament in the fourth and fifth centuries CE by the Antiochene Fathers, particularly as shaped by Theodore of Mopsuestia, sheds light on the exegetical environment of Late Antiquity in which these Jewish traditions were recorded. While criticizing Alexandrian allegory and emphasizing the historical interpretation of the Bible, the Antiochene Fathers argued that the Old Testament should be read within the historical context of its time rather than as a foreshadowing of New Testament events.[46] Jerome, who was familiar with and influenced by Antiochene scholars

---

42 Origen, *Cels.* 1.50 (Chadwick 1980, 47). The Greek is taken from Borret (1967, 212). Καὶ ἐπεὶ ἐν τοῖς ἑξῆς φησιν ἐν τῇ τοῦ Ἰουδαίου πρὸς τοὺς ἀπὸ τοῦ λαοῦ πιστεύοντας προσωποποιΐᾳ τὰς εἰς τὰ περὶ τούτου ἀναφερομένας προφητείας δύνασθαι καὶ ἄλλοις ἐφαρμόζειν πράγμασι, δεινῶς καὶ κακούργως τοῦτο λέγων. For Origen's use of the formula "τοῦ Ἰουδαίου προσωποποιΐαν" Cf. Origen, *Cels.* 1.32; 34; 2.1 (Borret 1967, 162; 168; 276).

43 Niehoff (2013).

44 Niehoff (2013, 168).

45 On Celsus' Jew, see also Baumgarten (2014).

46 See especially van Rompay (1997); Winn (2011, 68–85); On Theodore's exegesis, see Simonetti (2006); McLeod (2009, 17–22); Kofsky and Ruzer (2019). Theodore's hermeneutic position aligns with his Christological perspective, which emphasized Jesus' humanity and resisted either

such as Eusebius of Amasa and Diodore of Tarsus (Theodore's teacher), may have incorporated aspects of this Christian interpretive approach.[47] This trend also potentially mirrors the exegetical context of the Jewish interpretive traditions evident in Jerome's writings.

Similarly, Jerome's choice to present both the messianic and historical Jewish interpretations likely stems from his intention to offer a historical reading of the prophets. His focus on the historical interpretation may have led him to highlight this approach over the messianic one. However, there is no reason to assume that Jerome wanted to emphasize disunity among Jews. Rather, he presents both views as part of the richness of Jewish exegesis. This could reflect his broader goal of making Jewish knowledge accessible to a Latin audience and establishing his interpretive authority within Christian discourse.[48]

The factors discussed above underscore the fundamental insight that the historical reading of the consolation prophecies did not develop in isolation. Historical interpretation was an established approach both within and outside Jewish thought. Moreover, the continuity of this method over time suggests the potential coexistence of historical and messianic readings within Jewish thought. That said, the uniqueness of Jerome's Jewish comments remains undiminished. There is no doubt that the historical readings preserved by Jerome represent a singular phenomenon, notable for their scope and directness. Even if they may have originated in earlier approaches and hints can be found in rabbinic and Christian literature, the consistency and richness of the Jewish traditions recorded by Jerome are exceptional among surviving Jewish texts of the same period.

This raises an important question: What led to the revival of this interpretation at the turn of the fourth century? If we accept that the traditions Jerome records have Jewish origins, it follows that his informant must have been transmitting interpretations still extant in certain Jewish circles. Why, then, did this particular approach resurface so prominently at this time? Which factors might explain the renewed emphasis on historical interpretation?

4.3

Connecting this interpretive phenomenon—which, as noted, has early and diverse origins—to a specific historical context is challenging. However, certain events

abolishing or fully subordinating his human nature to his divine nature. See Bick (2022, 198–201) and the references there. For Theodore's Christological perspective, see Kofsky and Ruzer (2014).

47 Kamesar (1993, 126–175); Winn (2011, 37–41).

48 Newman (1997, 120).

may illuminate the period during which Jerome's Jewish informant conveyed the historical interpretation of the consolation prophecies. While this context may not fully explain the reason for his report, it can help us better understand the environment in which these traditions were transmitted.

Three major events occurred shortly before Jerome wrote his commentaries, potentially influencing this issue directly or indirectly: the Jewish revolt against Constantius Gallus in 351,[49] the episode with Julian and the failed restoration of the Temple in 362–363,[50] and the Christianization of public space in Palestine during the second half of the fourth century.[51] These events profoundly impacted Palestinian Jews. Both the revolt and Julian's initiative carried significant messianic implications, heightening messianic expectations among Jews.[52] A fascinating passage from Jerome's commentary on Daniel preserves an unknown Jewish interpretation that reflects exactly these aspirations. In Dan 11:34–35 we read:

> When they stumble, they shall receive a little help. And many shall join themselves to them with flattery, and some of the wise shall stumble, so that they may be refined, purified, and made white, until the time of the end, for it still awaits the appointed time.[53]

In his commentary on these verses, Jerome first presents Porphyry's interpretation, which explains the prophecy as referring to Mattathias Maccabeus and his sons. He then contrasts Porphyry with the Christian view, which interprets the prophecy as pointing to the future coming of the Antichrist, and states:

> Some of the Hebrews understand these things as referring to the princes Severus and Antoninus, who held the Jews in very high esteem. But others understand this of the Emperor Julian; for when they were oppressed by Gallus Caesar and had suffered much in the afflictions of their captivity, Julian rose up as one who feigned love for the Jews. He promised that he would even offer sacrifice in their temple. They would have a small hope of help from him.[54]

---

49 On the Jewish revolt see especially Schäfer (1986); Mor (1989); Irshai (2009, 402–410).

50 See especially Millar (2015, 121–146). For the Christian perspective, see Hansen (2024).

51 See Irshai (2009, 396–398) with some references to additional scholarship.

52 This topic merits a more in-depth discussion, which I will address in another place. In the meantime, see Irshai (2000) and Irshai (2013, 109–110).

53 Cf. *BHS*, Dan 11: 34–35: וּבְהִכָּשְׁלָם יֵעָזְרוּ עֵזֶר מְעָט וְנִלְווּ עֲלֵיהֶם רַבִּים בַּחֲלַקְלַקּוֹת׃ וּמִן־הַמַּשְׂכִּילִים יִכָּשְׁלוּ לִצְרוֹף בָּהֶם וּלְבָרֵר וְלַלְבֵּן עַד־עֵת קֵץ כִּי־עוֹד לַמּוֹעֵד׃

54 Jerome, *Comm. Dan.* 11:34–35 (trans. Scheck 2024, 143 [with some changes]), for the Latin text, see Glorie (1964, 924): *hebraeorum quidam haec de seuero et antonino principibus intellegunt, qui iudaeos plurimum dilexerunt. alii uero de iuliano imperatore: quod, quando oppressi fuerint a gallo caesare et in captiuitatis angustiis multa perpessi, ille consurgat, iudaeos amare se simulans et in templo eorum immolaturum esse promittens, in quo paruam spem habebunt auxilii.*

As Newman demonstrated, Jerome succinctly conveys the eschatological perspective of certain Jews who interpreted major political events in mid-fourth-century Palestine—the rebellion during Gallus' reign and Julian's failed attempt to rebuild the Temple—as signs heralding redemption at the end of time.[55]

Perhaps these events and their ultimate failure—combined with the fear of further catastrophe—spurred the revival of the historical approach. This may explain why Jerome's Jewish informant conveyed this distinctive Jewish perspective at the turn of the fourth century. On other occasions, we see that Jewish messianic views were reshaped in response to traumatic events, and a similar dynamic may be at play here. In a pioneering article published in 2007, Adiel Schremer emphasized the historical and theological background of a specific aspect of the rabbinic perspective on redemption: the militant *geula* ("הגאולה הלוחמת").[56] According to him, scholars often focus on two views of Jewish redemption—the revival of Judaism in the Land of Israel with autonomy, or redemption as a total catastrophe and destruction of the world.[57] There is, however, a third perspective in rabbinic literature: redemption as the time in which God will take revenge on his enemies (i. e., according to the rabbis, the enemies of the Jews). According to Schremer, this view became an important part of the rabbinic outlook of future redemption, especially in the generation after the Bar Kokhba revolt. But there was another aspect, dependent on the first one, that became an integral part of this view. As Schremer points out, along with the militant *geula*, the rabbis adopted a complementary motif, explaining that this militant attitude should not lead to deeds. Only God would take revenge on the enemies, in this case, Rome. Beyond the exegetical effect, this passive approach also has a political and practical impact. If God is the only one to take revenge, the Jews should not rebel, and their redemption will come at an unknown time. This last point, the postponement of the end to an unknown time, is well recorded in rabbinic literature. A considerable number of midrashim attempt to postpone the messianic era, saying that redemption is far, and its time is unknown.[58] Hence, we can conclude that within Jewish exege-

---

55 Newman (1997, 109). Rufinus, John Chrysostom, Gregory Nazianzus, Ephraem, and Sozomenus also document the messianic fervor among Jews following Julian's decision to rebuild the Temple. See Avi-Yonah (1970, 168). While their accounts may reflect an anti-Jewish perspective, the profound impact of this event on the Jewish communities in Byzantium is an established fact.

56 Schremer (2007).

57 See, especially, Herr (1985).

58 See, for instance, *y. Ta'an.* 4:5 (Guggenheimer 2015, 167) [with minor changes]: "Rabbi Simeon ben Yohai stated: Akiba my teacher used to preach, *there appeared a star out of Jacob* there appeared Koziba out of Jacob. When Rabbi Akiba saw Bar Koziba he said, this is King Messiah. Rabbi Yohanan ben Torta said to him, Akiba! Grass will grow from your jaws and still, David's son will not have come." *[=* תני ר׳ שמעון בן יוחי, עקיבה רבי היה דורש דרך כוכב מיעקב דרך כוזבא מיעקב. רבי

sis, there were interpretive, political, and theological trends that tried to channel the power of redemption from the people to God, along with a straightforward statement that this redemption is still far away.

The existence of a Jewish approach that adopts a passive attitude may shed light on the unique perspective reflected in Jerome's comments. Both approaches, in their own ways, can be understood as a rejection of contemporary messianism. Just as the "militant *geula*," following the failure of the Bar Kokhba revolt, shifted the focus of redemption to divine intervention—postponing it to an undefined future and rejecting immediate political aspirations—so too does the historical approach cited by Jerome. This approach emphasizes the historical dimensions of the biblical text rather than interpreting it as a prediction of the future, and it may be connected to the catastrophic events of the late fourth century.

Interestingly, a similar pattern of despair in human-led political redemption is evident in Rabbi Aha's words: "'The cords of death encompassed me' (Ps 18:5) [...] I turned here and there, and I have no redeemer but You."[59] Although this source is relatively late, it likely preserves an earlier tradition that faithfully reflects Rabbi Aha's perspective. In the fourth century, possibly as a response to Julian's failed attempt to rebuild the Temple,[60] Rabbi Aha appears to have adopted the same interpretive framework that developed after the Bar Kokhba revolt—one that emphasizes divine intervention and rejects political action. This hypothesis helps explain the context in which Jerome's Jewish informant preserved these historical interpretive traditions and why, at that particular time, the historical reading of biblical prophecies remained relevant. The realities of the late fourth century may have revived earlier interpretive traditions that had previously been overshadowed by messianic readings of the prophecies.

עקיבה כד הוה חמי בר כוזבה הוה אמר, דין הוא מלכא משיחא. אמר ליה רבי יוחנן בן תורתא, עקיבה יעלו עשבים בלחייך ועדיין בן דוד לא יבא/ R. Yohanan ben Torta renounces R. Akiba's messianic view on Bar-Kokhba, saying that "grass will grow from your jaws," that is long after you will be dead, and the Messiah, "David's son, will not have come."

59 *Midr. Ps.* 18.10 (Buber 1891, 139): אפפוני חבלי מות [...] נפניתי לכאן ולכאן ואין לי גואל אלא אתה. Michael Avi-Yonah linked several other sermons of Rabbi Aha to the events accompanying Julian's plan. See Avi-Yonah (1970, 171–172).

60 Urbach (1982, 621). For the rabbinic perspective on Julian's plan, see also Urbach (2002, 408–410).

Bibliography

Alexander, P. S. 2007. “The Rabbis and Messianism.” In *Redemption and Resistance: The Messianic Hopes of Jews and Christians in Antiquity*, edited by M. Bockmuehl and J. Carleton Paget, 227–244. London: T&T Clark.

Avi-Yonah, M. 1970. *In the Days of Rome and Byzantium.* Jerusalem: Bialik Institute. [Hebrew]

Baumgarten, A. I. 2014. “The Rule of the Martian in the Ancient Diaspora: Celsus and His Jew.” In *Jews and Christians in the First and Second Centuries: How to Write Their History*, edited by P. Tomson and J. Schwartz, 398–430. Leiden/Boston: Brill.

Bick, S. 2022. “The Bodies of the Law: Commandment’s Discourse in Late Antiquity.” The Hebrew University of Jerusalem. [Hebrew]

Braude, W. G., and I. J. Kapstein. 2002. *Pĕsiḳta Dĕ-Rab̠ Kahăna: R. Kahana’s Compilation of Discourses for Sabbaths and Festal Days.* 2nd ed. Philadelphia: Jewish Publication Society of America.

Buber, S., ed. 1891. *Midrash Tehilim (Schocher Tob): Sammlung agadischer Abhandlungen über die 150 Psalmen.* Vilna: Romm.

Cameron, J. 2016. “The Rabbinic Vulgate?” In *Jerome of Stridon: His Life, Writings and Legacy*, edited by J. Lössl and A. Cain, 117–129. London: Routledge.

Dunsky, S., ed. 1980. *Midrash Rabbah: Shir Ha-Shirim. Midrash Ḥazit*, Tel Aviv/Jerusalem: Devir. [Hebrew]

Elliger, K., and W. Rudolph, eds. 1997. *Biblia Hebraica Stuttgartensia.* 5th ed. Stuttgart: Deutsche Bibelgesellschaft.

Fishbane, M. 1998. “Midrash and Messianism: Some Theologies of Suffering and Salvation.” In *Toward the Millennium: Messianic Expectations from the Bible to Waco*, edited by P. Schäfer and M. Cohen, 57–71. Leiden: Brill.

Flusser, D. 2007. “Redemption.” In *Encyclopedia Judaica*, 2nd ed. Vol. 17, edited by F. Skolnik, 152. Detroit, MI/Jerusalem: Macmillan Publishers/Keter Publishing House.

Gafni, I. 2007. “Rabbinic Historiography and Representations of the Past.” In *The Cambridge Companion to the Talmud and Rabbinic Literature*, edited by C. E. Fonrobert and M. S. Jaffee, 295–312. Cambridge: Cambridge University Press.

Ginzberg, L. 1900. *Die Haggada bei den Kirchenvätern und in der apokryphischen Litteratur.* Berlin: S. Calvary.

Ginzberg, L. 1933. “Die Haggada bei den Kirchenvätern: V. Der Kommentar des Hieronymus zu Koheleth.” In *Abhandlungen zu Erinnerung an Hirsch Perez Chajes*, 22–55. Vienna: The Alexander Kohut Memorial Foundation.

Ginzberg, L. 1935. “Die Haggada bei den Kirchenvätern: VI. Der Kommentar des Hieronymus zu Jesaja.” In *Jewish Studies: In Memory of George A. Kohut*, edited by S. W. Baron and A. Marx, 279–314. New York: The Alexander Kohut Memorial Foundation.

Graves, M. 2007. *Jerome’s Hebrew Philology: A Study Based on His Commentary on Jeremiah.* Leiden: Brill.

Guggenheimer, H. W., ed. 2000. *Tractate Berakhot: Edition, Translation, and Commentary. The Jerusalem Talmud: Edition, Translation, and Commentary.* Berlin: De Gruyter.

Guggenheimer, H. W., ed. 2015. *Second Order Moed: Tractates Ta’aniot, Megillah, Hagigah and Mo’ed Qatan (Mašqin). The Jerusalem Talmud: Edition, Translation, and Commentary.* Berlin: De Gruyter.

Hansen, B. 2024. “An Improvised Apocalypse: The Rebuilding of the Jerusalem Temple from Julian to ʿAbd al-Malik.” *Studies in Late Antiquity* 8.2: 208–241.

Hayward, C. T. R. 1989. "The Date of Targum Pseudo-Jonathan: Some Comments." *Journal of Jewish Studies* 40.1: 7–30.

Hayward, C. T. R. 1995. *Saint Jerome's Hebrew Questions on Genesis.* Oxford: Clarendon Press/Oxford University Press.

Hayward, C. T. R. 2010. "Some Observations on St. Jerome's Hebrew Questions on Genesis and the Rabbinic Tradition." In *Targums and the Transmission of Scripture into Judaism and Christianity*, edited by C. T. R. Hayward, 318–338. Leiden/Boston: Brill.

Herr, M. D. 1985. "Realistic Political Messianism and Cosmic Eschatological Messianism in the Teaching of the Sages." *Tarbiz* 54.3: 331–346. [Hebrew]

Irshai, O. 2000. "Dating the Eschaton: Jewish and Christian Apocalyptic Calculations in Late Antiquity." In *Apocalyptic Time*, edited by A. I. Baumgarten, 113–153. Leiden: Brill.

Irshai, O. 2009. "Jewish Violence in the 4th Century – Reality and Imagination: On the Backstage of the Days of Gallus and Julian." In *Jewish Identities in Antiquity: Studies in Memory of Menahem Stern*, edited by L. I. Levine and D. R. Schwartz, 391–416. Tübingen: Mohr Siebeck.

Irshai, O. 2013. "The Earthquake in the Valley of Arbel: A Galilean Apocalyptic Tradition and Its Historical-Liturgical Context." *Jerusalem Studies in Hebrew Literature* 25: 107–132. [Hebrew]

Jerome. 1964. *Commentariorum in Danielem libri III (IV)*, edited by F. Glorie. Turnhout: Brepols.

Jerome. 1970. *Commentarii in prophetas minores: commentarii in prophetas Naum, Abacuc, Sophoniam, Aggaeum, Zachariam, Malachiam*, edited by M. Adriaen. Turnhout: Brepols.

Jerome. 1998. *Commentaires de Jérôme sur le prophète Isaïe: Livres XII–XV*, edited by R. Gryson and P. A. Deproost. Freiburg i. Br.: Herder.

Jerome. 2015. *Commentary on Isaiah. Including St. Jerome's Translation of Origen's Homilies 1–9 on Isaiah*, edited by T. P. Scheck. New York: The Newman Press.

Jerome. 2017. *Commentaries on the Twelve Prophets.* Vol. 2. Ancient Christian Texts, edited by T. P. Scheck. Downers Grove, IL: IVP Academic.

Jerome. 2024. *Commentary on Daniel*, edited by T. P. Scheck. New York: The Newman Press.

Josephus. 1937. *Jewish Antiquities.* Vol. 4: Books 9–11, translated by R. Marcus. Cambridge, MA: Harvard University Press.

Justin Martyr. 2005. *Iustini Martyris Apologiae pro Christianis. Iustini Martyris Dialogus cum Tryphone*, edited by M. Marcovich. Berlin/Boston: De Gruyter.

Kamesar, A. 1993. *Jerome, Greek Scholarship, and the Hebrew Bible: A Study of the Quaestiones Hebraicae in Genesim.* Oxford: Clarendon Press/Oxford University Press.

Kedar-Kopfstein, B. 1994. "Jewish Traditions in the Writings of Jerome." In *The Aramaic Bible: Targums in Their Historical Context*, edited by D. R. G. Beattie and M. J. McNamara, 420–430. Sheffield: Sheffield Academic Press.

Klausner, J. 1958. *The Messianic Idea in Israel: From Its Beginning to the Completion of the Mishnah.* Tel Aviv: Masada. [Hebrew]

Kofsky, A., and S. Ruzer. 2014. "Theodore of Mopsuestia's Hermeneutics: Transformed Theology in Response to Fourth Century Crises." *Vox Patrum* 34: 221–238.

Kofsky, A., and S. Ruzer. 2019. "Theodore of Mopsuestia: Rationalizing Hermeneutics and Theology." In *Rationalization in Religions: Judaism, Christianity and Islam*, edited by Y. Friedmann and C. Markschies, 74–102. Berlin/Boston: De Gruyter.

Kraus, M. A. 2017. *Jewish, Christian, and Classical Exegetical Traditions in Jerome's Translation of the Book of Exodus: Translation Technique and the Vulgate.* Leiden/Boston: Brill.

Krewson, W. L. 2017. *Jerome and the Jews: Innovative Supersessionism.* Eugene, OR: Wipf & Stock.

Lauterbach, J. Z., ed. 2004. *Mekhilta De-Rabbi Ishmael: A Critical Edition, Based on the Manuscripts and Early Editions, With an English Translation, Introduction, and Notes.* 2nd ed. Philadelphia: Jewish Publication Society.

Lieberman, S. 1995. *The Tosefta; according to Codex Vienna, with variants from Codex Erfurt, Genizah MSS. and editio princeps (Venice 1521), together with references to parallel passages in Talmudic literature, and a brief commentary. Order Zera'im.* New York and Jerusalem: Jewish Theological Seminary of America. [Hebrew]

Lieberman, S. 2001. *Tosefta Ki-fshutah: A Comprehensive Commentary on the Tosefta. Order Zera'im, Part I.* New York and Jerusalem: Jewish Theological Seminary of America. [Hebrew]

Lössl, J. 2002. "Hieronymus und Epiphanius von Salamis über das Judentum ihrer Zeit." *Journal for the Study of Judaism in the Persian, Hellenistic, and Roman Period* 33.4: 411–436.

Mandelbaum, B., ed. 1987. *Pesikta de Rav Kahana: According to an Oxford Manuscript.* New York: The Jewish Theological Seminary of America.

McCollough, C. T. 1984. *Theodore of Cyrus as Biblical Interpreter and the Presence of Judaism in Later Roman Syria.* PhD thesis, University of Notre Dame.

McLeod, F. G. 2009. *Theodore of Mopsuestia. The Early Church Fathers.* London: Routledge.

Milikowsky, C. 2013. *Seder Olam: Critical Edition, Commentary and Introduction.* Jerusalem: Yad Ben Zvi.

Millar, F. 2015. *Empire, Church and Society in the Late Roman Near East: Greeks, Jews, Syrians and Saracens. Collected Studies 2004–2014.* Peeters Publishers: Leuven.

Mor, M. 1989. "The Events of 351–352 in Palestine: The Last Revolt Against Rome?" In *The Eastern Frontier of the Roman Empire: Proceedings of a Colloquium Held at Ankara in September 1988*, edited by D. H. French and C. S. Lightfoot, 335–353. Oxford: BAR.

Newman, H. 1997. *Jerome and the Jews.* PhD thesis, The Hebrew University of Jerusalem. [Hebrew]

Newman, H. 2006. "The Birth of the Messiah on the Day of Destruction: Historical and Anti-Historical Comments." In *For Uriel: Studies in the History of Israel in Antiquity Presented to Professor Uriel Rappaport*, edited by M. Mor, J. Pator, I. Ronen and Y. Ashkenazi, 85–110. Jerusalem: The Zalman Shazar Center for Jewish History. [Hebrew]

Newman, H. 2018. "A Patristic Perspective on Rabbinic Literature." In *The Classic Rabbinic Literature of Eretz Israel: Introductions and Studies*, edited by M. Kahana, V. Noam, M. Kister and D. Rosenthal, 681–704. Jerusalem: Yad Ben Zvi. [Hebrew]

Niehoff, M. R. 2013. "Jewish Critique of Christianity from Second-Century Alexandria: Revisiting Celsus' Jew." *Journal of Early Christian Studies* 21: 151–175.

Niehoff, M. R. 2021. "Celsus' Jew in Third Century Caesarea: Tracing Hellenistic Judaism in Origen's *Contra Celsum.*" In *Social History of the Jews in Antiquity: Studies in Dialogue with Albert Baumgarten*, edited by M. B.-A. Siegal and J. Ben-Dov, 233–250. Tübingen: Mohr Siebeck.

Origen. 1980. *Contra Celsum*, edited by H. Chadwick. Cambridge: Cambridge University Press.

Origen. 1967. *Contra Celsum*, edited by M. Borret. Sources Chrétiennes 132. Paris: Éditions du Cerf.

Rahmer, M. 1861. *Die Hebräischen Traditionen in den Werken des Hieronymus: Durch Vergleichung mit den Jüdischen Quellen Kritisch Beleuchtet. Erster Theil. Die "Quaestiones in Genesim."* Breslau: Schletter'sche Buchhandlung H. Skutsch.

Reed, A. Y. 2014. "Messianism between Judaism and Christianity." In *Rethinking the Messianic Idea in Judaism*, edited by M. L. Morgan and S. Weitzman, 23–62. Bloomington: Indiana University Press.

Salvesen, A. 2013. "'Tradunt Hebraei': The Problem of the Function and Reception of Jewish Midrash in Jerome." In *Midrash Unbound: Transformations and Innovations*, edited by M. Fishbane and J. Weinberg, 57–86. Liverpool: Liverpool University Press.
Schäfer, P. 1986. "Der Aufstand gegen Gallus Caesar." In *Tradition and Re-Interpretation in Jewish and Early Christian Literature: Essays in Honour of Jürgen C. H. Lebram*, edited by J. W. van Henten, H. J. de Jonge, P. van Rooden, and J. W. Wesselius, 184–201. Leiden: Brill.
Schäfer, P. 1998. "Diversity and Interaction: Messiahs in Early Judaism." In *Toward the Millennium: Messianic Expectations from the Bible to Waco*, edited by P. Schäfer and M. Cohen, 15–35. Leiden: Brill.
Schremer, A. 2007. "Midrash and History: God's Power, the Roman Empire, and Hopes for Redemption in Tannaitic Literature." *Zion* 72.1: 5–36. [Hebrew]
Simonetti, M. 2006. "Theodore of Mopsuestia." In *Handbook of Patristic Exegesis: The Bible in Ancient Christianity*, edited by C. Kannengiesser, 799–828. Leiden: Brill.
Sussman, Y. 2001. *Talmud Yerushalmi: According to Ms. Or. 4720 (Scal. 3) of the Leiden University Library, with Restorations and Corrections.* Jerusalem: Academy of the Hebrew Language. [Hebrew]
Urbach, E. E. 1982. *The Sages.* Jerusalem: Magnes Press. [Hebrew]
Urbach, E. E. 2002. "Cyrus and His Proclamation in the Eyes of the Sages." In *From the World of the Sages*, edited by E. E. Urbach, 403–410. Jerusalem: Magnes Press. [Hebrew]
Van Rompay, L. 1997. "Antiochene Biblical Interpretation: Greek and Syriac." In *The Book of Genesis in Jewish and Oriental Christian Interpretation*, edited by J. Frishman and L. Van Rompay, 103–123. Leuven: Peeters.
Williams, M. H. 2006. *The Monk and the Book: Jerome and the Making of Christian Scholarship.* Chicago: University of Chicago Press.
Williams, M. H. 2008. "Lessons from Jerome's Jewish Teachers: Exegesis and Cultural Interaction in Late Antique Palestine." In *Jewish Biblical Interpretation and Cultural Exchange: Comparative Exegesis in Context*, edited by N. B. Dohrmann and D. Stern, 66–86. Philadelphia: University of Pennsylvania Press.
Winn, R. E. 2011. *Eusebius of Emesa: Church and Theology in the Mid-Fourth Century.* Washington, D.C.: Catholic University of America Press.

Index of Biblical References

 https://doi.org/10.1515/9783112225981-007

Index of Rabbinic Sources

 https://doi.org/10.1515/9783112225981-008

Index of Greco-Roman Sources

https://doi.org/10.1515/9783112225981-009

General Index (in selection)

 https://doi.org/10.1515/9783112225981-010

The following volumes have been published in this series:

Volume 2
Detel, Wolfgang. *Subjektive und objektive Zeit: Aristoteles und die moderne Zeit-Theorie*. Berlin/Boston: De Gruyter, 2021.

Volume 3
Singer, P. N. *Time for the Ancients: Measurement, Theory, Experience.* Berlin/Boston: De Gruyter, 2022.

Volume 4
Gertzen, Thomas L. *Aber die Zeit fürchtet die Pyramiden: Die Wissenschaften vom Alten Orient und die zeitliche Dimension von Kulturgeschichte.* Berlin/Boston: De Gruyter, 2022.

Volume 6
Zachhuber, Johannes. *Time and Soul: From Aristotle to St. Augustine.* Berlin/Boston: De Gruyter, 2022.

Volume 7
Golitsis, Pantelis. *Damascius' Philosophy of Time.* Berlin/Boston: De Gruyter, 2023.

Volume 8
Defaux, Olivier. *La Table des rois: Contribution à l'histoire textuelle des ›Tables faciles‹ de Ptolémée.* Berlin/Boston: De Gruyter, 2023.

Volume 9
Fischer, Julia (ed.). *Zwiegespräche über die Zeit: Dialoge in der Berlin-Brandenburgischen Akademie der Wissenschaften aus Anlass des sechzigsten Geburtstags von Christoph Markschies.* Berlin/Boston: De Gruyter, 2024.

Volume 10
Walter, Anke (ed.). *The Temporality of Festivals: Approaches to Festive Time in Ancient Babylon, Greece, Rome, and Medieval China.* Berlin/Boston: De Gruyter, 2024.

Volume 12
Sieroka, Norman. *Zeit-Hören: Erfahrungen, Taktungen, Musik.* Berlin/Boston: De Gruyter, 2024.

Volume 13
Birk, Ralph/Coulon, Laurent (eds.). *The Thebaid in Times of Crisis: Revolt and Response in Ptolemaic Egypt.* Berlin/Boston: De Gruyter, 2025.

Volume 14
Pallavidini, Marta. *(A)synchronic (Re)actions: Crises and Their Perception in Hittite History.* Berlin/Boston: De Gruyter, 2025.

Volume 15
Nosch, Marie-Louise Bech. *Time and Textiles in Ancient Greece.* Berlin/Boston: De Gruyter, 2025.

Volume 16
Klinger, Jörg. *Das Erfassen von Zeit im Kontext der Vergangenheit.* Berlin/Boston: De Gruyter, 2026.

Volume 17
Zachhuber, Johannes. *Time and History in Denis Pétau. Philosophy, Science, and Religion in Early Modern France.* Berlin/Boston: De Gruyter, 2026.

Volume 18
Ossendrijver, Mathieu. *Conceptions of Cyclicity in Babylonian and Greco-Roman Scholarship.* Berlin/Boston: De Gruyter, 2025.

Volume 19
Schumacher, Lydia. *From Eternal to Everlasting: God and Time in Franciscan Thought.* Berlin/Boston: De Gruyter, 2026.

Volume 20
Wiedemann, Felix. *The Modern Hammurapi: An Old Babylonian King in Imperial Germany.* Berlin/Boston: De Gruyter, 2026.

www.ingramcontent.com/pod-product-compliance
Lightning Source LLC
LaVergne TN
LVHW010904110826
845149LV00005B/1462

* 9 7 8 3 1 1 2 2 2 5 9 7 4 *